Italy in Uncertain Times

Foreign Policies of the Middle Powers

Series Editors: Giampiero Giacomello, University of Bologna &
Bertjan Verbeek, Radboud University, Nijmegen

This series publishes studies that offer sophisticated theorizing about middle powers and cutting edge empirical analysis of middle powers in action, today as well as in distant history. It seeks to fill a major gap in our understanding of world politics. The International Relations discipline has traditionally centered on the security policies of the great powers. This resulted in a theoretical neglect of middle or secondary powers. Middle powers often aspire to be great powers or happen to be "demoted" great powers. This discrepancy between ambition and recognized status makes them difficult and often dangerous states to deal with. Global middle powers can also be regional great powers, enjoying leverage over regional security, diplomacy, economy, and technology. Middle powers can also be great powers in specific policy domains. A limited, traditional focus on the great powers prevents us from observing important power relations. In the twenty-first century, the "ranks" of middle powers have swollen to a size never seen before in international affairs. Nevertheless the topic of middle powers remains understudied and underestimated. This series seeks to remedy this issue.

Titles Published

Italian Foreign Policy During Matteo Renzi's Government: A Domestically-Focused Outsider and the World by Fabrizio Coticchia and Jason W. Davidson
Italy in Uncertain Times: Europeanizing Foreign Policy in the Declining Process of the American Hegemony by Carla Monteleone

Italy in Uncertain Times

Europeanizing Foreign Policy in the Declining Process of the American Hegemony

Carla Monteleone

LEXINGTON BOOKS
Lanham • Boulder • New York • London

Published by Lexington Books
An imprint of The Rowman & Littlefield Publishing Group, Inc.
4501 Forbes Boulevard, Suite 200, Lanham, Maryland 20706
www.rowman.com

6 Tinworth Street, London SE11 5AL

Copyright © 2019 The Rowman & Littlefield Publishing Group, Inc.

All rights reserved. No part of this book may be reproduced in any form or by any electronic or mechanical means, including information storage and retrieval systems, without written permission from the publisher, except by a reviewer who may quote passages in a review.

British Library Cataloguing in Publication Information Available

Library of Congress Cataloging-in-Publication Data Available

ISBN: 978-1-4985-8183-7 (cloth)
ISBN: 978-1-4985-8185-1 (pbk)
ISBN: 978-1-4985-8184-4 (electronic)

Contents

Introduction 1

1 The Europeanization of Italian Foreign Policy in the US-led World Order 13
2 Analyzing Europeanization at the United Nations 43
3 In the General Assembly 73
4 In the Security Council 109
5 The Challenge of Crises: Toward a De-Europeanization? 141

Conclusions 165

Bibliography 171

Index 193

About the Author 199

Introduction

Widening an already deep rift with the European Union (EU) on an issue of crucial importance for its European allies and provoking their vehement reactions, on 5 November 2018, the United States (US) re-imposed sanctions on Iran with bruising effects on all countries buying Iranian oil. Only eight countries were temporarily exempted. Italy was among them, in recognition of its recently renewed allegiance to the US. Once again, Italy was caught in between the US and the EU.

Tension between loyalty to the EU and loyalty to the US has become an increasingly recurring condition in Italian foreign policy since the end of the Cold War, and more evidently since the 2000s. Considering that the US and Europe, together with multilateralism, have been longstanding pillars of Italian foreign policy and that they were all adopted to signal Italian allegiance to the US authority in a hegemonic order, this condition may appear as a paradox. In fact, this condition is the result of how two processes combine: on the one hand, the evolution of the US-led hegemonic order and, on the other hand, Italy's interpretation of its role within that order as a member of both the US-led dominant coalition and a coalition of European states that since the 1970s has progressively institutionalized its foreign policy cooperation. The result of these two courses is what this book focuses on.

Within this framework, variations in the European pillar of Italian foreign policy are themselves particularly puzzling. On the one hand, the advanced institutionalization of foreign policy cooperation among EU member states would lead to expect Italy to be bound by common positions reached at the EU level. On the other hand, Italy periodically claims and gains margins of maneuver. Not surprisingly, the evidence on the Europeanization of Italian foreign policy has led to contradictory interpretations: Italy has been taken as a case of both Europeanized and de-Europeanized foreign policy. Clarifying the composition of these processes is important for theories on hegemonic orders, because it sheds light on the little-explored aspect of political support; on the Europeanization of foreign policy, because it looks at the relevance for the phenomenon of international factors; and on Italian foreign policy, because it contributes to clarifying a puzzle that has attracted great attention but has so far led to inconclusive results. The object of study is indeed situated at the center of interconnected and intersecting processes.

To analyze the interplay of these processes in their evolution, Italy seems to be a useful case study. The Italian perspective is important not only because Italy is a big and founding member of the EU, but also because the Italian case can be representative of middle power behavior.

This design, however, requires some analytical and methodological choices that it is useful to clarify at this early stage. First of all, to better understand Italian behavior in the context of the evolution of the US-led hegemonic order, requires adapting existing definitions of foreign policy Europeanization, so far more focused on the transformation in the construction processes of national foreign policies, to better highlight the coalitional behavior of EU member states in the international system. Building on Hill and Wong (2011: 211) and their ideal-typical Europeanized foreign policy, it is here proposed that for Italy Europeanizing meant adapting its foreign policy to be part of a coalition made of EU states, here called the European formalized coalition. Secondly, the European formalized coalition is here defined as a coalition of EU member states that has progressively strongly institutionalized foreign policy cooperation and formalized collective decision-making processes, whose members are guided by a negotiated convergence of interests and strategies and have developed norms to overcome internal disagreements and that tends to present itself as a stable single unit over time to the point of creating expectations on members' behavior. The European formalized coalition is a subset of the US-led dominant coalition and is nested into it. It has been originally promoted by the US and has traditionally acted in support of the global leader and its organization of the international political system.[1]

It is here argued that, because of its collocation, the European formalized coalition is not only influenced by intra-European dynamics, but also by international systemic pressures and modifications in its bargaining environment, and this helps explain variations and fluctuations over time in the Europeanization of Italian foreign policy. Within the European formalized coalition Italy played the role of facilitator, that is, it supported not only the creation but most importantly the maintenance of the European formalized coalition, in support of the US-led hegemonic order. Although it is the initiator of a coalition that normally gets most attention, in the long-term evolution of hegemonic processes facilitating the maintenance of a coalition in support of the hegemon and preventing or reducing defections is extremely important too, because the initial enthusiasm of coalition members is subject to progressive reduction but that support is vital for legitimizing the authority of the hegemon and for its capacity to deal with potential challenges. Facilitating the European formalized coalition allowed Italy to gain leverage and use it to support the US-led hegemonic order, in a strategy that gave the country advantage in the competition for status with other middle powers and was consistent with its identity and strategic culture. The possibility of politics of scale inherent to leveraging on the European formalized coalition progressively allowed the country to amplify its weight and initiate a more active foreign policy. This is all the more relevant in multilateral contexts, and in particular in the United Nations (UN), not only because they are traditional forums for middle powers, but also because multilateralism is a declared feature in the identity of both the EU and Italy, and it has been a key component of the hegemonic order promoted by the US after World War II with the support of its Western European allies.

To analyze the Europeanization of Italian foreign policy in a declining hegemonic order, it is here proposed that variations in the Europeanization of Italian foreign policy can be tested through an empirical analysis of the Italian coalitional behavior at the UN in the period 2000–2017, that is the period in which the fluctuations have become more apparent and that is considered by hegemonic theorists as the one in which tensions within traditional coalitions may explode and lead to a reshuffling. Moving the analysis to the UN allows to overcome some methodological issues indicated in the Europeanization literature and to have a more accurate picture of variations over time. While literature so far has analyzed the position of a state focusing mostly on voting behavior in the UN General Assembly (UNGA), it is here proposed to analyze also sponsoring behavior and to extend the analysis to the Security Council (UNSC). The analysis of sponsoring behavior and the stress on the importance of the UNSC are not commonly used, but it is here believed that they better reflect the coalitional behavior of a country at the international system level. The analysis focuses on whether Italian coalitional behavior at the UN reflects a willingness to adapt its foreign policy to belong to the European formalized coalition and facilitate its existence, and assesses the Italian cohesion with its traditional ally, the US, and the so-called rising powers (China, Russia, India, and Brazil) to see whether this behavior is used to increase Italy's structural opportunities and status as a country contributing to international system maintenance or is used in opposition to the US. A focus on cases of Italian convergence and divergence from the European formalized coalition to better understand Europeanization processes is also present.

Moreover, a focus on the changing context is proposed to see whether the EU crises had an impact on Italian coalitional behavior.

The main result of the analysis is to have demonstrated a still elevated level of Europeanization of Italian foreign policy especially on important issues and to have confirmed the role of Italy as coalition facilitator within the European formalized coalition in support of the US and its order. Once the rising powers appeared as a potential challenge to the US-led hegemonic order, Italy increased its level of loyalty to the US while maintaining its elevated level of cohesion with the European formalized coalition. However, elements of weakness in the strength and cohesion of the European formalized coalition are present on less prominent issues and, following the EU crises since the late 2000s, they translated into higher volatility in the Italian coalitional behavior in relation to its traditionally preferred coalition members.

To understand the relevance of this result, some background context is now appropriate as well as an introduction to some specificities of the Italian case.

The end of World War II was a turning point and a founding moment for Italy's status and role in the international system, and for Italian foreign policy more generally (Diodato and Niglia 2017). Despite its cobelligerent status after 1943 and all attempts at distancing itself from the fascist experience, Italy was treated as a loser: it could not really negotiate the peace treaty and had to accept rather unfavorable terms (Ferraris 1998: 5). Its isolation became apparent with the exclusion from the 1945 San Francisco Conference that set up the UN. Since then Italian membership of the UN became a major foreign policy goal, symbolizing the country's readmission to the international community, and the policy of internationalism became a sort of external constraint or the only way in which Italy could promote national goals and interests (Diodato and Niglia 2017: 55; Nuti 2011a: 30; Panebianco 2015: 231–232). It is within this context that, once the Cold War was looming, Italy matured its most important foreign policy choices: the choice for a strong alliance with the US and the Western camp, in the European region taking the form of European integration, and the choice for multilateralism.

It is difficult to disentangle the influence that the international and domestic levels had on Italian foreign policy in such a turning point (Attinà 1979: 73 and 1983: 106; Panebianco 1977, 1982, and 1986; Pasquino 1974). In hierarchical relations, the great power shapes both the domestic institutional structure and the foreign policy choices of the subordinate state (Lake 2013; McDonald 2015). This happened in Italy too. At the beginning of the Cold War the choice for the Western camp re-legitimized Italy internationally, and the alliance with the US was used as a leverage to regain some of the country's previous standing (Nuti 2011a: 31; Coralluzzo 2000: 45). US assistance through the Marshall Plan and later Italian membership of NATO were crucial to the Italian post-war recovery and international rehabilitation. They were also ways of supporting a domestic coalition that had signaled its intention to preserve the hierarchical relationship with the US (McDonald 2015: 565).

Elections in 1948 exposed that the East-West cleavage at the international level was reproduced and amplified domestically in the political competition between the Christian Democrats (DC) and the Italian Communist Party (PCI), since the former found a political referent and support in the US and the latter in the Soviet Union. Linking the domestic political system to the international one created the impossibility to rule for the PCI, legitimized the Christian Democrats and crystalized their advantage (Panebianco 1977: 862–863). But the important presence of the PCI meant that "every general election became a referendum on whether Italy should stay in the Atlantic alliance and the EEC" (Varsori 2015: 293). To preserve the existing domestic political equilibria the pro-Western choice was presented as something that could not be debated, and public opinion was led to delegate foreign policy to the government or to international actors through a blank check (Panebianco 1977: 863 and 868). Italy internalized external constraints and externalized domestic constraints (Isernia 1996: 150), but in order not to jeopardize its domestic order it had to adopt a "low profile" and an inactive foreign policy style, minimizing the impact of the commitments it had entered (Isernia and Longo 2017: 116; Panebianco 1982; Pasquino 1974: 171).

Over time the parties that were allowed access to government increased, but their legitimation passed by their assent to the Western camp choice (Panebianco 1977: 867; Pasquino 1974: 166 and 171; Panebianco 1982: 19; Nuti 1999).[2] Eventually, also the PCI in the late 1960s and more explicitly in 1977, acquiesced to the pro-Western foreign policy choice, so bipartisan foreign policy priorities emerged (Brighi 2013: 106). The convergence process among Italian parties translated into a heterodox foreign policy exploiting all room for maneuvering that the Atlantic alliance allowed (Andreatta 2001: 48). At times several conflicting foreign policies could coexist and be pursued by different government members (Panebianco 1997: 232), resulting in difficult to reconcile positions: orthodox loyalty to the US, including a permissive presence of military bases and nuclear weapons on Italian soil, but also low military expenses, no involvement of Italian military troops abroad and close commercial and diplomatic relations with the Soviet Union (Andreatta 2008a: 204–205; Andreatta 2001: 49). Italian foreign policy oscillated continuously between full subordination and the search for autonomy from the US. Italian governments muddled through, at times finding selective elements of relative autonomy (especially in the Mediterranean area[3] but also in the relationship with the Soviet Union) and presenting Italy as a bridge or mediator between opposing instances in international politics, somehow accommodating existing domestic cleavages and intra-party divisions.

For the PCI the European integration process was more acceptable than the alliance with the US (Parsi 2011: 257), but initially the PCI opposed it too because of its strict association with the Atlantic choice. The European integration project was promoted by the US through the Marshall Plan, and it was a way for the Italian government to express its choice for the Western camp in favor of the American administration while gaining recognition from it (Varsori 2010: 38–42). The European choice was also a way for Italy to regain status, to redefine a new national identity following the melting down in World War II, and to create an external constraint to force the country into modernity and economic progress, legitimizing unpopular reforms that Italian elites were not strong enough to impose (Panebianco 1997: 247; Diodato and Niglia 2017; Varsori 2010: 405). It was such an important choice that it became part of the Italian constitution (Carlassare 2013: 12). It was also the foreign policy issue that created the least controversy among the Italian public (Varsori 2010: 416–417; Isernia 2008) especially since the 1980s, when leftist parties saw it as a sort of third way, more acceptable and therefore worth promoting.[4] This unanimous support continuously registered over time created a passive acceptance of the European integration process (Coralluzzo 1994 and 2000).

Convergence was possible also on multilateralism. This pillar of Italian foreign policy too is strictly related to the US and its choice to promote multilateral institutions after World War II (Attinà 2009; Brighi 2017; Caffarena and Gabusi 2017: 133–134; Ferraris 1998: 293; Ratti 2011; Romero 2016; Rosa 2016; Ruggie 1993). The main parties enshrined multilateralism in article 11 of the Italian constitution in the belief that supranational projects could help denationalize post-fascist Italy and avoid potential nationalist temptations (Mammarella and Cacace 2010: 146; Santoro 1991: 186).[5] For Italian decision makers multilateralism was also a way to be reaccepted by the international community and to play a role in the organization of the international system, a nonconfrontational way to gain status and to guarantee the anchorage of Italy to the West (Ratti 2011: 125).

The convergence trend transformed Italian foreign policy from a position issue to a valence issue (Isernia 1996: 157).[6] In the context of improvements at the international level in the relationship between the US and the USSR, in the 1980s this transformation allowed Italy to initiate a more active foreign policy, although legitimation from the UN remained indispensable for Italian military troops to intervene abroad (Panebianco 1997: 235).

The end of the Cold War was another turning point for Italian foreign policy, although not as defining as the previous one. The dramatic change at the international level was paralleled by a similarly dramatic change in the Italian domestic political system. Previously frozen political forces both in the extreme right and in the extreme left found new legitimacy (Hill and Andreatta 2001). The collapse or transformation of traditional parties and the emergence of new ones led toward a political system characterized by the alternation in government of two large but fragmented and fragile coalitions, center-left and center-right. Both coalitions adopted a pro-Western stance, but the high fragmentation of the Italian party system, with small parties capable of black boxing coalition governments, led to continuous risks of non-confidence votes. In such a context, foreign policy became relevant again as an intra-coalitional issue capable of threatening the existence of a government.

The more permissive international environment exposed Italian limits (Andreatta 2008a; Cladi and Webber 2011), but changes in the international context made the traditional inactive foreign policy style no longer sustainable (Isernia and Longo 2017: 118). Reacting to the presence of areas of instability in its neighborhood, Italian foreign policy became much more active, both in terms of presence in different areas and in the difficult domain of military interventions within multilateral frameworks. Italian governments also assertively engaged in reform processes of existing multilateral institutions to improve the Italian position within them. Elements of neo-nationalism resurfaced (Aliboni and Greco 1996). Europe became a partisan issue (Andreatta 2008b; Brighi 2006).

Multilateralism provided a legitimizing framework for the more assertive Italian foreign policy actions. Italy very actively contributed to peace operations and committed its troops abroad within—and under the cover of—multilateral frameworks (Attinà 2009; Ignazi et al. 2012), moving from the position of security consumer to the one of security provider (Walston 2007). A strategy of "active multilateralism," including proposals to adapt the existing international organizations and raise Italy's international profile within them (Hill and Andreatta 2001: 252), became at times opposed to a more opportunistic strategy of "effective multilateralism" (Brighi 2013: 132), but both strategies transpired pragmatism and assertiveness. Born together, the destiny of the US and Europe as pillars of Italian foreign policy seemed to diverge during the 1990s and even more the 2000s, but the divergence never became a zero-sum-game (Brighi 2007 and 2013; Croci 2008). The fundamental choices of Italian foreign policy were never called into question, but they were differently interpreted by center-left and center-right governments. The uncertainty divided scholars between those who denounced deep changes in Italian foreign policy (Ignazi 2004; Romano 2006; Walston 2007) and those who stressed elements of continuity and the holding of the traditional pillars (Croci 2005; Parsi 2011).

Foreign policy images and discourses were restructured (Brighi 2013: 131). The center-right espoused the idea that Italy could enjoy greater freedom to assert its national interest. This translated into the advancement of Italy's profile in international politics through active bilateralism and "effective multilateralism," a less deferential attitude toward the process of European integration and the strengthening of economic diplomacy. The center-left maintained the traditional anchoring to international frameworks, provided an international cover to Italian foreign policy and adopted a different set of policy guidelines: firm internationalism, "active multilateralism" and enhancement of Italy's profile and contributions in multilateral frameworks, and centrality of European integration for Italy's national interests (Brighi 2013: 133).

According to some scholars, the revolution in the Italian political system led to a significant instability that inhibited collaboration between the two confronting coalitions, because next to a general convergence on a pro-Western orientation and a higher military profile, there was also a more open dissent over foreign policy issues, with cleavages also running within parties (Andreatta 2001 and 2008b). Other scholars have argued that, despite appearances, Italian foreign policy has been characterized by bipartisanship on the most important choices involving national security, as attested by the parliamentary rescue of fragile majorities with opposition votes in several crucial instances (among them, the Operation Alba, the ratification of NATO enlargement, and participation in UNIFIL II), or by the bipartisan support—widening the existing majority—to ISAF in Afghanistan or to the post-Saddam Hussein stabilization mission in Iraq (Parsi 2011: 263–266; Walston 2004).

Following the financial crisis, in the 2010s, according to some scholars a post-ideological foreign policy has emerged (Brighi and Giugni 2016; Brighi 2017). Overall the gap between previously opposing coalitions and their alternative foreign policy visions has narrowed, and the competing coalitions have toned down their differences on the traditional pillars of Italian foreign policy, allowing Italy to remain faithful to its positioning within the Atlantic alliance, the EU, and the UN. The Italian government was at times vocal with the EU on the management of the economic and migration crises and on sanctions against Russia, but eventually never defected from the common European position.

The 2018 election led to the rise of a new coalition government made of the Five Star Movement (M5S) and the League,[7] both openly bringing more nationalist, Eurosceptical, and filo-Russian positions and promising radical changes in Italian foreign policy. Among the first foreign policy actions the new government has confirmed the pro-Atlanticist line and has explicitly excluded an Italian exit not just from the EU but also from the Eurozone. So far, the pro-Atlanticist line has been maintained, even at the cost of reversing positions expressed during the electoral campaign (among others, on the F35 program, the TAP in Apulia, and the MUOS in Sicily),[8] and the close relationship with President Trump has been in display.[9] The vehement Italian call for an end of sanctions against Russia has not led to defecting, in this showing continuity with previous governments. A loud anti-EU rhetoric has been in display especially in the first months of government, but eventually has been toned down, when the Italian government negotiated with the European Commission changes to the Italian 2019 budget. However, the government has openly distanced itself from its traditional partners in the EU, France, and Germany above all, and so far, the search for alternative European partners has proven unsuccessful. As for multilateralism, the first speech of the Italian Prime Minister at the UNGA was a mixture of support for effective multilateralism and the strengthening of the UN as a pillar of the international system, on the one hand, and sovereignism, on the other (Vaccara and Nobis 2018). However, in a reversal of a consolidated trend that had seen the country using its position as a top contributor to gain influence, Italy has reduced its financial contribution to the UN budget (*La Repubblica* 2018). It remains to be seen whether this mixture of continuity and change will affect the traditional pillars of Italian foreign policy.

The Italian attitude toward the use of force is another factor influencing Italian foreign policy that needs to be introduced (Rosa 2014, 2016, and 2018). The capitulation and the dramatic consequences of World War II led to the emergence of a strategic culture that rejected nationalism, unilateralism, and offensive strategies. Italy assumed strict limits to the use of force in its constitution, reorganized its armed forces based on a conscription army and, certain that its actual defense would have been guaranteed by the US, it rescaled its military-industrial complex. To distance itself from the fascist rule, it created self-justifying myths to promote the image of a country reluctant to fight (Rosa 2014; Rosa 2016: 70–73 and 77). All of this contributed to the stabilization of a nonmilitarized strategic culture that was widely shared and translated into an antiwar attitude and into the possibility of using military force only in a defensive or multilateral framework.

After the end of the Cold War, Italy became increasingly involved in international crises showing greater activism, and its armed forces moved from conscription to a professional army. Nevertheless, changes occurred "within the parameters determined by the strategic culture, sometimes pushing these parameters to their limits, but never breaking them" (Rosa 2016: 109). The Italian involvement in multilateral peacekeeping missions has increased (Attinà 2009; Rosa 2016), but the nonmilitarized strategic culture still transpires in the need to identify the military operations in which Italy has been involved as international policing or peace operations, and in the caveats and limitations in the use of force that are intentionally imposed (Ignazi et al. 2012; Rosa 2016). Important limits exist, among which the frequent hiding behind the multilateral institution that approved the mission rather than assuming political responsibility for the intervention (Coticchia 2013: 14). However, this is in line with the Italian idea that peacekeeping operations are intended as a contribution to reconstruction and pacification and with the Italian nonmilitarized strategic culture (Rosa 2016).

Some of the traditionally defining elements of Italian foreign policy have shown their limits over time. Established after World War II, at times they seem to play against each other. These elements are certainly influenced by the domestic processes previously described. But they are also the result of wider interconnected processes, including the evolution of the international hegemonic order and the process of foreign policy coordination at the European level, that exert an influence on domestic choices. The attempt here is to bring the variations emerged after the Cold War into a longer-term perspective and a wider context to see the interplay of processes that originated together but then occasionally diverged along the way. The focus on the 2000–2017 period—that is, when the crisis of the international hegemonic order and of the US authority within it became apparent—can help in understanding the contradictions exploded and the variations registered, but also the tensions to which Italy is exposed due to the significant variations in its bargaining environment.

The book unfolds in five chapters. In the first one, the object of study is introduced, and its functioning theorized. The chapter presents the theoretical framework and introduces Italy as a status-seeking middle power in a hegemonic world order and the Italian membership of both the US-led dominant coalition and the European formalized coalition. It focuses on changes in the Italian opportunity structure and theorizes coalition facilitation as a strategy used by Italy for system maintenance and status competition, and Europeanization as part of this strategy. Focusing on the importance of the evolution of political coalitions at the international level, it explains how structural changes may affect the bargaining environment of both the dominant coalition and the European formalized coalition. It then describes the most distinctive traits and processes of the Europeanization of Italian foreign policy.

In the second chapter, the object of study is located at the UN. It is explained why it is useful to explore the Europeanization of Italian foreign policy within this setting, and a methodological proposal to study Europeanization within the UN context is advanced. A specific focus on changes in the incentives and constraints for Italian foreign policy within the UN is present.

Because of the significant institutional differences between the General Assembly and the Security Council, the two organs are explored in separate chapters. Based on an original dataset of UNGA roll call votes in regular sessions and sponsoring activity built specifically for this study, the third chapter provides a quantitative analysis of Italian behavior (voting and sponsoring) in the UNGA in the period 2000–2017, and of Italy's capacity to be part of and maintain the European formalized coalition. It highlights not only variations in Italian behavior in relation to the EU majority, but also which EU member states are more or least likely to be in a coalition with Italy. It also explores whether the coalitions Italy forms are in support of or in opposition to the US and whether variations in the Italian coalitional behavior might include the search for alternative coalitions in the so-called BRIC countries (Brazil, Russia, India, and China). The chapter includes the analysis of two case studies of issues considered indicators of Europeanization in the literature to explore convergence (human rights) and divergence (disarmament and nuclear issues) in Italian behavior in respect to the majority position of EU member states.

The fourth chapter focuses on Italian behavior in the Security Council in the period 2000–2017 and explains how Italy plays the role of member of the European formalized coalition within that forum with a focus on the "split term" with the Netherlands in 2017, result of a competition between the countries, but presented as a sign of European unity. It presents both a quantitative analysis based on a dataset of Italian sponsoring and voting behavior in the UNSC built for this research, and case studies on issues on which: divergence with European coalition members was registered and uploading failed, but critical in the Italian quest for status (Security Council reform); Italy managed to upload its national interests successfully (Libya and Somalia); downloading took place on an issue relevant for the European identity (human rights).

The fifth chapter introduces the issue of crises in the EU and in the organization of the international system and of variations in the Italian domestic political system and assesses whether they have caused a de-Europeanization of Italian foreign policy in the most recent years of the analysis. The chapter identifies continuity in Italian behavior but also potential challenges due to changing incentives and constraints at the domestic, regional, and international levels.

In the conclusions it will be explained that under changing structural conditions it is becoming more difficult for Italy to interpret its traditional role.

This book has been in the making for quite some time, and as it is often the case, I am indebted to a large number of colleagues and friends. First of all, the whole group of the 2012 national research project on Italian foreign policy, and in particular Fulvio Attinà, Francesca Longo, and Pierangelo Isernia. Secondly, the research group on the impact of the economic and financial crisis on the de-Europeanization of the foreign policies of EU Mediterranean states, and in particular Stelios Stavridis. Thirdly, the group on the role of the US in the spatially fragmented contemporary international system and, in particular, Marco Clementi. Those research experiences contributed to developing some of the ideas that are now part of this book. I am grateful for their insightful comments to Andrea Locatelli, to all the discussants of the conferences at which parts of this book were presented, and to the anonymous referees who helped me to improve this book. I am particularly indebted to Laura Azzolina, who always made time to read the most difficult parts of this book and gave me the most helpful comments. This book is dedicated to my parents.

NOTES

1. The terms organization and order will be used interchangeably.
2. In the final period of the Cold War the socialist party (PSI) even tried to legitimize itself as the new guarantor of the Western position of Italy (Panebianco 1982: 14).
3. By some scholars considered among the pillars of Italian foreign policy (Santoro 1991).
4. As Varsori (2010: 418) puts it, it was the only foreign policy area on which all parties could agree even when strong tensions existed on other foreign policy issues.
5. Article 11 of the Italian constitution states: "Italy rejects war as an instrument of aggression against the freedom of other peoples and as a means for the settlement of international disputes. Italy agrees, on conditions of equality with other States, to the limitations of sovereignty that may be necessary to a world order ensuring peace and justice among the Nations. Italy promotes and encourages international organizations furthering such ends." See also Lugato (2013).
6. A position issue is one in which parties diverge on the most fundamental choices. A valence issue is one in which parties diverge on how to implement shared goals.
7. Previously Northern League.
8. The F35 program concerns the Italian commitment to produce and buy F35 military aircrafts, opposed because of its excessive costs and the fighting posture of the aircraft. TAP stands for Trans Adriatic Pipeline, a pipeline that will convey gas from the Caspian Sea to Europe through Apulia and is opposed because of its environmental impact. MUOS is part of a crucial US military satellite communication system and is opposed mostly because of health concerns.
9. The populist nature of both governments has been underlined and appreciated by Trump on several occasions (De Giovannangeli 2018).

Chapter One

The Europeanization of Italian Foreign Policy in the US-led World Order

ITALY IN A HIERARCHICAL WORLD ORDER

A Middle Power Searching for Status

The literature on Italian foreign policy concurs on the definition of Italy as a middle power searching for—when not obsessed by—status (Santoro 1991; Giacomello and Verbeek 2011; Hill 2011; Nuti 2011a; Romero 2016; Valigi 2017). Despite some weaknesses, Italy was a major power in the period 1860–1943,[1] but following capitulation in 1943 it lost status and ranking, and it is the only continuing state that has lost its status of major power permanently (Volgy et al. 2011: 5). According to Hill (2011: xii), this led Italy to start lamenting a disadvantaged position, betraying its difficulty to get over that defeat, and gave origin to two "collective neuroses": seeing international affairs through the lens of personal relations and image, and an obsession with rank evident in constant fear of exclusion. This neurosis became noticeable since the 1980s, when, thanks to its economic growth, the country became a leading industrial power. The rhetoric of Italy as a "great country" gained strength and the middle power foreign policy model consolidated, leading to a new international activism and to a greater military contribution to peacekeeping to enhance the country's voice in multilateral forums (Romero 2016).

Defining middle powers is controversial (Robertson 2017; Valigi 2017: 38–41), but over time the notion originally proposed by Cooper et al. (1993: 19) has prevailed and middle powers have been associated with pursuing multilateral compromises, engaging in acts of "good international citizenship," and promoting coalition building (Neack 2017). Middle powers are believed to display "a specific pattern of statecraft," as they all have displayed coalition-building and cooperation-building behaviors, entrepreneurial or technical leadership, and facilitator attitudes (Cooper 1997: 9). They are also believed to benefit from international institutions because it is there that middle powers can exert a greater bargaining power. International institutions provide "the most solid fulcrum and appropriate forum for middle power diplomacy" and for middle powers membership in the UN Security Council is an "institutional prize" (Henrikson 1997: 47 and 53).

Because narrative on middle powers emerged in a period in which the organization of the international political system combined US hegemonic role with multilateralism, and since then a growth in the number of multilateral institutions has been registered, and because within multilateral institutions middle powers can create coalitions that allow them to multiply their force, over time middle powers became more and more associated with multilateral institutions (Neak 2017). In the current international system states that have traditionally been defined middle powers have supported the US hegemonic order and the Western political vision of stability, taking the lead in system maintenance activities such as coalition building, mediation, facilitation, and peacekeeping to support the order (Neack 1995 and 2014).

These activities are useful to gain or to keep status, which confers additional influence internationally and additional support domestically (Volgy et al. 2011: 10). Welch Larson et al. (2014: 7) define status as "collective beliefs about a state's ranking on valued attributes," highlighting that it transcends individual state perceptions, it is subjective in that it depends on others' perceptions that manifest it through voluntary deference, and it is measured relative to other states. They also point out that it is socially scarce, hence competition for status in a hierarchical social system. But some status markers exist, among which membership in elite clubs (such as the G7 or G20), permanent membership of the Security Council, and leadership positions in international organizations.

That status is not just positional and relational but also socially attributed is evident within international institutions, which should be considered as *"arenas in which states strive for status"* (Welch Larson et al. 2014: 23). Partnership in multilateral organizations is one of the preferred avenues to look for status attribution (Volgy et al. 2011). Moreover, status attribution is associated with compliance with existing uncontested international norms, among which multilateralism (Miller et al. 2015). As pointed out by Wohlforth et al. (2018), in a hegemonic order, support to the hegemon and to the hegemonic system and even more support to the orderly maintenance of the system, particularly in the field of peace and security, allows to be perceived as a "good power" and therefore to be distinguished from other smaller powers. As

Giacomello and Verbeek (2011: 18) put it, it provides "middle power credit points." So, a competition on getting status through system maintenance activities is particularly evident in multilateral settings that originated with the hegemonic order. Status is associated with the adoption of fundamental values, so status-seeking behavior can result in cooperative behavior contributing to the maintenance of the international order (Duque 2018: 13), but also international engagement in activities such as mediation and peacekeeping can help status seeking states to occupy a more central position in networks of diplomatic and alliance relationships (Baxter et al. 2018). The possibility of advancing actions that increase the status of a country might vary over time as status is also related to domestic identity, global norms, and international systemic pressures (Wohlforth et al. 2018: 536).

Despite no longer being a major power and despite its limited capabilities, Italy has a high status for a middle power (Duque 2018: 7). Applying the findings on middle powers and status to the Italian case suggests that reasons pertaining to the international political system were relevant in the main foreign policy choices of Italy since the end of World War II and that the three pillars of Italian foreign policy are all in line with what is to be expected from a middle power trying to gain leverage within and through institutions. As Giacomello and Verbeek (2011) note, Italy's role as a founding member of the European communities and a major engine of European integration bolstered the country's self-esteem. The loss of status experienced over time with the accession of other important players in the EU was somehow compensated through its membership in the G7, and then, over time, the G20. More importantly, the increasing role of international institutions in the post–Cold War period tied nicely with what was by then an established Italian strategy: gaining influence through multilateralism (Giacomello and Verbeek 2011: 23). A strategy that suits middle powers well (Wohlforth et al. 2018: 533; Cooper et al. 1993; Ravenhill 1998: 312).

Looking at Italian foreign policy only as a status-seeking middle power, however, provides us with a static picture that does not fully explain variations that have occurred over time in the weight accorded to the three pillars, and more generally in the style of foreign policy adopted by this specific middle power especially since the end of the Cold War. It leaves unexplained why since the end of the Cold War Italy has adopted a more active foreign policy but has also expressed meaningful variations in the European and multilateral pillars of its traditional foreign policy, without ever renouncing to them. The literature on middle power and status tends to strictly connect them to the existence of a specific hierarchical order (the US-led one) and to its specific institutional structure (based on multilateral institutions). This aspect is explored by the hegemonic theories of international relations.

On Hegemonic Theories

The changes in the foreign policy choices of Italy as a status-seeking middle power have been influenced by the evolution of the hierarchical world order emerged after World War II and by the role that Italy has played within it.[2] Attention to hierarchies and hierarchical relationships (Bially Mattern and Zarakol 2016; Zarakol 2017) has brought attention on the authority contracts that states can create and that allow the dominant state to provide a political order that is valued by the subordinate states in exchange for their subordination and legitimacy (Lake 2009 and 2017). Subordinate states benefit from political order because their security and territorial integrity are enhanced, the transaction costs of international exchanges are reduced, and general standards of international behavior are defined and enforced (Lake 2009: 8–9). The security guarantee of the dominant state also favors domestic leaders of the subordinate state over internal challengers (Lake 2013; McDonald 2015).

Hegemonic orders embody hierarchical relations and are associated with the existence of a single state with extraordinary capabilities that controls or leads less powerful states thanks to its capacity to dominate the rules and agreements through which relations among states are conducted (Gilpin 1981; Goldstein 1988: 281; for a review Norloff 2017). The hegemon has the will and capacity to impose its preferences thanks to its coercive capabilities, but also to its capacity to produce satisfaction and approval, normally through the provision of public goods. It creates social structures and international institutions that, reflecting its interests and ideology, also amplify its power.

Some regularities or patterns have been highlighted in the hegemonic cycle. For Gilpin (1981) a great power is legitimated to rule based on its victory in the previous hegemonic war, during which the dominant state(s) and the challenger(s) and their respective supporting states clash. The war adjusts the system to the new distribution of power and determines who will rule and whose interests will be served by the international order. Over time, the growth in number and strength of potential rivals forces the hegemon to spend more to maintain its position, while revenues generated by the system decrease. At this stage, the costs for the hegemon of maintaining the status quo override the benefits deriving from the hegemonic order, leading the dominant power to political and economic decline, and weakening the foundations of the order. The resulting disequilibrium forces the hegemon to increase the resources destined to system maintenance or reduce its commitments and decreases the potential cost of system change for challengers. The principal mechanism of change in history has been a hegemonic war. The US after World War II imposed Pax Americana, but signs of decline were already evident in the 1980s.

For Gilpin (1981) the distribution of power among competing coalitions decides who will govern the international system and whose interests will be favored. A preponderant weight is attributed to military coalitions and to the collective mobilization of military resources, because the right to rule depends on victory in a hegemonic war and the constituted order remains stable only as long as the distribution of power does not change. This may only partly apply to the Italian case, because Italy sided with the US only after 1943 and it came out from World War II as a loser, it was never treated as an ally, as it became evident when the peace treaty was signed. Moreover, Italy emerged devastated from World War II and with very limited military capabilities that made of it an unpalatable military partner for the US, and, also because of its strategic culture, once it could, it rejected requests for a military rearmament, delegating its defense to the American ally, and preferred to invest its limited resources in its economic reconstruction (Mammarella and Cacace 2010: 178 and 189). Italy could be useful for installing military bases more than for its own military contribution, but that was not an imperative strategic need for the US (Nuti 1993a and 1993b). Finally, Italy could not be fully relied on, because to keep its fragile domestic order it could only enter into inconsequential commitments (Isernia and Longo 2017: 116).

More relevant for the Italian case is the political role that coalitions supporting a hegemonic order can play, on which more emphasis is placed by global leadership theorists (Modelski 1987, 1990, 1999, and 2008; Modelski and Thompson 1999; Thompson 2001; Attinà 2008 and 2011). The global leader (or hegemon) is selected through a systemic, collective process occurring in political cycles, each of which goes through four phases.[3] During the agenda-setting or delegitimation phase some characteristics of the international order and of the global leadership are contested. New problems and dissatisfaction toward the old alignments rise to prominence. During the coalition-building or de-concentration phase the global leader is weakened and multipolarity emerges. Established coalitions are reshuffled, flexibility of alignments emerges, and the alliance systems are restructured around defense versus opposition to the existing global order. During the macrodecision or global war phase at least two coalitions, each bringing its own rival political agenda, clash to decide which agenda should be executed and the leadership composition for the following "term of office." During the execution or global power phase, the winner of the previous phase, whose weight and influence are unquestioned, together with its dominant coalition creates an institutional structure more responsive to the needs of the global system, and the post-war settlement can help to mold an order (Modelski 1999: 20).

According to global leadership theorists, the current is an American cycle. The execution or global power phase lasted from 1945 until approximately

1973, and in this phase the US was at the peak of its power and legitimacy. The agenda setting or delegitimation phase lasted approximately from 1973 until 2000 and saw the Europeans openly dissociate themselves from the Americans on some issues, while new states emerged from the decolonization process started challenging elements of the order. The current period is a phase of coalition-building or deconcentration and has seen the appearance of the so-called rising powers asking for reforms of the current institutions to accommodate their newly gained influence. This phase is expected to last until the next decade, when it will be followed by a macrodecision phase. While in the past macrodecision has taken the form of a generation long global war, this should not necessarily be the case for the next selection, because the evolution of world politics is deeply influenced by ongoing global processes such as the information revolution, the diffusion of a global economy, the dissemination of democratic practices, and the emerging of a world public opinion (Modelski and Thompson 1999; Modelski and Perry 2002; Thompson and Zakhirova 2017).

The global leader is expected to create institutional structures that innovate on previous ones and are responsive to global problems and processes. New forms of global institutions whose agenda is centered on building a democratic base for global governance have gradually been introduced.[4] Emerged in the ninth century, the diffusion and widespread acceptance of multilateral institutions are strictly connected to the US-led order (Ruggie 1993). Multilateral institutions have become forums in which the global leader and its potential challengers compete for support. The spread of a rule-based order and of multilateral practices is promoting long-term changes toward a democratic order, but the international system is not democratic yet (Modelski 2008). In the processes leading to structural changes and aimed at finding organizational and institutional forms that are more responsive to global problems coalitions are crucial: they support the global leader and recognize its political organization and authority as legitimate, or they oppose the global leader and its organization and propose alternatives. Not all states comply with and legitimize the government structure of the global political system in the same way, so they assume different systemic roles in the global political competition: leader, allied of the leader, free rider, opponent, and challenger (Attinà 2009: 11 and 13). The interpretation of these roles may vary over time, subject to structural changes, but global coalition theorists have devoted little attention to processes of coalition formation and variation, and to the role that individual countries could play within them.

Ikenberry (1998, 2001, 2011, 2015a, and 2015b; Ikenberry and Kupchan 1990) has concentrated on the post-1945 US-led hegemonic order and has underlined its coalition-based character. According to Ikenberry (2001), the organization of the international political system emerged at the end of World War II and promoted by the US with the support of its main Western allies represented an innovation in that it promoted American interests and values but, to link other states to the order, it was based on leadership sharing, a system of rules and multilateral institutions of a universal type (the UN, the IMF, the World Bank, the GATT) that introduced voluntary restraints and made the hegemon's behavior more restrained and therefore more acceptable. This gave a constitutional character to the US-led international order. The settlement was remarkable in the use of multilateral institutions linking Americans and Europeans. As Ikenberry (2001: 165) notes, "European integration and reconstruction became the critical component of securing a wider open multilateral order." The greatest American fear was European weakness, that could lead to communist European governments, but the Europeans could only accept a stronger Germany within a wider and more integrated Europe strictly linked to the US (Ikenberry 2001: 165–166). For the State Department it was also important to strengthen the ideological Western orientation of European leaders and only European unity appeared suitable to do that, so the US started pushing for a united and more economically integrated Europe. The Marshall Plan was administered in a way that would promote European unity (Ikenberry 2001: 180–183) and European countries accepted European integration and German remilitarization in exchange for American engagement and institutional moderation (Ikenberry 2001: 212).

Ikenberry (2011) stresses the liberal character of the US-led hegemonic order and the importance of the support it received from a coalition of Western democracies. With its expansion from the Western world where it was built to a global level after the end of the Cold War, but especially in the 2000s, the international liberal order entered a crisis of authority. The emergence of the so-called rising powers, the financial crisis, and the disputes with the European allies over American unipolar ambitions are all signs of the ongoing crisis. The old order may be staying, but its governance may change. The coalition of Western liberal democratic states that has supported the US-led order so far and that is the ultimate guardian of rules, institutions, and values of the order is no longer enough (Ikenberry 2011: 136). Moreover, in the 2000s the Bush administration and now the current Trump administration seem to challenge the fundamental characters of this order through the promotion of unilateralism and of ad hoc coalitions of the willing. For Ikenberry it is politically important that states coalesce to legitimate and support the hegemonic order both during its foundation and when it enters a crisis. In this case too, however, how coalitions vary remains unexplained.

The importance of ideological support to the hegemonic order is emphasized by Cox (1983 and 1992). Building on Gramsci, Cox notes that what characterizes the hegemon is not its dominance, but its capacity to build a structure of values and understandings about the nature of order that is perceived as relatively stable and unquestioned and appears as the natural order.[5] This order is underpinned by a structure of power, but the dominance in itself is not sufficient to create hegemony: hegemony needs to be legitimized through social practices and ideologies. Supporting states are therefore crucial because they share the hegemon's social practices and ideology.[6]

The hegemonic theories mentioned concur on indicating that the hierarchical order built by the US with the support of its allies at the end of World War II is now weakened.[7] Next to the material dimension, the political and ideological dimensions are highlighted. Even when the hegemon is at the peak of its power, hegemony is not mere dominance by one state over the others, because it needs to be legitimized by the subordinate states. Hegemony is therefore a relational concept and the hegemonic order is a collective enterprise. The coalition's support and legitimation of the order and of the authority of the hegemon is a crucial element of the order. Support and legitimation vary over time, subject to structural changes. All the above-mentioned hegemonic theorists would concur on the description of the period 1945–1960s as the one in which the strength of the US and of its hegemonic order was at the apex, and on the post-Cold War period, especially since the 2000s, as a period of crisis. Even the so-called unipolar moment is a sign of the crisis of the US-led hegemonic order, because hegemony is not dominance, so when dominance prevails, the hegemon loses support, and this creates the conditions for the weakening of its authority (Ikenberry 2011). But the hegemon's willingness to lead is important too, and the reduction of gains determined over time by structural variations can cause strains with subordinate countries, asked to contribute more to the order maintenance. However, how coalitions supporting the hegemonic order vary over time, has not received much attention.

Italy and the EU Member States in the Hegemonic Order

The political and ideological support provided by Italy as a coalition member to the US-led hegemonic order is a function of the role that Italy plays within that order and of its collocation within the government structure of the global political system (Attinà 2009: 4). The crisis of that order and structural variations within coalitions especially evident after the 2000s can affect variations in the foreign policy of coalition members.

In the post-World War II organization, the US combined its hegemonic role with multilateral institutions that allowed it to share transactional costs and give the structure greater stability (Attinà 2011: 97). The UN, the IMF, the World Bank, and the GATT were all quintessential to the US-led hegemonic organization. Once established, multilateral institutions introduced formal procedures in the government of the global political system, transforming the hierarchical order into an institution-based leadership organization (Attinà 2008: 125).[8] Within this organization, the US benefitted from the material and political support of its Western European allies and promoted the European integration process as a strategy to strengthen the hegemonic order by diminishing potential conflicts among them and increasing their potential contribution to its maintenance. The US and its Western European allies created a very cohesive dominant coalition capable of controlling the decision-making processes of the main multilateral institutions despite Soviet opposition. The European integration process was part of the order and led initially reluctant countries to institutionalize their relations and share their functional sovereignty in some areas, while favoring an economic growth that was needed domestically to legitimize the ruling political elites and internationally to legitimize the US-led order and contribute to it.

Over time, divergences between Americans and Europeans arose. The US had a harder time controlling multilateral institutions' decision-making processes and hegemonizing them, something that became particularly evident in the UNGA. Occasionally the US has played the role of great power more than the one of hegemon (Cronin 2001) and role tensions have reverberated on the organization of the international political system.[9] The end of the Cold War exposed this tension more than in the past, as the emergence in the US of parochial groups and veto players opposing multilateralism became obstacles to American engagement within multilateral institutions and the US started showing greater inclination toward unilateralism or minilateral solutions (Skidmore 2005 and 2012; Patrick 2014 and 2015). The European integration process, on the contrary, led to a further deepening of the institutionalization process that highlighted the importance of multilateralism and multilateral institutions for EU member states. In the 1970s their foreign policies started being coordinated, initially loosely and then in a more systematic way, leading to a progressive Europeanization of the foreign policies of EU member states that translated into their capability to act more often as a bloc within multilateral institutions, but also to occasionally become competitors of the US especially on economic matters. Within the GATT and then the WTO, negotiation rounds started being structured around competing positions between the US and the EU. At the UN, the distance between Americans and Europeans (on the Middle East above all) grew over time and was in evidence on occasion of the 2003 US invasion of Iraq, when France and Germany strongly opposed the US decision. Transatlantic rifts on security issues became more frequent, spurring a growing literature on the end of transatlantic relations and therefore of the West (Kagan 2003; Cox 2005). The limits of the EU were also exposed, as its member states, torn between European institutionalized solidarity and political allegiance to the US, had troubles finding a common position.

The 2007 financial crisis and the emergence of the so-called rising powers (Brazil, Russia, India, and China—also known as BRIC) exposed further limitations in the capacity of the US-led hegemonic order to hold and adapt to the ongoing power shift, eventually adjusting to emerging instances of fragmentation (Clementi et al. 2018; Stephen 2014 and 2017). Not only the BRICs started asking to be more influential, especially after the financial crisis, leading to (limited) reforms of some of the universal multilateral institutions, but their dissatisfaction with the results led to the creation of regional organizations (such as the Asian Infrastructure Investment Bank and the New Development Bank) indicating a potential regional fragmentation of the international order. While some scholars minimize the contestation element of the new institutions (Brooks and Wohlforth 2016; Ikenberry 2015a and 2015b), others believe that they represent a challenge to the existing pecking order (Kupchan 2012) and a sign of the increasing fragmentation of the international order (Barma et al. 2007, 2013, and 2014) and that we already live in a decentered, complex, and multidimensional world (Acharya 2014). Limitations in the capacity of the dominant coalition to hold emerged when Brexit, the financial crisis and the migration crisis hit the European integration process and the Trump administration started identifying the EU as "a foe" on trade and forcefully calling for NATO allies to increase their contribution (CBS News 2018).

By choosing the alliance with the US as the first pillar of its foreign policy after World War II, Italy played the role of the allied actor of the world government leader not only because it entered into the North Atlantic Pact, and later into NATO, but also because it chose to be a member of the Western dominant coalition and to back the US-led organization of the world system (Attinà 2009). Though initially a marginal one, Italy's role within the Western coalition increased over time thanks to the loyal relationship with the coalition leader and the incremental contribution of Italian governments to the preservation of the world system organization. Although domestic reasons were certainly relevant, the choice of multilateralism and European integration was also a way for Italy to legitimize and support the world political organization promoted by the US and the dominant coalition, of which it wanted to be part. Over time, Italy increased its contribution to system maintenance not so much in relation to the military alliance, where it contributed through the concession of its soil for American military basing (Monteleone 2007; Nuti 2011a), but mostly through its activities in support of the European integration project and of multilateral institutions. Despite its efforts, Italy was not a big contributor in material and financial resources (Coralluzzo 2000; Tosi 2010), but its political support to the institutions was important. When occasional tensions and disagreements within the dominant coalition arose, Italy always preferred to side with the US (Nuti 2003).

With the end of the Cold War, the Italian contribution to multilateralism intensified and became more effective. The size of the Italian participation to UN peacekeeping operations increased, leading the country to be among the top contributors, and many energies were spent to support the Italian proposal for the reform of the Security Council. Additionally, as the European integration process progressed, and EU member states started coordinating their voting behavior within the UN, Italy proved to be responsive, regularly being in the majority coalition in the 1990s. It did so even when EU countries' voting cohesion started decreasing and despite the greater freedom of maneuver and possibility of assertiveness provided by the end of the Cold War (Laatikainen and Smith 2006a: 11; Luif 2003). However, disagreements between the US and Europe emerged more often, and the different policy lines adopted by the Berlusconi and Prodi governments are an indication of the loss of strength and cohesiveness of the dominant coalition.

After 2001, the tensions between Americans and Europeans within the dominant coalition experienced in the previous phase became more acute, with divergences materializing in various forms. While keeping the traditional pillars of Italian foreign policy, variations in their relative weight have emerged, and a growing distance between Italy and its main traditional allies has become apparent. In this period, it has also more clearly emerged a self-ascribed role that has traditionally characterized Italian foreign policy: the role of mediator (Caffarena and Gabusi 2017) or coalition-builder or, as we will call it here from now on, facilitator. Indeed, the worsening of tensions after 2001 has increased the possibility for the country to play this role, eventually enhancing it. Italy has played this role, for instance, in relation to tensions between the West and Russia, Israel and Palestine, Iran and the West, in a way that is consonant to a more general vision of this self-ascribed role particularly relevant in a context of fraying alliances (Caffarena and Gabusi 2017: 138).

The role of facilitator has been a traditional trademark for Italy (Varsori 2010: 42 and 71; Foradori and Rosa 2008: 184). As already seen, it is a consonant role for a middle power, one that, especially when played within multilateral institutions to perform system maintenance functions, has traditionally provided greater leverage, and led to status gains, another goal of Italian foreign policy. If the two preferred avenues to collective status recognition have traditionally been assertive foreign policy moves and partnership in multilateral organizations (Corbetta et al. 2011), the former option was precluded to Italy because of its relatively scarce resources and even more because of its strategic culture, while the latter option was consonant to both. Moreover, Italy had to compete with the other middle powers supporting the US-led hegemonic order in its quest for status, but during the Cold War it could not do it in a way that altered its domestic order and the separation between domestic politics and foreign policy, and after the Cold War it could not guarantee greater bargaining credibility due to the need of Italian governments to rely on help from the opposition in Parliament on major foreign policy issues.

It is here proposed that, as EU member states furthered the European integration process and progressively institutionalized their foreign policy cooperation, the Europeanization of Italian foreign policy, that is the progressive coordination with the other EU member states and adaptation of its foreign policy in order to be part of and be seen as acting with the rest of EU states or at least its majority group, became a strategy that Italy adopted to gain an advantage in its competition for status with other middle powers. Acting with other EU member states gave the country the possibility of exploiting the leverage that the support of a coalition provides within multilateral institutions and Italy used this leverage to be more effective in its support to the US-led hegemonic order. This strategy gave Italy high visibility, provided the country with the possibility to play this niche role consistently with its identity and strategic culture, and increased Italy's structural opportunities and status. Furthermore, Italy had the opportunity to delegate the most politically sensitive foreign policy decisions to an external actor (in this case the EU or the European allies) and to internalize an external constraint, bypassing domestic controversies. The politics of scale, which is inherent to a Europeanized foreign policy, has progressively allowed the country to amplify its weight and to increase its activism. However, as EU member states have progressively institutionalized their coordination and Europeanized their foreign policies, they have also been socialized to acting as a group.

THE EUROPEANIZATION OF FOREIGN POLICY

On Europeanization

The Italian case has been taken as an example of Europeanization (Rosa 2003) and, more recently, de-Europeanization (Brighi 2011) and incremental Europeanization with signs of renationalization (Dobrescu et al. 2017). The contradictory results are evidence of the methodological challenges that analyzing Europeanization in the case of foreign policy carries. Among the mechanisms that have been identified to explain the Europeanization of

Italian foreign policy, the idea of belonging to a group, the possibility of exploiting the European network for a projection beyond Italy's capabilities (politics of scale), and the creation of a new opportunity structure play a key role. However, the recurring crises in the EU have shaken the idea of European solidarity at the very basis of the existence of a group and have reduced resources to play an active role. This could potentially drive Italian foreign policy in conflicting directions.

The many existing definitions of Europeanization are evidence of the difficulty in conceptualizing and identifying indicators for such a process.[10] Over time, Europeanization has become associated both with a bottom-up process of institution formation and governance structure, and with a top-down process of influence of the new European institutions on the national and subnational level of EU member states (Radaelli 2003; Risse et al. 2001). Europeanization is a process that does not necessarily lead to policy convergence, but convergence can be a consequence of Europeanization (Radaelli 2003: 33). Both the logic of consequences and the logic of appropriateness are followed in the Europeanization process: EU member states see Europeanization as "an emerging political opportunity structure which offers some actors additional resources to exert influence" (Börzel and Risse 2003: 63), but they are also "guided by collective understandings of what constitutes proper, that is socially accepted behavior in a given rule structure" and strive to fulfill social expectations (Börzel and Risse 2003: 65–66). Uncertainty about preferences or strategy options might make EU states more likely to follow the logic of appropriateness, while well-defined preferences and strategy options might make the logic of consequences prevail (Börzel and Risse 2003: 74).

Due to its specificity doubts have been cast as to whether it is possible to talk about Europeanization processes in the foreign policy field at all. This is the area that traditionally characterizes states and their sovereignty, the one that states have never fully delegated to a supranational body. Not surprisingly, the EU decision-making mechanisms chosen in this field have always been within the tradition of intergovernmentalism: EU member states are always fully responsible for making the decision. Europeanization has also been applied to the foreign policy field, because, as noted by Major (2005: 182), "would not Europeanisation in such a sensitive area as foreign and security policy be the ultimate sign of a growing penetration of the European dimension into the national arena?" However, the analysis of the Europeanization of foreign policy has a different take than the literature on the Europeanization of other policies, ending up in a category of its own.

As Featherstone (2003: 10) notes, the use of the term Europeanization by International Relations scholars has reflected the evolution of EU foreign policy coordination, that is, the construction of new methods of governance and of the EU as an international actor as well as the reorientation of the foreign policies of the member states especially after the coordination input provided by the European Political Cooperation (EPC) in the 1970s and later by the Common Foreign and Security Policy (CFSP). Manners and Whitman (2000) have explored how through EU membership states adapt their foreign policy and whether the EU is a constriction on their choices or an opportunity to amplify their actions. Their comparative analysis of 14 EU member states concluded that it is no longer possible to analyze the foreign policy of an EU member state without considering the impact of and adaptation to the EU (Manners and Whitman 2000; see also White 2001; Larsen 2009).

Analysis of the Europeanization of foreign policy has betrayed that the term has been used to refer to national adaptation, as well as to national projection, identity reconstruction, modernization, and isomorphism (Wong 2005). Tonra's seminal definition (2000: 229) of Europeanization as "a transformation in the way in which national foreign policies are constructed, in the way in which professional roles are defined and pursued and in the consequent internalization of norms and expectations arising from a complex system of collective European policy making" opened the way to this field of study and indicated the importance of a broader understanding of adaptational pressures. It has been noted that, despite the lack of enforcement mechanisms, since the time of the EPC an increasingly binding set of behavioral standards has emerged, and norms of behavior have been progressively reinforced (Ginsberg 2001; Tonra 2003; Major 2005). The presence of alterations in the opportunity structure for domestic actors that the EU provides points to the existence of a causal link (Ladrech 2000: 190).

In Tonra's analysis (2000), policy makers value the international weight and higher profile that EU membership provides, because it confers greater influence on, and access to, otherwise inaccessible decision-makers in third countries and institutions. They also acknowledge that the access to an otherwise more limited wealth of shared information that EU membership provides has an impact on national foreign policy discussions. Moreover, the mere existence of the common policy makes its presence felt because decision makers know that they must take it into account and prepare for it, and because the foreign policy agenda itself is influenced and broadened by participation in EU level decision-making processes, while a degree of collective identification develops. This creates habits of taking into consideration the views of European partners in the national formulation of foreign policy.[11] While these developments do not eliminate national concerns and interests, their definition goes through a process that takes into account interactions at the European level, because a substantial portion of national foreign policy is now formulated through a European context and national and European interests are not perceived as a zero-sum game, but they are defined together as a result of a collective identification (Tonra 2000: 231). Indeed, several analyses have pointed out that national officials in Brussels have been socialized, becoming more European and displaying a coordination reflex (Wong and Hill 2011: 10).

In successive works, Tonra (2001) remarked the existence of a learning process. Besides the automatic reflex of consultation with European partners before defining national positions, participation to a common process leads to the habit of thinking in terms of consensus, that translates into a psychological process of narrowing differences, and to a European reflex, that is the internalization of the practice of defining a national position not independently but in relation to others' expectations. Through participation in the European foreign policy decision-making process, decision makers change the formulation and outputs of national foreign policies. However, Europeanization should not be confused with the homogenization of the foreign policies of the member states or with convergence to a single EU point, as varying paths of adaptation might exist (Tonra 2015: 188).

While it is generally acknowledged that national foreign policies of EU member states have been transformed, some methodological issues in relation to Europeanization have been raised. As Tonra (2015) reconstructs, Europeanization has been studied as both an independent and a dependent variable. At the same time, it is the specific nature of this field that makes a case for some distinctions. National decision makers are not adapting to a hierarchical order, but out of a system of informal information sharing they have progressively changed their attitudes and preferences to adapt to a corporate body of European values and norms that has developed over time (Ginsberg 2001: 38). At the same time, the two logics of consequences and appropriateness identified in the general literature on Europeanization have been present in the field of foreign policy as well. Scholars highlighting the presence of a rationalist logic point out that, following the logic of consequences, the evaluation of costs and benefits by the state will determine the degree of their foreign policy adaptation or exploitation of the common EU structures. The strategic calculation that common European action will maximize a state's foreign policy preferences or help a state reach a goal is a form of Europeanization, although arguably a thin one, and may lead to a variety of actions and strategies to make sure that the European structures are involved in national foreign policy making (Moumoutzis 2011: 617; Tonra 2015: 189). Scholars highlighting a logic of appropriateness in Europeanization will focus on mechanisms of socialization and learning, with the goal of identifying EU-level practices, procedures, and norms that can be related to changes in national foreign policy (Moumoutzis 2011; Tonra 2015: 189).

Within the last strand, despite acknowledging serious methodological difficulties inherent to the analysis of Europeanization in the field of foreign policy, and particularly to the detection of causality relations (Major 2005; Moumoutzis 2011), mechanisms typical of horizontal Europeanization have been identified. Major (2005) stresses that Europeanization is a process of constant and gradual transformation in which misfit and vertical pressure do not apply. On the contrary, the process of transformation at the domestic level is voluntary and non-hierarchical, and it is useful to take into consideration, when analyzing it, also the domestic and the international levels to properly isolate the impact of Europeanization. Major points out that Europeanization is also a way to rescue the nation state, in that it is a process through which states multiply their power and influence on the international scene to cope with their challenges, be they coping with their decline or, more relevant for the Italian case, overcoming their past. According to Moumoutzis (2011: 608 and 625), Europeanization takes place because of the choice of national policy makers to incorporate EU norms, practices, and procedures either because they believe that it is appropriate within the EU context or because they believe it is in their interest to do so. However, to identify cooperation as an observable implication of Europeanization, especially if associated with the socialization logic, expressed through the coordination reflex, this should be pursued consistently, across issues, and over time. Alecu de Flers and Müller (2012), suggest that both policy projection and policy adaptation are indicators of Europeanization, although of different dimensions, and domestic factors such as the size of the EU member state, the extent of its foreign relations network, its national identity, and strategic culture influence national Europeanization experiences. They also underline that Europeanization is not an irreversible process and de-Europeanization is always possible.

Other methodological problems have been identified in the heavy reliance of this kind of research on interviews with national officials in Brussels, who might be potentially biased in favor of Europeanization, in the limited number of studies testing the longitudinal impact of the EU on national foreign policies on a sufficiently long number of years, and in the difficulty of controlling for other causal variables deriving from the international level (Wong and Hill 2011: 11–13).

Another important methodological issue is related to convergence as an outcome. Indeed, while Europeanization per se is not expected to lead to convergence, it is in this specific policy field, where the possibility of politics of scale (Ginsberg 1989) for states that have lost their prominence and the *réflexe communautaire* push in that direction, although not irreversibly (Wong 2005). Europeanization is therefore expected to lead to a process of interests and identity convergence that will bring European interests and identity to exist alongside national interests and identities, co-shaping national policies (Wong and Hill 2011: 2). Europeanization manifests itself as policy convergence and as national policies amplified through EU policies (Wong and Hill 2011: 4), although in some cases convergence has been found to be superficial and more procedural than substantive (Tsardanidis and Stavridis 2005).

While methodological contributions have highlighted the many problems and difficulties in the analysis of the Europeanization of foreign policy, even the scholars that are most critical of the use made so far of Europeanization in this policy area point out that, when incorporated into national foreign policy, substantive EU foreign policy norms can change national foreign policy goals, EU practices can change national policy instruments and their use, and procedural EU foreign policy norms can affect the national foreign policymaking process and even the actors involved (Moumoutzis 2011: 619).[12] In this respect, the Europeanization approach indicates the existence of a *negotiated* convergence and of a policy reorientation (Wong and Hill 2011: 12).

Processes and Modes

Several attempts have been made at identifying factors and conditions facilitating or impeding Europeanization, but so far, they have not been systematically operationalized (Tonra 2015: 190). Smith (2000) proposed to look at: 1) élite socialization; 2) bureaucratic reorganization; 3) constitutional change; and 4) the increase in public support for European foreign policy. Looking just at domestic adaptation, however, risks ignoring other dimensions and processes of Europeanization. More recently, three processes or dimensions of the Europeanization of foreign policy have been identified (Wong and Hill 2011). The first, called downloading, can proceed top-down and refers to "changes in national foreign policies caused by participation over time in foreign policymaking at the European level" (Hill and Wong 2011: 4). The focus is on EU member states' adaptation to EU demands and cross-national policy convergence is expected over time, as members harmonize to adapt to EU needs. Wong and Hill (2011: 7) identify as indicators of this adaptation the increasing salience of the European political agenda to the EU member states, their adherence to common objectives, the priority they accord to common policy obligations, their internalization of EU membership, and the organizational and procedural changes in national bureaucracies in response to EU demands.

The second process, named uploading, proceeds bottom-up and refers to "the projection of national preferences, ideas and policy models onto the level of the European Union" (Wong and Hill 2011: 4). The focus is on the capacity of EU member states to project from the national to the EU level and it can be detected looking at states' attempts to increase their national weight, to influence the foreign policies of other member states, to use the EU as a cover or to use the EU level as an influence multiplier (Wong and Hill 2011: 7).

The third process, called cross-loading, proceeds in a bi-directional way, and refers to "a negotiated convergence in terms of policy goals, preferences and even identity between the national and the supranational levels" (Wong and Hill 2011: 4). This is expected to lead to a process of interest and identity convergence and to convert into the attempt to find a middle position and to promote common EU interests. Indicators of cross-loading in national foreign policies have been identified in the emergence of shared norms and values among elites regarding international politics, in shared definitions of European and national interests, and in the coordination reflex and pendulum effect, that is, the reconciliation of the more extreme positions via interactions at the bilateral or EU level (Wong and Hill 2011: 7).

According to Wong and Hill (2011: 12) Europeanization should not be seen as a movement toward coordination and cooperation by EU member states on all issues, but rather as a negotiated convergence between extreme positions (Tsardanidis and Stavridis 2005) and as a process of reorientation in the reference points of EU member states from extra-European ones to EU ones. They also point out that some facilitating factors help to promote the Europeanization of national foreign policies (Hill and Wong 2011: 220–224). The first is the presence of institutions and treaties of the EU that help to shape the choices of EU member states and create incentives to cooperate within an already established framework. Socialization is another facilitating factor, since it fosters a sense of common purpose among foreign policy decision makers. Likewise, leadership, that is the wish to exert a decisive influence, can facilitate Europeanization because states capable of leadership (normally the biggest EU members) can mobilize the EU behind their initiatives. A fourth facilitating factor has been identified in the presence of external federators, like the US at the beginning of the European integration process, but also in the perception of a common external threat. Politics of scale (Ginsberg 1989), that is the perceived advantage deriving from the multiplier effect of acting together in international politics, therefore increasing power and influence, can be a very potent facilitating factor. The legitimization of a global role for European states, whose individual activism would be negatively perceived because of their past, can also be a facilitating factor. Finally, a sense of geo-cultural identity may encourage the existence of a common set of preferences. On the other hand, Hill and Wong (2011: 225–226) also identify factors countering Europeanization in the ideological hostility at the domestic level against further integration, in domestic politics ebb and flow, in the pulling away from Europeanization exerted by international forces, and in special relationships.

In such a setting, Hill and Wong (2011: 227) argue, the two-level game (Putnam 1988) no longer holds, as a third level is present, that of the collective EU foreign policy-making process, and possibly another half, that has to do with the community-based external relations. This points to a European foreign policy system, based on the continuous interactions across many levels between its actors, their domestic pressures, and the EU institutional structure, in which convergence on the main lines and basic assumptions of foreign policy exists, although divergences remain on how to implement them.

Hill and Wong (2011: 211) define the ideal type Europeanized foreign policy as one which: 1) "Takes common EU positions, whether formally or informally established, as its major reference point, despite operating in multilateral forums"; 2) "Does not generally defect from common positions even when they cause difficulties for the state concerned"; 3) "Attempts to pursue its national priorities principally (but not exclusively) through the means of collective EU action"; and 4) "Subscribes positively to the values and principles expressed by the EU in its international activity." Europeanization should be thought of in terms of degrees while de-Europeanization, that is a change of direction to achieve greater freedom of maneuver, always remains a possibility (Hill and Wong 2011: 214).

Hadfield et al. (2017a) point out that EU member states can follow several foreign policy modes, and that variation in their foreign policy coherence is often to be attributed to the location of competence and to the state's sensitivity to policy transfers to the EU. Different modes of Europeanization coexist depending on the area. EU member states can operate within an EU framework in a deeply institutionalized and potentially supranational fashion (mode I) or according to intergovernmental mechanisms (mode II); they can act bilaterally or multilaterally with other EU member states but outside established EU frameworks (mode III); or they can operate with non-EU member states (mode IV). The first two modes are the most Europeanized and indicate a strongly integrated foreign policy making that reinforces Europeanization, but, although commensurate to EU policy objectives, the latter can also reinforce national preferences. Modes III and IV are typical of a less integrated foreign policy making, one that prioritizes national preferences. However, while modes II, III, and IV attest the willingness to assert national agendas, they do not necessarily indicate a de-Europeanization (Hadfield et al. 2017a: 15). This contribution is particularly effective in pointing out that, depending on the foreign policy area, variations in Europeanization may occur also *within* an EU member state, and that, although within an ever more complex foreign policy system whose opportunities and constraints they cannot ignore, member states remain central. Most importantly, it points to the existence of a hybrid system of foreign policy making (Hadfield et al. 2017b: 266).

The Italian Case

White's (2001: 6) remark that national foreign policies had significantly changed in the process of participating to European level policy making has been followed, according to Tonra (2015), by the empirical analysis of several case studies, that turned Europeanization into a growing scientific field. Interestingly, though, while many EU member states have been thoroughly analyzed, attention to the Italian case has been limited.

While a pillar of Italian foreign policy, through which Italy affirmed its loyalty to the West, initially the European integration process was also seen as a way to define the domestic political competition space. Only in the 1970s and 1980s it became a consensual issue (Cotta et al. 2005: 11–12) and support was so wide that the change started from the electorate of the PCI and only later reached the party (Ammendola and Isernia 2005; Isernia 2008). At least until the 1990s, Italian elites held a positive view of European integration, and developed a pro-European culture, while public opinion polls kept registering great support for the European project (Fabbrini and Piattoni 2008: 5). But while during the Cold War European integration was an international anchorage ("vincolo esterno") and a myth of modernization that could be instrumentally used to get the approval of domestic reforms that otherwise would not have had any chance of being approved, it contributed to the international standing of the country, and it received affective support from Italian public opinion also as a result of a Europeanized Italian identity, after the Cold War this anchorage changed nature (Diodato and Niglia 2017; Lucarelli 2015). Difficulties in the consolidation of Italy as a competitive democracy became evident with the implementation of the Maastricht treaty and the sacrifices to join the euro group. The perceived increase in EU competences and powers led to the politicization of the debate on European institutions and to the growth both in interest and contestation of the choices made by EU institutions (Della Porta and Caiani 2006). The common trend adopted by national governments to justify restrictive policies in the name of Europe focalized attention on the consequences of European integration. This took Euroscepticism into the Italian public debate and signaled the end of permissive consensus toward the EU, which was based on the effectiveness of European policies, and on the rise of critical attitudes toward the European integration process (Della Porta and Caiani 2006: 62).

In this context, the growth of unleashed nationalist attitudes opened the way to the possibility that Italy could be more assertive and promote its national interests also outside the European framework. This became particularly evident in Italian foreign policy decision making (Diodato and Niglia 2017: 91–92). As effectively synthesized by Diodato and Niglia (2017: 93), "What put Italy in difficulty was the contradiction between the instability of domestic and international structures, on the one hand, and the strengthening of the European constraints, on the other." This reduced the possibility of using the myth of the *vincolo esterno* and progressively transformed the permissive consensus on Europe, that is, the acquiescent attitude of Italians toward the national government's engagement with the integration process, into a more critical one. The change became evident in the 2000s, causing disenchantment and a soft Euroscepticism, which is dissent on specific policy areas but not on the Italian membership in the EU, as well as a more politicized debate on the EU (Lucarelli 2015). As Lucarelli (2015: 58) puts it, "Europe as a dream has made way for an image of Europe as a political space in which different views compete in a context of uneven power."

Despite the previously described important changes, however, very few analysts have attempted to analyze the Europeanization of Italian foreign policy and its variations over time.[13] Rosa (2003) has provided the most in-depth analysis of the Europeanization of Italian foreign policy so far, describing the many ways in which Italian foreign policy and actors at all levels have been deeply affected by the Europeanization process. The first evidence indicated by Rosa is elite socialization. The high number of interactions between officials from the Ministry of Foreign Affairs and their European counterparts has become a standard procedure and working together has become a habit that influences Italian officials in the regular creation of transgovernmental coalitions between Italian officials and their European colleagues. From Rosa's interviews it emerges that this socialization process has two important effects. Policy makers get the hang of other countries' foreign policy positions, so it has become customary for Italian diplomats, when they first analyze an issue, to ask themselves how their European partners are positioned on that specific issue, and how far Italy can push with its requests without damaging the EU cohesion. Knowing the partners' position influences the position that Italy finally adopts, as it helps in reducing deviant behavior in a context in which isolation is perceived negatively. Furthermore, a common culture develops on most of the issues on the agenda. This should not lead to believe that European interests substitute Italian ones. On the contrary, Rosa's interviews with Italian diplomats draw attention to the awareness that the EU is clearly an instrument to strengthen Italian foreign policy, not a burden to Italian interests. None of the diplomats interviewed seem to believe that

Italy's weight could be the same without the EU. The Ministry of Foreign Affairs supports a progressive communitarization of the Common Foreign and Security Policy and Italian policy makers consider it difficult to act outside the EU and consider the EU an added value. They deem it important to present Italian actions as European actions and to be part of European initiatives even when what the EU does is not fully in line with Italian positions (Rosa 2003: 223). Italy consults with its European partners on all the most important international issues, even those that are of strict national interest, systematically and regularly consulting its European partners before its American ally even in case of tough decisions (Rosa 2003: 228).

In Rosa's analysis, Europeanization is present also in the bureaucratic reorganization over time of the Ministry of Foreign Affairs to adapt to the growing needs of European foreign policy, particularly important after the Amsterdam treaty, and in the changes in the working style of the Italian foreign policy community, now giving greater responsibilities to peripheral units in the formulation of policy guidelines, in line with the need to coordinate positions as quickly as possible. Rosa values the growth of public support for the European foreign and defense policy. Italian public opinion on this issue moved from well below the EU average to well above the EU average. A similar pattern is registered in top decision makers' opinion polls, markedly in favor of an EU decision-making process in foreign policy (Rosa 2003: 231).

Finally, Rosa stresses that the EU created the opportunity for a bipartisan compromise from the 1970s, it gave Italian governments the opportunity to run under the EU umbrella actions that otherwise were considered as contentious, and it strengthened Italy's image and influence abroad. Despite showing greater assertiveness in foreign policy, after the Cold War, Italy preferred to put its foreign policy actions within a European framework, even when they were crucial to the national interests. Likewise, Italy has at times (for instance, in relation to the issue of the so-called rogue states) chosen to slow down its actions and even change its orientation when its EU partners had different perceptions, because the Italian willingness not to break European solidarity weighs on its national choices (Rosa 2003: 234). As one of the officials interviewed by Rosa remarks, "it is not only in pursuing the national interest that there is an effect, there is [an effect] in the very formulation of national interest [. . .] The EU factor is already built-in during policy-making [. . .] more and more we are part of this European framework and this determines the formulation of our policy, not just its implementation" (Rosa 2003: 233, ft 40).

Analyzing Italian foreign policy a few years later, Brighi (2011: 57–58) reached quite different conclusions. Brighi points out that for all the talk about Italy as devoted to the European cause, the Italian strategic document *Rapporto 2020* (Ministero degli affari esteri 2008) betrays an instrumental vision of "Europe" (what the EU is often called in Italy). In other terms, Europe turns into an opportunity for Italy, an instrument of Italy's external action, and a venue in which to be reassured regarding the Italian status, "Europe *for* Italy," not vice versa (Brighi 2011: 57). Admitting that this de-Europeanization takes place because Italian foreign policy was already Europeanized, Brighi notes that since the end of the Cold War Italy has abandoned its traditional habit of passively relying on the EU and has started to free ride, if necessary contributing to divisions among EU member states, and to have an opportunistic and instrumental attitude toward the EU. Brighi finds that, in the context of a changing strategic scenario and of increasing EU crises, and therefore of different calculations regarding the EU as an opportunity structure, the change in the party system, and in particular the alternation of center-right and center-left coalitions, has led to fluctuations toward Europe, in terms of foreign policy style, discourse, and choices. This means that, although all Italian governments have kept their commitment to the US and the EU as pillars of Italian foreign policy, they have also exercised more freedom of maneuver. When faced with divisions between the US and the EU, center-right governments have been particularly keen to take side with the US and avoid pressures coming from Brussels. The case of relations with Russia is particularly interesting. While Rosa (2003: 235–236) noted that the importance of respecting human rights as a pillar of European foreign policy affected Italian relations with Russia to the point of becoming an obstacle in establishing closer relations, Brighi (2011–2064) notes that on Russia "centre-right governments have been more inclined to break the European unity on politically sensitive issues, such as human rights." Likewise, in the Mediterranean and the Middle East, areas of traditional interest for Italy, when the EU has lagged behind (for instance, on Albania in 1997 and on Lebanon in 2006), Italy has not hesitated to take the lead without trying to build a consensus among the EU members (Brighi 2011: 67). However, in other sensitive areas, such as defense, Italian cooperation with the EU has been solid and stable, because Italian policy makers have realized that European integration is in Italy's interest, since the country is an overcommitted middle power with a shrinking defense budget (Brighi 2011: 65).

According to Brighi (2011: 69), "Italy's traditional concerns over rank and exclusion [. . .] are still alive and kicking" and Italy's mode of Europeanization is "rather opportunistic and instrumental." This is not to say that there is no Europeanization of Italian foreign policy, but that Europeanization takes place when it is most convenient for the country, and that Italy otherwise is willing to explore other options. Interestingly, though, it is when the EU is divided that Italy strays from EU positions (Brighi 2011: 70). Despite acknowledging variations in the degree of Europeanization in different foreign policy areas and issues, and that Europeanization is still pushed by the Italian foreign policy establishment, Brighi concludes that Italian foreign policy is resistant to substantial change in terms of its objectives and identity and that ultimately it is a case of de-Europeanization. Hill and Wong (2011: 218) take Brighi's results to classify Italy as both a case of a state engaged in the Europeanization process but on a slow process and a case of de-Europeanization.

A third recent contribution comes from Dobrescu et al. (2017) who analyze the Italian case since 2001 in the wider context of Southern European countries. Starting from the assumption that all the countries under consideration are Europeanized countries, both in the top-down dimension of being capable of adaptation, and in the capacity to project their national preferences to either influence the positions of other EU states or contribute to the shaping of a common stance, the scholars dispute that uploading national problems necessarily amounts to a successful Europeanization, because this uploading might as well be a form of renationalization. In the case of the analyzed countries, according to the authors, uploading was understood not as trying to speak with a single voice or in advancement of EU values and norms, but as national foreign policy stances that, once transferred to the EU level, make national preferences more rigid, thus weakening the EU foreign policy actorness and effectiveness. According to the authors, Italy has not changed its goals but has changed its means. It is trying to keep a high profile within the EU and to keep performing the role of bridge, but it does it with greater difficulties. Overall, the Italian case is considered one of incremental Europeanization with signs of renationalization.

Rosa (2003), Brighi (2011), and Dobrescu et al. (2017) reach three different conclusions. Both Brighi (2011) and Dobrescu et al. (2017) examine a selected and small number of cases in an overlapping period. According to the former Italy is a case of resistance and de-Europeanization. The latter, on the contrary, considers Italy a case of incremental Europeanization with signs of renationalization. Rosa (2003) and Brighi (2011) too analyze overlapping periods and come to different conclusions. Interestingly, although Brighi (2011) and Dobrescu et al. (2017) point out limitations or an inversion of the trend, they somehow refer to an already Europeanized Italian foreign policy. This makes the case for further exploring the roots and modalities of the Europeanization of Italian foreign policy, and for more systematically analyzing variations in Italian foreign policy behavior over an extended period.

ITALY AS COALITION FACILITATOR

Both the logic of consequences and the logic of appropriateness are at play according to the existing literature on the Europeanization of Italian foreign policy. The common thread is that, both instrumentally and for identity reasons, and consistently with the Italian strategic culture, the EU is an added value to Italy's foreign policy. The EU widens the opportunity structure of Italian foreign policy, an indication of the causality nexus of Europeanization (Ladrech 2000: 190). It gives Italy the opportunity to expand its influence by providing additional resources and by legitimizing its most assertive initiatives. It does so in terms of politics of scale and has traditionally done so in relation to its domestic need to delegate its foreign policy to a superior authority, although in the post–Cold War period this aspect has also been a cover for a renewed assertiveness. The logic of appropriateness is also present in the "we-feeling" that leads Italian actors involved in the foreign policy decision-making process to continuously redefine Italian interests and not to defect, therefore contributing to the possibility of achieving a consensus. This is consonant with the highlighted attempts at keeping a high profile and at playing a role consonant with its status of middle power: the role of facilitator.[14] Italy regularly played a role during European crises and conflicts, to the point of being considered the "indispensable broker," and its capacity to mediate among different positions gained it influence, while helping the country to promote its own preferences (Fabbrini and Piattoni 2008: 5 and 18). The Italian facilitating capacity is an important asset, particularly in a compound and multilevel polity like the EU (Fabbrini and Piattoni 2008: 19), and Italy has traditionally been very comfortable in using it (Foradori and Rosa 2008: 184).

By allowing Italy to facilitate the negotiated convergence among EU member states, Europeanization has thus been key to Italian foreign policy. It has enabled the country to play a niche role that suits particularly well a middle power in a way that is consistent with its identity and strategic culture, and that increases Italy's structural opportunities and status. Through the politics of scale inherent to acting with the other EU states the country could amplify its weight and initiate a more active foreign policy. But the role of facilitator played by Italy has also been important for the EU, because it has allowed EU member states to act on initiatives that may not have been started by Italy but on which Italy helped to facilitate the negotiated convergence and therefore the creation of the needed support.

This is particularly relevant because the characteristics of the ideal type of Europeanized foreign policy described by Hill and Wong (2011: 211) lead to the expectation that, in respect to third parties and in particular in multilateral contexts, through a collective decision-making process EU member states whose foreign policy has been Europeanized will tend to develop a negotiated convergence of interests and strategies that allows them to present themselves as a single unit with other EU member states (they should take "common EU positions, whether formally or informally established as [. . .] major reference point, despite operating in other multilateral forums"). This unit should persist over time and despite the absence of enforcing mechanisms, even when some members of the unit have little stake in the outcome ("not generally defect from common positions"). To be clear, the existence of this unit does not exclude that EU member states might occasionally defect but discourages more autonomous foreign policy lines by modifying their opportunity structure. EU member states in this unit do not act together just because they share homogeneous preferences, although this is certainly relevant. They act together because they create internal bonds and expectations on how members of the unit should behave, and they develop an organizational distinctiveness and procedural norms to manage conflicts and disagreements that allow them to overcome their original preferences (they should "attempt to pursue [. . .] national priorities principally (but not exclusively) through the means of collective EU action" and they should subscribe "positively to the values and principles expressed by the EU in its international activity, to the extent of becoming part of a shared image and identity, in the eyes of both other Europeans and outsiders").

In fact, EU member states whose foreign policies are Europeanized show a behavior typical of coalition members at the international level (Coleman 1970; Attinà 2011: 68; Monteleone 2015: 45–46). In the foreign policy area relations among EU states have been formalized over time, with the progression of the institutionalization process, but they are not as binding as an alliance, because the costs of severance of their relationship or failure to honor an agreement are rather limited. The European treaties and the enormous amount of coordination meetings certainly help EU member states to act more cohesively and even push toward that direction. But defections remain a common and tolerated occurrence.

EU member states can be said to act in the international system as a European formalized coalition, that is a political coalition of EU states that has persisted over time and whose members are guided by a negotiated convergence of interests and strategies, normally act as a single unit despite the absence of enforcing mechanisms or of important stakes in the outcome, have created expectations on members' behavior, have developed norms to overcome internal disagreements, and have also strongly institutionalized and formalized their collective decision-making process. The European formalized coalition is a subset of the US-led dominant coalition and is nested into it. It has been originally promoted by the hegemon and it has traditionally acted in support of the global leader and its organization of the international political system, helping the global leader to be decisive within institutions, that is, to control the decision-making outcomes and agenda on issues that the coalition identifies as most important. Because of its position, it is not only influenced by intra-European dynamics, but also by systemic pressures, and this helps explain variations and fluctuations over time in its cohesion. Competition among members to enter the more selected but influential "cabinet" of the dominant coalition should be expected. In this respect, it would not be realistic to expect the Europeanization process to be insulated from ongoing dynamics in the international system, and indeed even the ideal type Europeanized foreign policy described by Hill and Wong (2011: 211 and 225–226) allows margins of ambiguity and the occasional defection or pursuance of national foreign goals through other means and recognizes that the international system can introduce countering factors in the Europeanization process. This confirms the methodological difficulties in analyzing the impact of Europeanization as separated from other ongoing processes at the international level.

It is here proposed that the evolution of the European formalized coalition is influenced by the evolution of the international hegemonic order, in support of which it was originally created, and that this explains variations in Italian foreign policy. Within a hegemonic order, coalitions are important because they provide support to the global leader and recognize its political organization and authority as legitimate, or they oppose the global leader and its organization of the system and propose alternatives. The political dimension of coalitions is therefore extremely important and has been highlighted especially by global leadership theorists. Nevertheless, processes of coalition formation and variation remain little explored.

Building on Monteleone (2015) it is here proposed that coalition formation and variation is affected by bargaining power, that is the resources controlled, but also by the bargaining environment, that includes institutional rules, but can also refer to distribution of power, previous coalitional experiences, presence of credible alternative coalitions, competition levels and ideological polarization levels, mechanisms of global leadership change, and the competitiveness of the international system. Variations in the European formalized coalition could therefore be related to structural variations and be strictly connected to the evolution of the dominant coalition. In the framework of the phases of global leadership identified by Modelski (2008), this would explain why immediately after World War II, when the strength and cohesion of the dominant coalition were high and increasing, the US created incentives for European states to coalesce to increase their support to the hegemonic order. Since the 1970s, the global leader's power progressively deconcentrated and the dominant coalition lost strength and cohesiveness, losing part of its supporting coalition, while states gathered around new problems. It is in this phase that European states increased the institutionalization of the European formalized coalition and chose to build a more autonomous identity in front of the others. EU states started autonomous actions from the global leader but kept close coordination with the US and established through the EU a wide cooperative relationship with the US (the New Transatlantic Agenda) that allowed them to be seen not only as sharing the burden of maintaining the hegemonic order, but also as having assumed the responsibility of doing so (Monteleone 2003).

In the current phase, that started approximately in 2000, it is expected that the rise of multipolarity and lower concentrations of power, and an increase in levels of competition and ideological polarization, might favor flexibility of alignments and the creation of new coalitions based on common proposals for the restructuring of the global political system that aspire to challenge the dominant coalition. Old coalitions are expected to reshuffle and prioritize new issues, while requests and divergences should materialize. The strength and cohesion of the dominant coalition are expected to be low. Indeed, both the rise of the so-called BRIC countries and their so far volatile and unsuccessful attempts at coalescing, and ups and downs in transatlantic relations and in US support toward multilateralism, particularly evident under the current US administration, are consonant with this phase (Monteleone 2015). This may represent a challenge for the Europeanization of the foreign policy of Italy. American hegemony is delegitimized, and the leadership of the US on its European allies is declining, leading to the weakening of the old dominant coalition. New potential challengers arise, bringing up new issues on which they attract attention and gain support, further destabilizing the old dominant coalition. Born in support of the US-led hegemonic order, the European formalized coalition too might be weakened by the systemic pressures that are present in this phase and lead coalition members to disaggregate. The European formalized coalition has reached a high level of institutionalization, reducing room for maneuver and increasing the cost of defection, but it may be subject to reshuffling too. However, over time, the bonds between core members of the dominant coalition should strengthen, and under increasing levels of competition and ideological polarization, the cohesiveness and strength of the core members of the dominant coalition should progressively increase to face the existence of coalitions capable of challenging the dominant one.[15]

Should they be confirmed, the previously described variations in the systemic coalitions would have important implications for Italy's foreign policy. The three traditional pillars of Italian foreign policy were all based on the assumption that Italy was (or wanted to become) a member of the dominant coalition. This implied not only support to the US, but also to its organization, that included multilateral institutions and the European integration process. Supporting them was therefore a way to support the hegemon. Considering the limitations of its resources, the internal political divisions, and the strategic culture, for Italy Europeanizing its foreign policy meant using the support of other European states as a leverage to increase its influence and as a way to expand its room for maneuver. Europeanization for Italy therefore meant adapting its foreign policy to be part of the European formalized coalition. And joining that coalition gave Italy the possibility of an increase in status while contributing to support the US-led hegemonic organization. However, in the current phase, the strength and cohesion of both the dominant coalition and the European one are expected to be low and for Italy leveraging on the European formalized coalition may no longer be an effective strategy in a weakened order, while the costs of facilitating consensus among members of the coalition might increase. Most importantly, when the European formalized coalition diverges from the US, this may create tensions and incoherent behavior. However, under increasing levels of competition and ideological polarization, the core members of the dominant coalition should increase their cohesiveness and strength. This may increase the value of Italy as a coalition facilitator among the core members of the reorganizing dominant coalition.

Given the relevance that has been attributed or self-attributed to the Italian role as a bridge or mediator, it is to be expected that the Europeanization of Italian foreign policy translates into the role of coalition facilitator. That is, Italy should value presenting itself as a member of the European formalized coalition, whenever one can create, and contribute to facilitating its coming into existence or maintaining it, if necessary adapting its foreign policy in order to be part of it. However, for Italy this coalition remains a way of supporting the organization of the international system and gain recognition and ultimately status for it, so it should not be done in opposition to the US.

This is all the more relevant in multilateral contexts, and in particular in the UN, not only because they are traditional forums for middle powers, but also because multilateralism is a declared feature in the identity of both the EU and Italy, and it has been a key component of the international order promoted by the US after World War II with the support of its Western European allies. It is therefore useful to turn to that forum to systematically analyze whether the expected variations in the Europeanization of Italian foreign policy in the declining process of American hegemony are confirmed.

NOTES

1. Correlates of War project, State System Membership (v2016), Major 2016, available at http://www.correlatesofwar.org/data-sets/state-system-membership (accessed on 07/04/2018).
2. On roles in the international system, see the seminal work of Holsti (1970).
3. The reconstruction of the phases is based on Modelski (1999).

4. On this see also Pouliot and Thérien (2015).

5. "Hegemony frames thought and thereby circumscribes action" (Cox 1992: 140).

6. More recent scholarship has also highlighted the relevance of identity in the hegemonic challenge (Allan et al. 2018) and of the possession of a plurality of meta-capital (Nexon and Neumann 2018).

7. It would be beyond the scope of this book to make an exhaustive review of hegemonic theories, for which Norloff (2017) is an excellent starting point.

8. This innovation was consistent with US preferences (Ruggie 1993), but it was also the result of an environment in which norms of self-restraint in the use of force by states, democratic practices, a world public opinion, norms of sovereign equality, and universal participation, and the principle that legitimate authority is based on reciprocally binding agreements that should be equally applied to all members started being diffused (Ikenberry 2001; Modelski 2008; Finnemore and Jurkovic 2014; Reus-Smit 1997; Hurd 2007; Pouliot and Thérien 2015).

9. The US has always tried to avoid real restraints on its autonomy (Ikenberry 2003) and, despite being the promoter, has always used multilateral organizations instrumentally or pragmatically (Foot et al. 2003).

10. The term Europeanization has been used progressively since the 1990s, but its meaning has been diversified in relation to different disciplines (Featherstone 2003: 5–6). Ladrech (1994: 69) defined Europeanization as "a process reorienting the direction and shape of politics to the degree that EC political and economic dynamics become part of the organizational logic of national politics and policy-making." Because the focus here is on the Europeanization of foreign policy, and there is wide agreement that there are major differences with the Europeanization of other policies, the literature on Europeanization will only be introduced in aspects that might be of interest for the analysis of foreign policy.

11. As one of the diplomats interviewed by Tonra (2000: 230) notes, "there is a lot of soul searching all the time about our profile, that is [the Union's] profile, at the UN."

12. Along the same lines, Bicchi (2014: 254) has highlighted the importance of information sharing and knowledge construction taking place in missions abroad among European diplomats in defining national positions: all EU member states value information and knowledge about what the collectivity believes, and this constitutes a crucial component of their assessments.

13. Analysis of the Europeanization of Italian development cooperation is excluded because it is a subfield with specific technical aspects (among others, Carbone and Quartapelle 2016).

14. Or bridge, or mediator, or coalition builder. These terms should be considered as synonymous in the context of this work.

15. It is not possible to say whether the transition will take place through a hegemonic war, but on the topic see also Allison (2017).

Chapter Two

Analyzing Europeanization at the United Nations

WHY LOOKING AT THE UN

Scholars disagree about the Europeanization of Italian foreign policy in the post–Cold War period. To someone it is a strong case of Europeanization (Rosa 2003); to others a case of either de-Europeanization (Brighi 2011) or something in between (Dobrescu et al. 2017). It is indeed difficult to assess the Europeanization of the foreign policy of a country, a process triggered and reversed by changes at the domestic, European, and international levels. It is also hard to agree on how Europeanized the foreign policy of a country is, because Europeanization is neither a dichotomous variable nor a linear process (Hill and Wong 2011). Lastly, scholars warn about methodological issues like the importance of accounting for multiple levels to properly isolate Europeanization as an independent variable (Major 2005), of identifying cooperation as an observable consequence of Europeanization only when it is consistently pursued across issues and over time (Moumoutzis 2011), of going beyond interviews with national officials in Brussels, of testing the longitudinal impact of the EU on national foreign policies on a sufficiently long number of years, and of controlling for other causal variables (Wong and Hill 2011: 11–13). The ideal type of Europeanized foreign policy defined by Hill and Wong (2011: 211), however, provides a useful indication on how to proceed because it makes of EU member states' behavior within multilateral forums a hard test of Europeanization.

    Multilateral forums are a hard test for Europeanization to display its effects because the principle one state one vote creates more incentives to defect than to cooperate, so states are encouraged to act independently or to opportunistically coalesce to obtain outcomes consonant with their established national preferences. Studies on the UN have revealed that acting within a group could be disadvantageous, because the state loses visibility and maneuverability, while the group position could be the lowest common denominator and a suboptimal choice. Moreover, the group common position may be too difficult and time-consuming to reach, and, once reached, it may introduce an excessive rigidity that harms the negotiating process and creates polarization (Laatikainen and Smith 2017). Regular and persisting coordination to ensure behavioral cohesion is normally the result of the political will to be—and be perceived as—members of a group.

Acting through groups within multilateral forums like the UN has advantages too: it helps to gather the votes needed in view of reaching a majority or a blocking minority, it enables to increase influence and accomplish results, it allows access to greater information, and avoids isolation (Laatikainen and Smith 2017). Indeed, several groups exist at the UN and recent literature has brought attention to the importance of group politics in that forum (Laatikainen 2017). However, states are simultaneously part of competing groups, so they are subject to different and often incoherent requests and pressures. This makes defection a concrete possibility. Group cohesion is often the result of coordination processes among group members. The group itself reflects the interests and identities of its members, but also contributes to shaping them, especially considering that the state representatives involved may not receive clear guidelines or red lines on all the issues on the agenda (Laatikainen and Smith 2017: 103; Panke 2017a: 8). In such a context, coalition politics heavily structures UN hierarchies of standing and holding brokerage positions confers status (Pouliot 2016: 4 and 141–144).

Looking at the UN to detect the Europeanization of the foreign policy of EU member states is useful also because multilateralism, and particularly the UN, is a crucial element in the security strategy of the European Union (2003 and 2016) and the repeated references to it underline its importance for the identity of the EU. To emphasize the importance of the UN for the EU and its identity, on 9 May 2017 High Representative Mogherini in front of the Security Council stated: "The European way is also the United Nations' way." The 2003 EU security strategy dedicated an entire section to "An International Order Based on Effective Multilateralism," identified in the UN Charter the fundamental framework for international relations and indicated an EU goal in the development of a stronger international society, well-functioning international institutions, and a rules-based international order (European Union 2003). More importantly, it determined that the strengthening of the UN is an EU priority that should lead to greater support to the organization. The 2016 EU security strategy went even further, identifying the EU as the promoter of a rules-based order "with multilateralism as its key principle and the United Nations at its core" and, having in mind a reformed global governance more adequate for the contemporary situation, it declared that "the EU will strive for a strong UN as the bedrock of a multilateral rules-based order" (European Union 2016). The strategy also expressed the European Union's determination to reform the UN, including the Security Council, and called for greater cohesion among EU member states at the UN and for principled actions in the UNSC.

EU member states' cohesion at the UN represents one of the most important goals and a strategic priority, because the UN is an integral component of the organization of the international system that the EU promotes. The EU prescribes a specific action for its member states. They have been called by the treaties to coordinate their action in international organizations and at international conferences, and to uphold EU common positions in such forums (Article J.2[3] of the Maastricht Treaty), to share information on matters of common interests with other members who are not present in the institution, and when in the Security Council to concert and keep the other members fully informed (Article J.5[4] of the Maastricht Treaty). Although limitations toward greater autonomy are included, permanent members of the Security Council are called to "ensure the defence of the positions and the interests of the Union" (Article J.5[4] of the Maastricht Treaty). The commitment has been included in successive EU treaties like the Amsterdam treaty (Article J.9) and is present also in the 2016 Consolidated versions of the Treaty on the European Union and the Treaty on the Functioning of the European Union (Article 34). Moreover, support to the UN and the principles of the UN Charter are considered a fundamental EU guiding principle in the treaties (see Article 21[1] of the 2016 Treaty on the European Union and the Treaty on the Functioning of the European Union). However, the treaties include provisions limiting EU member states' commitment to coordination and unitary action and leave ample room for defection, ultimately leaving decisions in the hands of each member state. How EU member states act within the UN, whether they act cohesively or defect and how often, and whether they are guided in their behavior by these common guiding principles and strategies or not, is therefore an important test of their willingness to adapt their foreign policies in support of a visible presence as EU member states and not just as independent states, and to promote EU principles and follow common strategies. That is, it is an important threshold that helps to analyze their degree of Europeanization.

Moreover, although some internal dynamics have to be taken into account and isolated when generalizing from the institutional level to the international level (more on this later in the chapter), this forum allows the analysis of EU member states' behavior for consistent periods of time and on an extremely large spectrum of issues, in the case of the Security Council all the most important security issues. It is therefore possible to identify variations in the behavior of EU member states, overcoming some of the methodological weaknesses highlighted in literature, and through the analysis of coalitional behavior assess their degree of Europeanization. As it is so important for the EU that its member states act cohesively within and in support of the UN, a consistent—that is, across issues and over time—active participation to the creation of the European formalized coalition, made of at least the majority of EU member states, within the UNGA and even more within the UNSC should be taken as an indication of Europeanization, while a consistent defection should be taken as an indication that the EU member state does not feel bound enough and is not willing to adapt its stance to present a unified EU position.

Analyzing the Europeanization of foreign policy at the UN is also appropriate in the case of Italy because multilateralism was a critical choice for the country and is still perceived by Italian decision makers as a cornerstone of the international order (Attinà 2009; Caffarena and Gabusi 2017). Initially excluded, Italy fought hard to become a UN member, eventually succeeding only in 1955 after several attempts. Considering UN membership an essential political goal, it even shaped its constitution so as to facilitate accession to the organization. Membership in a supranational institution like the UN for Italy meant distancing itself from its fascist past and being readmitted into the international community as a peer, so it also had implications for the Italian identity and strategic culture and for the Italian status. Italy has always been strongly committed to the UN. It has become a top contributor both to the regular budget (8th top contributor in the 2018 scale of assessments with 3.748 percent [United Nations Secretariat 2017]) and to peacekeeping operations (8th top financial contributor to peace missions and top Western supplier of troops).[1] In Italy the UN became a "myth" consonant with its more neutralist and pacifist stances, on which during the Cold War all political forces could find common ground and to which, with the end of the Cold War, Italian governments could delegate authority and receive a political cover for their most assertive actions in the security field (Orsini 2005). The UN also became a battleground for Italy. Reform of the organization to increase its effectiveness became a consolidated and constant feature of its post–Cold War foreign policy. Reform of the UN Security Council has certainly been one of the top issues on the foreign policy agenda of all governments, and great resources have been invested to avoid marginalization. The UN is therefore an important arena for Italy and one in which Italy may be found at odds with other EU member states on issues that are of foremost importance for Italian national interests, so it is certainly worth exploring Italian foreign policy behavior in this forum.

Looking at the Europeanization of Italian foreign policy at the UN is also consonant with Italy being a status seeking middle power. As mentioned in the previous chapter, it is in multilateral institutions that middle powers tend to exercise middle power diplomacy (Wohlforth et al. 2018; Cooper et al. 1993; Ravenhill 1998: 312), and the UN has traditionally played an important role in the post–World War II US-led hegemonic order, so it is a forum where Italian foreign policy behavior can be related to system maintenance activities and to the self-ascribed role as coalition facilitator. Not surprisingly, the website of the Italian Permanent mission to the UN claims Italy's role in narrowing differences in positions and broadening consensus within that forum.[2] Considering that it has been observed that multilateral practices lend themselves to pecking order dynamics reflecting hierarchy in the system (Pouliot 2016), and that the current organization of the international system is based on multilateral institutions, in this forum it is also possible to observe whether and to what degree the Italian behavior in relation to other EU member states is independent or related to other factors that might affect the Italian opportunity structure such as its relationship with the US and the growing importance of the BRIC countries.

Finally, the UN has become the standard forum in which state preferences, coalitions in the international system, and their variations are detected (Alker 1964; Alker and Russett 1965; Bailey et al. 2017; Kim and Russett 1996; Monteleone 2015; Voeten 2000). Analyzing the Europeanization of Italian foreign policy through its coalitional behavior in this forum is therefore in line with a longstanding research tradition in International Relations.

Accordingly, it is here proposed that the degree of Europeanization of Italian foreign policy and its variations can be assessed through an empirical analysis of the Italian behavior at the UN in the period 2000–2017. The analysis will focus on whether the Italian coalitional behavior at the UN reflects a willingness to adapt Italian foreign policy to be part of and be seen as belonging to the European formalized coalition, here intended as at least the majority of EU member states, but also to facilitate its creation and maintenance. The analysis will also focus on whether Italy adopts this behavior to increase its structural opportunities and status as a country contributing to international system maintenance and explore whether the Italian participation to the European formalized coalition has become alternative to Italian support to the US.

Given that the expected changes in the international system in the analyzed period, and in particular the delegitimation of the US and the reshuffling of old coalitions, may pressure Italy to search for alternative coalitions, the Italian distance from its traditional ally, the US, and the so-called rising powers (China, Russia, India, and Brazil) will also be assessed.

THE THREE PILLARS

Multilateralism

To use the UN for analyzing variations in Italian foreign policy, it is useful to see whether and how the three fundamental pillars of Italian foreign policy are present and reflected in this forum.

Variations in Italian supporting activities at the UN can provide direct indications regarding multilateralism as a pillar of Italian foreign policy. The exclusion from the group of initial UN members raised the alarm for the country, indicating its initial post–World War II isolation. UN membership became a symbolic goal to which all forces should be dedicated, because it meant a reengagement with the international community. Moreover, as Salleo and Pirozzi (2008: 95–96) put it, the UN was a realistic choice for a middle power. It was consonant with the new accommodationist strategic culture and with the aversion to the power politics typical of the fascist period, and it was in line with the prevailing internationalist attitude among political forces and with public opinion's belief that through the UN Italy could solve its structural problems. Except for right-wing parties, political forces easily converged on constitutional norms that indicated aversion to power politics, promotion of pacifism, freedom, and democracy, and most of all international cooperation. UN membership became such an important goal for Italy that it allowed sovereignty limitations to reach it (Costa Bona and Tosi 2007: 152–153). Finally, the UN, and its Security Council, were perceived as bearing primary responsibility for dealing with international security and, in line with the Italian constitution, the organization was considered the only source of legitimacy for the use of force (Salleo and Pirozzi 2008: 96).

Italian participation in UN activities was not disconnected from the international context. On the contrary, it was strongly related to its role as allied of the US in the organization of the international system. Italy was invited to submit its application to gain UN membership from the US Department of State in 1947, immediately after the Truman doctrine was formulated, in what was in fact an invitation to join the US and the Western bloc at the UN (Costa Bona and Tosi 2007: 159). The Italian application was presented by the US and supported by the United Kingdom (UK) and France. It was rejected because of Cold War dynamics. After the second failed attempt, in 1947 Italy became an observer at the UN. Only in 1955, after several attempts and much diplomatic effort, Italy became a UN member. This immediately spurred great Italian activism within the organization. In a confirmation that status issues were still relevant, the admission encouraged immediate thoughts that Italy should become a candidate for a nonpermanent seat of the Security Council (Costa Bona and Tosi 2007: 182).

UN membership was important also for domestic reasons. During the Cold War, it allowed the country to strengthen its status in the international system and gain some margin of maneuver, while avoiding domestic controversies and an excess of politicization, since the pro-UN position was strongly supported by public opinion and shared by the PSI, the PCI, and a large sector of the DC (Costa Bona and Tosi 2007: 206). Italian activism at the UN grew over time and, in recognition of the strong Italian commitment to the organization, Italy was elected nonpermanent member of the Security Council for the period 1959–1960 and an Italian (Fanfani) was elected president of the UNGA in 1965. Italy became the eight-top contributor to the UN regular budget already in 1968 (Costa Bona and Tosi 2007: 189, 193, and 209). Always trying to act within the UN framework, in the 1960s Italy became more active in the greater Mediterranean area and in relation to Third World countries. Indeed, the UN increased Italian autonomy while allowing the country to be solidly anchored to its allies, so it became the forum in which the country could increase its role and status while playing as a peer (Costa Bona and Tosi 2007: 188, 194, 206, and 216).

Italy remained highly active at the UN (among other things, it was elected nonpermanent member of the Security Council for the periods 1971–1972 and 1975–1976), always discussing the most difficult issues within this multilateral framework and acting as a bridge between North and South, and declared in the UNGA in 1976 that the three pillars of Italian foreign policy were European integration, the Atlantic alliance, and the UN. However, in the 1970s Italian governments started putting forward the issue of UN reform, including reform of the Security Council, to increase the effectiveness of the organization, whose salience had decreased over time (Costa Bona and Tosi 2007: 232–233, 237, and 246). In the 1980s, Italy kept claiming that the UN was an essential forum for dialogue and cooperation (and was elected for the fourth time as nonpermanent Security Council member for the period 1987–1988), but it showed greater autonomy and assertiveness in foreign policy also outside the UN context, initiating a more ambivalent course (Costa Bona and Tosi 2007: 256).

With the end of the Cold War, in the 1990s, the Italian willingness to play a greater role in the international system translated into a renewed interest and support for the UN, where Italy displayed a much greater activism, including on the issue of UN reform and in particular on reform of the Security Council, where Italy asked to be represented in consideration of its growing commitment to the organization and increased role (Costa Bona and Tosi 2007: 281). Particularly important was the Italian decision to shift from being a security consumer to becoming a security provider, and therefore contributing more to the peacekeeping activities of the UN (Tercovich

2016: 686). Italy became an important contributor to UN peace operations and a top contributor to the UN regular budget (the fifth top contributor to the regular budget and the third top troop contributor for UN peace operations in 1999 and 2000), and this commitment gained it the fifth mandate in the Security Council for the period 1995–1996. On this occasion, also holding the EU Presidency, Italy tried to bring the EU position to the Security Council and to extensively coordinate with the other EU members (Costa Bona and Tosi 2007: 307 and 319). Although the initiative received lukewarm acceptance, when not open opposition, in the second half of the 1990s Italy's action for Security Council reform focused on upgrading the relevance of the European foreign and security policy. Italy tried to promote a higher level of information sharing among EU member states and constantly referred to EU positions in its interventions. It also strongly opposed the creation of new permanent seats, in this conflicting with Germany, to avoid its own marginalization (Salleo and Pirozzi 2008: 99).

In the 1990s Italy tried to raise its profile within the UN system. It won 27 elections to UN bodies, increasing its presence, it strengthened its contribution in the field of peacekeeping, it assigned more Italian officers to the UN Secretariat in New York, it welcomed the UN Staff College to train UN personnel in Turin and a UN Logistic Base for operations support in Brindisi. In recognition of this commitment, two Italian generals were appointed as commanders of two major UN operations and a multinational force under UN mandate in Albania under Italian command was launched (Salleo and Pirozzi 2008: 99–100). However, willing to count more because of its contribution to the UN, Italy proposed its candidature close to the previous mandate but lost support from some European members. The intra-EU clash on UNSC reform led to lack of support for a Security Council mandate for the period 2001–2002 and for the appointment of an Italian as UN High Commissioner for Refugees (Costa Bona and Tosi 2007: 319–320).

In recognition of its commitment to UN activities, and particularly to UN peacekeeping, Italy received the Security Council mandate again for the period 2006–2007 (Tercovich 2016: 688). Among the initiatives undertaken, particularly important was its campaign to make "European use" of its seat to favor a progressive harmonization and the emergence of an EU profile (Salleo and Pirozzi 2008: 106–107). It is in this period that one of the Italian long-term goals most consonant with EU values, the moratorium on death penalty, was promoted in close coordination with the EU Presidency and approved by the UNGA (Salleo and Pirozzi 2008: 107).

The UN was also traditionally seen by Italian decision makers as a forum through which more autonomous actions from the Atlantic alliance could be advanced while preserving domestic equilibria (Fois and Pagani 2008: 85).

With the end of the Cold War, however, some domestic differences emerged on the role that the UN should play in Italian foreign policy given the growing distance between the US and the UN. This became evident in relation to the Italian engagement in UN peacekeeping, whose fluctuation has been related to changes in domestic government coalitions (Tercovich 2016: 689). Center-right governments expressed a preference to follow the US in case of clash between the US and the UN, while center-left governments kept the traditional pro-UN line. But even then, Italy always tried to reconcile its close relationship with the US with its support to the UN, both central to its foreign policy (Fois and Pagani 2008: 85–86). Moreover, actions outside the UN framework under US request took place also under center-left governments (on Kosovo under the D'Alema government, for instance), showing that differences were not as wide as depicted (Ratti 2011: 129).

The recent rationalization of the Italian involvement in missions that are strategic for Italy, together with the availability to further engage in UN peacekeeping (especially in strategic areas like Libya) and the launch of the "blue helmets of culture," a specialized unit aimed at preserving cultural heritage in crisis areas to which Italy can provide a significant contribution thanks to the expertise of its Carabinieri, confirm the Italian commitment to the UN but also a more pragmatic approach (Tercovich 2016: 695; Foradori 2017). In cooperation with Germany, in 2014, during its EU Presidency, Italy promoted the EU-UN Cooperation in Crisis Management and Peace Operations to increase collaboration in this field between the two organizations (Tercovich 2016: 697).

After forcing the Italian candidature to the Security Council for the period 2017–2018, following a stalemate in the competition between Italy and the Netherlands, the two countries decided to split the term in a sign of European unity. It is worth noting that this election makes Italy the country of the Western European and Others Group (WEOG) that has served most terms (seven) in the Security Council, remarking how important the UN is in Italian foreign policy as a forum in which Italy can be an important player and avoid marginalization.[3] The election mechanism to the most prestigious body of the organization generates competition and makes sitting in the Security Council one of the highest privileges at the UN. Even though the voting power of nonpermanent members is minimal compared to permanent members', and even though a single nonpermanent member can be easily outvoted, "the jump in status is huge" (Hurd 2002: 44). Accordingly, Pouliot (2016: 219), considers that in relation to this factor Italy is in the top tier of the UN member states' pecking order,[4] and including a wider range of factors it remains in the upper-to top group of the UN pecking order (Pouliot 2016: 235). Among the wider range of factors contributing to the Italian position in the UN pecking order particularly important are its leadership of the Uniting for Consensus group in relation to the issue of Security Council reform, its contributions to peacekeeping and development, its permanent mission size, and its voting alignments with the US in the UNGA (Pouliot 2016: 213). This suggests that Italian activism at the UN translates into status and influence, but also that this is an important forum where Italy can gain them.

The US

The relationship with the US and its hegemonic organization of the international system, the most important pillar of Italian foreign policy since the end of World War II, is also evident at the UN. The US promoted it and determined its structure, because the UN was essential to the US-led organization of the international system (Puchala 2005: 573). Many at the State Department considered that the UN was crucial for the institutionalization of US leadership and for the promotion of US values in the new post–World War II order (Cronin 2001: 115). The UN was a forum in which the Cold War was played and allegiance to the US by bloc members was requested. Italian membership of the UN was strongly encouraged and supported by the US to strengthen the Western bloc, and as for other members of the dominant coalition Italy's allegiance to the US was requested and expected.

During the first Cold War years, the US instrumentally recurred to the UN on all the most important international crises to receive international legitimation to its actions (Puchala 1982–1983). A Western bloc made of the US and its traditional allies among which Western European states, Canada, Australia, and Japan was identifiable both in the UNGA and in the Security Council. Within that coalition exchange of information, attempts at coordination and even a socialization process took place, encouraged by the perspective (now remote in the UNGA) of controlling the decision-making outcome and key positions. Until the sudden growth in UN members produced by the decolonization process, the US, despite Cold War dynamics, managed to mobilize consistent support within the organization, thanks to European and Latin-American states (Puchala 2005: 573). However, from the 1970s onward, a new majority formed in the UNGA, and the US lost control of its decision-making processes and was frequently isolated. The loss of control of the UNGA and the incapacity to create supporting majorities and gain consensus in the organization created a cleavage between the UN and the US. The change was evident in the Security Council too, where the US was forced to use its veto power more regularly to stop resolutions against its interests. Nevertheless, as Puchala (2005: 573) observes, the US managed to strongly influence the agenda of the organization and prevent reforms that could have reduced its influence. To do that, it had to rely on the support of its allies, whose backing was more and more important to control the organization. Whether its allies voted like the US was under scrutiny and reports on voting practices in the UN became an instrument to check allegiance that bore important consequences.[5] How Italy voted at the UN, and whether it voted like the US, became particularly important for the Italian relationship with the US, because defections on important votes could damage it. The relationship between Italy and the US at the UN can therefore be explored looking at the Italian voting coincidence with the US, on which the State Department regularly produces reports for the Congress since 1983, and whose data are publicly available (see figure 2.1).

In the 1980s, in line with its more activist foreign policy, Italy occasionally allowed itself a little room for maneuver, but on votes that were deemed important by the US, it confirmed its close alignment. With the end of the Cold War, the US started reconsidering the UN as a prime venue for its foreign policy and asked for UN legitimation of its most important foreign policy initiatives. In the 1990s the Clinton administration associated the slogan "assertive multilateralism" to its foreign policy, signaling that multilateralism was again central to American foreign policy. The UN became much more active, especially in relation to peacekeeping operations, and the US regained wide support in the UNGA and was better able to control UN

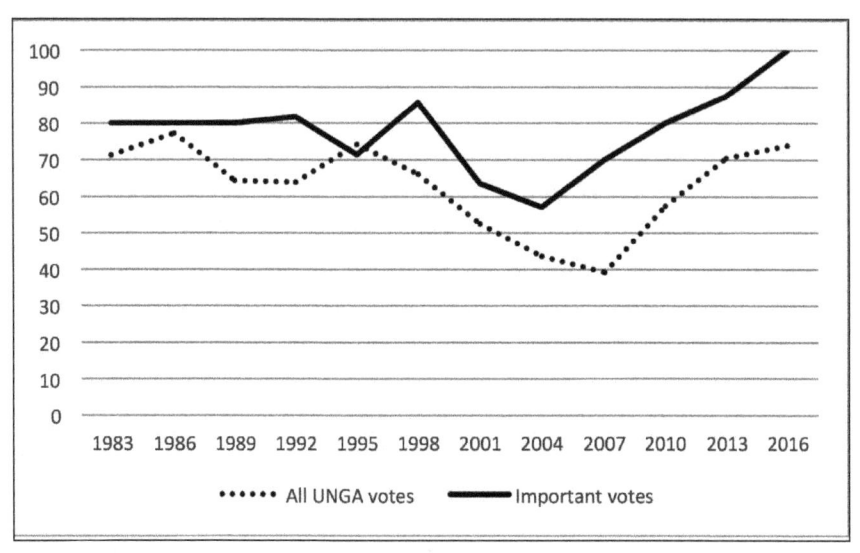

Figure 2.1. Italian voting coincidence with the US in the UNGA on roll call votes (percentage), 1983–2016.
Source: United States Department of State 1984–2017 (elaboration by the author).

decision-making processes, although this was more evident in the Security Council. The US also made a priority of UN reform, launching a request that has persisted across different administrations. In this period Italian greater autonomy from the US and foreign policy activism and assertiveness translated into a wider gap between voting coincidence with the US on all votes and voting coincidence on important votes in the UNGA.

The 2000s saw an important change in the US commitment to multilateral institutions and the promotion of unilateral initiatives that proved highly divisive across the Atlantic, including the Iraq war. While Italy under the Berlusconi government positioned itself close to the Bush administration, diverging from other European countries, the issue was deeply divisive, and the conflict strongly felt. Although voting cohesion on important votes between Italy and the US was always above 50 percent, a significant cohesion drop was registered. The situation improved only with the reengagement with multilateral institutions under the second Bush administration (Patrick 2015).

In the 2010s, the Obama administration put US reengagement with multilateral institutions at the center of its program. Rebuilding and reform of multilateral institutions, thanks to the US capacity to widen support toward them, was presented as an integral element of US leadership (Obama 2007).[6] Obama (2008) referred to the need to have global institutions that work to face global challenges, and to the UN as being indispensable and imperfect.

The US still had troubles getting its initiatives approved, and often found itself in a minority group. A different situation existed in the Security Council, where the US, supported by its European allies, increased its control of the agenda (Monteleone 2015). For the US, being able to count on its traditional European allies to perform system maintenance activities within the UN proved to be particularly appreciated. Accordingly, the Italian voting cohesion with the US in the 2010s has dramatically increased to reach 100 percent of important votes in 2016 (figure 2.1).

The Trump administration has severely challenged the usefulness for the US of the existing international order and its institutions. Its relationship with the UN is still rather uncertain. For all the talk about abandoning existing universal multilateral institutions, so far, the US seems to have chosen selective engagement, and it is within the UN framework that the most important crisis of the period, the one over North Korean nuclear proliferation, has been managed, also engaging China and Russia. The Trump administration has also prompted harsher conflicts with European allies, no longer necessarily acknowledged as important, and from whom a greater burden-sharing is expected. Although the information is not immediately comparable because of changes in the way the report is made, in the only year (2017) of the Trump administration for which data are available at the moment of writing, Italian voting cohesion on votes considered important by the US administration dropped to 62 percent (United States Department of State 2018), indicating difficulties for Italy to adjust to the new American perspective on the organization of the international system.

The EU

Support to European integration as a pillar of Italian foreign policy can also be explored at the UN, because the EU has institutionalized its relationship with the organization and has attempted to increase its presence (Laatikainen and Smith 2006b; Blavoukos and Bourantonis 2017; Laatikainen 2015). Three types of Europeanization can be seen at play at the UN: the development of institutional capability for coordinating the policies of EU member states; the adaptation of EU member states to ensure consistency and effectiveness to the EU voice; and an external diffusion process of European ideas and institutions (Laatikainen and Smith 2006a: 9). However, the aspect that has attracted the most attention is the creation of an EU voice, analyzed through EU member states' voting behavior in the UNGA. Voting cohesion studies reflected an interest in the Europeanization of EU member states' diplomacy at the UN (Laatikainen 2015: 705).

With the European Political Cooperation in the 1970s, the attribution to the EU of the status of permanent observer in 1974, and then even more with the Maastricht treaty and the CFSP in the 1990s, EU member states have made increasing attempts not only at consulting each other but also at institutionalizing their consultations at the UN. The 1999 Framework Agreement between the UN and the EU stressed the importance ("It is vital") for the EU of speaking at the UN with one voice and of coordinating. In 2011 the EU obtained an "enhanced" observer status, and in 2017 the Council of the EU (2017) in its *EU priorities at the United Nations and the 72nd United Nations General Assembly* identified upholding, strengthening, and reforming the UN as an EU key priority. The EU's political choice for an effective multilateralism with at its heart a strong UN makes EU member states' coordination at the UN important not only as a political goal per se but also instrumental to supporting UN effectiveness.

At the UNGA, EU member states belong to three different regional groups: the majority to the WEOG, the rest to the Eastern European Group and one (Cyprus) to the Asian Group. Acting as a single political group is a choice that creates another institutional layer for EU states, one that is not formally recognized but that is perceived by the other UN member states. At the UN EU member states are expected to act as a unified actor (Paasivirta and Porter 2006: 35). Interviews at the UN headquarters reveal that "the growth of the

EU as an actor at the UN is such that representatives from other UN member states charge that nothing gets accomplished in many UN bodies unless the Europeans are on board" (Laatikainen 2004: 4). Coordination at the UN, especially in the UNGA, is particularly intense, as more than 1,300 meetings in New York are held every year to develop a common EU stance (European External Action Service 2017). The EU member states' diplomats working in the subject area of the resolution meet and, on the basis of their national instructions, negotiate a common stance. This means that "Debate about the particular policy question or agenda item is continued until all members of the EU group without any exception agree to the direction and wording of the policy to be endorsed" (Dedring 2004: 2). Seeing EU states acting as a single actor has become "a familiar sight to all partners at the UN and is the pattern of behavior which is now expected of the EU" (Paasivirta and Porter 2006: 47). But in the end coordination among EU member states at the UN works so well not only because it is "ingrained in the working habits" of EU diplomats in New York and is supported by common rules and a common space, but also because there is "a substantive and realistic judgment that more is achieved by the EU's Member States when acting together than any state could manage alone" (Paasivirta and Porter 2006: 48). This situation has been only slightly changed with the entry into force of the Lisbon treaty, which led the EU delegation to the UN to progressively assume the role of the rotating Presidency and to be responsible for the day-to-day coordination of the EU position, and with the upgrading in 2011 of the EU's status in the UNGA.

Europeanization has been recorded at the UN through the analysis of EU member states' voting cohesion in roll call votes, the most politicized ones, in the UNGA (Jin and Hosli 2013; Panke 2017b). The increase in EU member states' voting cohesion in the UNGA is generally considered in literature as evidence of the coordination results, as it has been repeatedly pointed out that until the 1990s EU members rarely voted as a bloc, unless the level of disagreement in the UNGA was high (Luif 2003; Laatikainen 2004; Paasivirta and Porter 2006; Burmester and Jankowski 2014). When a cohesive vote by EU member states was unlikely to change the outcome of a resolution, the coordination process seemed to be limited and specific national interests could prevail over the majority position of the EU. However, since the 1990s, coordination efforts in the UNGA drove to a marked increase in EU states' voting cohesion. EU member states since the second half of the 1990s have managed to increase the level of unanimous votes to around 80 percent and drastically reduce two-way splits and three-way splits to around 10 percent (Johansson-Nogués 2004: 72; Jin and Hosli 2013; Panke 2017b). As Panke (2017b) has shown, also EU group coherence (i.e., the percentage of EU member states sharing the majority preference of the EU) in the UNGA in the period 1990–2010 is high and indicates that in about 95 percent of all resolutions in the analyzed period EU member states voted in the same way, and this is to be attributed to their coordination in New York. Moreover, the trend is stable. EU member states' voting cohesion in the UNGA is not significantly higher than other regional organizations (Jin and Hosli 2013), but the EU is the only regional organization that since the 1980s has acquired such a high level of coordination and strategic voting behavior that it has become capable of increasing its level of voting cohesion in contested votes (Burmester and Jankowski 2014).

The willingness of EU member states to be perceived as a bloc is indicated by the increase in the number of statements and documents made in the name of the EU (Laatikainen 2004). Analyzing all EU oral interventions in the UNGA bodies from the 64th to the 69th UNGA sessions, Blavoukos et al. (2016) show that the EU delegation has increased its interventions from three in the 64th session to 82 in the 69th session. However, their analysis also shows that this trend was reversed in the 69th session and that interventions by EU member states to support the EU position are quite high, indicating that EU member states still cherish their own visibility.

There is still considerable variation in the degree of adaptation of EU member states toward an EU diplomacy (Laatikainen and Smith 2006a) and remarkable differences have been registered on some issues (Luif 2003; Jin and Hosli 2013; Panke 2017b). EU member states tend to defect when it comes to vital national issues, and the content and flexibility of individual states' win-sets, the ability of national diplomats and the red lines imposed through instructions by their ministries of foreign affairs can be important factors when negotiating a common EU stance (Panke 2017b). National capitals, the instructions they send, and the flexibility allowed can determine the negotiating space for diplomats involved in negotiations in New York. The more politicized the issue the less probable reaching a common stance becomes.

Burmester and Jankowski (2018) have shown that vote defection from the EU majority has been increasing since the 1990s. The older EU members tend to defect less, and agreement between the EU majority and the US on an issue that is important for the US reduces defection too. On the contrary, contentious issues such as colonialism and nuclear proliferation and disagreements between the EU majority and the US increase the probability of a deviating vote, because showing loyalty to the US is perceived as important by EU member states, especially on resolutions that are important to the US. States like France and the UK have been deviating more often even when the proportion of deviators was low, while smaller states only deviate together with other states. Burmester and Jankowski (2018) also point out the German case as a major EU player whose behavior resembles that of EU smaller states because of its specific historical background and dominant discourse that the EU interest is in the German interest. While not exploring the case, they also show that Italy, another big EU member, deviates much less than Germany and is at the bottom of the list of deviators. Only Lithuania, Bulgaria, Luxembourg, Estonia, Denmark, Slovakia, and Slovenia, all small states, deviated from the EU majority less than Italy in the period 1991–2011 (Burmester and Jankowski 2018).

The Italian attitude in relation to the creation of a common position of EU member states has been touched upon in previous studies. Although analyzing voting coincidence only, Laatikainen and Smith (2006a: 11) recorded very high levels of Italian voting with the EU majority in the UNGA in the period 1991–2003, regardless of the EU overall cohesion registered. However, their data also show that, starting from the 54th session (1999–2000), both the Italian cohesion and the EU overall cohesion started to decline slightly, and that the decline was more marked in the latter case. Luif (2003) also indicated that the distance Italy had from the EU majority in the UNGA during the 1990s and at the beginning of the 2000s on crucial issues such as the Middle East, security and disarmament, decolonization and human rights was minimal: Italy did belong to the existing EU majority regardless of the issue. The 1990s even registered an improvement on the already excellent record of Italy as a European country, while the early 2000s saw a little distance from the EU majority on the issue of human rights, a critical issue for the Europeanization of foreign policy because strongly linked to the EU identity. Young and Rees (2005) also note that, while at a great distance from the UK and France, in the period 1990–2002 Italy occasionally used isolated voting, but, compared to the other EU members, it avoided voting in minority groupings, suggesting a stronger commitment to EU cohesion.

In the Security Council, EU member states make a fundamental contribution to the implementation of resolutions thanks to their financial and personnel resources (Blavoukos and Bourantonis 2011: 735). The EU has no status, but two permanent members (the UK and France) and at least two more non-permanent members normally have a seat. This allows a potentially strong European influence on UNSC matters, as EU members occupy about a third of the available seats. Although the two EU permanent members normally defend their role and have traditionally shown not to be very keen on sharing their information and consulting with the other EU members (Hill 2006), the UK and France have over time acquired a more accommodating attitude on informing and consulting the other EU member states (Dedring 2004: 3).

While in the 1990s no meaningful coordination among EU member states took place, from the 2000s pragmatic arrangements have allowed an increased coordination and information sharing and therefore an increased EU presence (Drieskens et al. 2007; Marchesi 2010; Blavoukos and Bourantonis 2011). Consultations among EU members take place in New York on a regular basis, and the quality of these consultations has improved over the years, with EU members sitting in the Security Council briefing the other EU members on Council activities (Verbeke 2006: 55; Marchesi 2010). EU member states sitting in the UNSC do not just provide information to the other members but have also proven to be receptive to their opinions on matters under consideration in the Security Council. This activity has resulted in a progressive increase of EU speeches and statements during the 1990s and in the first half of the 2000s (Laatikainen 2004). However, the coordination level of EU member states in the Security Council remains much lower than the one registered in the UNGA and, being vital national interests more likely to be at play in such a forum, they can always prevail on EU states' attempts at coordination. Divisions among EU member states remain particularly evident in the case of Security Council reform, where "the member states' different status in the UN system and their diverging political aspirations predispose against [. . .] a uniform approach" (Blavoukos and Bourantonis 2011: 738).

In the Security Council, Italy has been characterized by a very Europeanized outlook, trying to give its mandates a European dimension, unsuccessfully proposing an EU laboratory within the Security Council (opposed by France and the UK), giving an extensive interpretation to EU treaty articles dealing with EU coordination in international forums and even declaring during its 2007 term that the Italian seat would be an EU one (Salleo and Pirozzi 2008; Drieskens et al. 2007). However, Italy has also invested consisting resources in defending its national interests, fighting mostly with non-European countries against EU member states, to prevent a reform that would significantly reduce the Italian status (Blavoukos and Bourantonis 2011). Moreover, the Italian proposal for an increased EU presence and coordination has been seen as a way of framing a conflicting strategy within a pro-European rhetoric (Marchesi 2010: 106).

The divisions on Security Council reform as well as the analysis of EU member states' defection from the EU majority in the UNGA remind us that national interests are still present and that intra-EU divisions are always possible. This is confirmed by analyses of the Europeanization of EU member states' foreign policy in the Human Rights Council, in which, according to Smith (2017), EU states are keen to preserve their autonomy and capacity to act on a national basis, in a case of arrested Europeanization.

A CHANGING OPPORTUNITY STRUCTURE AND POTENTIAL CHALLENGES

The traditional pillars of Italian foreign policy emerged after World War II within the framework of an organization of the international political system in which multilateral institutions and the European integration process were strictly connected to the hegemonic organization of the international political system promoted by the US. Supporting the UN and performing system maintenance activities building on a European coalition of states—what is here called the European formalized coalition—was therefore an effective way for Italy to play its role in the international system and gain prestige and status for its support. The assumptions on which Italian foreign policy was based, however, are no longer solid, and this might change incentives and constraints of Italian actions, leading to decreasing returns in case of continuation and making room for potential deviations from the traditional foreign policy pillars.

While it would not be possible to mention all the relevant changes that might affect Italian foreign policy options, a few ones are worth pointing out. The first has to do with the UN itself and its legitimacy. The UN is in line with a long-term trend toward inclusive security institutions (Pouliot and Thérien 2015). However, it is also the universal multilateral institution that attracts almost universal requests for reform to update it to the current international context. This is particularly true of the Security Council, on which reform debates started in the 1990s and are not any more advanced today than they were back then (Bourantonis 2005). The capability of the Security Council to legitimize the use of force is seen as a form of political reassurance about the consequences of the proposed action (Voeten 2005). However, the deep changes in the 1990s, signaled by the enormous increase in the number of peace operations, in the number of non-state actors involved, and in the intrusive type of interventions, brought about new questions. The organization most responsible for preserving peace, the UN, "was no longer simply viewed as an incremental tool for the improvement of security at the margin, but as responsible for protecting human rights even when states failed or refused to do so. Increasingly, it was held responsible for inaction as well as action" (Keohane 2006: 63). Put otherwise, the UN capacity to solve contemporary global problems, its responsiveness and performance are important to determine the support that it will receive (Gilley 2009: 38). To be perceived as legitimate, institutions must provide a comparative benefit, that is, they must supply those important public goods that cannot be achieved without them and that were invoked to justify the constraints that they impose (Buchanan and Keohane 2006), and they must be responsive to the evolving political expectations of the underlying political community regarding the existence of a common good against which performance can be measured (Gilley 2009: 4; Easton 1965). Next to the procedural aspects (input legitimacy), the achievement of the substantive purposes of the organization or its effectiveness (output legitimacy) is an important source of legitimacy (Scharpf 1999). Doubts regarding the legitimacy of the organization reflect on the decisions approved, but reviving performance is a way to exit from a legitimacy crisis (Gilley 2009). In the case of the UN, requests for a thorough reform express not just power struggles, but most of all dissatisfaction with the existing institution, uttered both by the leading global power and by states that feel left out of the decision-making process. As the agenda of the Security Council is controlled by Western countries and Russia and China more frequently exert their role as veto players (Monteleone 2015), concerns for representativeness have become a common thread in reform requests (Pouliot and Thérien 2015).

This has also led to wonder whether we are undergoing a crisis of global institutions (Newman 2007) and whether the UN is still capable of addressing the major contemporary global problems. It has also led to ask what role the US, originally the main proponent of the UN, will keep playing at the UN, and, conversely, whether the UN is still relevant for the US. The issue is quite an important one because the US is the main contributor to the UN, but the UN has traditionally legitimized US policies (Attinà 2003). An increasingly sovereigntist Congress (Drezner 2012) has forced even an administration that attributed a strategic role to multilateralism, the Obama administration, to recur to a sort of stealth multilateralism (Kaye 2013), making it more convenient for US administrations to invest in forms of informal cooperation or minilateralism, rather than engage in far-reaching reforms of the existing universal multilateral institutions (Skidmore 2012; Patrick 2014 and 2015). While the Obama administration pledged to continue to embrace the post–World War II institutional architecture, seen as essential and still crucial (White House 2015), and adopted a defensive stance of the existing institutions, the current Trump administration has been highly critical, considering the UN too feebly responsive to US interests, and has already cut funds to some of its programs. The issue is relevant in that the US is by far the largest contributor to the UN. In 2018 its contribution was 22 percent of the UN regular budget, against China's 7.921 percent and Russia's 3.088 percent (United Nations Secretariat 2017), and 28.4344 percent of the UN peacekeeping budget, against China's 10.2377 percent and Russia's 3.9912 percent (United Nations General Assembly 2015). A significant reduction in the US contribution would therefore be enough to undermine the UN.

It remains to be seen whether a real US disengagement from the UN will take place. Under the Trump administration the US has withdrawn from the

UN Human Rights Council, but its actions are not unprecedented. The first Permanent Representative to the UN appointed by the Trump administration, Nikki Haley, has promoted a political line of engagement toward the organization that so far has not been publicly disavowed. Moreover, the increasing attention of the US administration to the analysis of voting coincidence in important votes, next to rather explicit threats of negative consequences, suggests that the UN is still an important forum for the US, in which it creates coalitions and tests allegiances (Landler 2017; Sengupta 2017). Especially considering the importance attributed to the Security Council by China and Russia as a forum for confrontation and competition among great powers, it should not be ruled out that the Trump administration may keep selectively engaging as long as it controls the decision-making process in the Security Council and other countries increase their contributions to relieve the US burden. On the contrary, should the US disengage from the UN, this would affect the Italian opportunity structure. Given the role of the UN as the main pillar of the post–World War II US-led international order and the Italian role as ally of the US in that order, variations in the American attitude toward the UN could have effects on the Italian support to the UN as a strategy to strengthen the hegemonic order. Likewise, a loss of legitimacy of the UN could reduce incentives for Italy to act through the UN and play a discernible supporting role there as a way of increasing its status. Under these conditions, the Italian traditional middle power strategy of investment in the UN and multilateralism could produce decreasing returns that might discourage pursuing it (Romero 2016).

The need to achieve the substantive purposes of the organization has requested new actors to support the UN and make it more effective. Both the EU and the so-called rising powers (BRIC) have opted for supporting the UN and acting through it.

As already shown, the EU has made of the UN an important forum with which it cooperates and in which EU member states are expected to become proactive and to coalesce in support of the organization. The economic and financial crisis, Brexit, the migration crisis, and the rise of Euroscepticism in many European countries may affect the capacity of EU member states to coordinate, act cohesively, present themselves as speaking with a single voice, but also to be effective. This too might decrease for Italy incentives to act at the UN through the European formalized coalition and work to facilitate its coming into being and maintenance. However, both the logic of consequences and the logic of appropriateness can be seen at play in Europeanization processes, so belonging to a European community may still be a driver leading Italy to align with and support the creation and maintenance of the European formalized coalition. On the other hand, with its actions on

Security Council reform and its creation of a wide variegate coalition in the UNGA, Italy has proven to be capable of acting together with non-European states to prevent actions that would damage its interests.

Another international factor influencing Italian foreign policy at the UN is the rise of the so-called BRIC countries. Their growth has been reflected in requests for reform of the existing multilateral institutions to take into account their new weight. However, none of the BRIC countries challenges the existence of the UN. On the contrary, China's contribution to its activities has dramatically increased over time both in terms of budget and peacekeeping personnel (United Nations Secretariat 2017), showing support to the activities of the organization. Moreover, China and Russia have become (again, in the case of Russia) extremely active in the Security Council, making frequent use of their privileges. Although the two countries are not yet capable of influencing the agenda setting phase, they have become effective as veto players (Monteleone 2015). The two countries are also active defenders of their privileges and therefore of the status quo, refusing any option that might create limitations to their veto power use, and in general any change that might alter their position. Interestingly, India and Brazil too have long aimed at a permanent seat in the Security Council, but despite efforts at concerting positions with Russia and China they have not received any significant support from them.

The strong presence at the UN of the BRIC countries might affect Italian foreign policy. Given the close relationship between Italy and Russia, considered by some (Brighi 2011) an element of de-Europeanization, the rising presence of Russia and the BRIC group at the UN might attract Italy and provide an alternative to its traditional strategy by aligning with them.

The last notable change that affects Italian opportunities and constraints is a domestic one and has to do with the rise of Euroscepticism in Italy, also reflected in public opinion polls showing a greater distance between Italy and the EU, increasingly perceived as a constraint rather than an opportunity (Lucarelli 2015). Although existing analyses have shown that the attitudes of governments toward the EU do not significantly affect their deviation from an EU majority at the UN (Burmester and Jankowski 2018), the lack of support from public opinion may affect the red lines in the indications sent from the ministry of foreign affairs in the coordination phase, reducing the chances of agreement and increasing the chances of deviation from the EU formalized coalition.

The previously indicated factors point toward broader changes in the US-led hegemonic order. It is therefore worth analyzing whether the low cohesion and strength of both the dominant coalition and the European formalized coalition in this phase of crisis of the order expected by hegemonic theories have taken place, reducing the possibility for Italy to use acting with the European formalized coalition as a strategy to gain status. However, the limited attention so far dedicated by hegemonic theorists to political coalitions is at the basis of a shortage of systematic analyses and of a consolidated methodology to empirically test expectations in relation to their creation and variation. This is an important limitation of hegemonic theories.

HOW TO ANALYZE THE EUROPEAN FORMALIZED COALITION MEMBERSHIP AT THE UN

To overcome this limitation, it is necessary to identify how to empirically analyze the creation and variation of political coalitions. It is here proposed that variations in the Italian attitude to be part of the European formalized coalition can be analyzed through an empirical analysis of Italian voting and sponsoring behavior at the UN. Investigating the combination of Italian voting and sponsoring will allow to empirically explore a niche role that Italy has consistently attempted to play in its quest for status, the one of coalition facilitator, that is the capacity of Italy to facilitate the creation or support the maintenance over time of a political coalition, the European formalized coalition, that is nested into the dominant coalition and supports the US-led hegemonic order. The analysis will focus on whether Italian coalitional behavior at the UN reflects a willingness to adapt Italian foreign policy to be a member of the European formalized coalition. It will also assess whether this behavior is used to increase Italy's structural opportunities and status as a country contributing to international system maintenance. It will therefore look at the modes/styles in which Italy, as many middle powers, has attempted to increase its status by acting—and being perceived—as a member in good standing of the dominant coalition in the US-led hegemonic order, providing system maintenance and therefore supporting the existing organization of the international system. Especially considering the mounting challenges to the existing US-led hegemonic order, among which a potential fragmentation triggered by the advance of the so-called rising powers and a reduction in US support to the existing multilateral institutions, this aspect of Italian foreign policy deserves further exploration. It is here argued that the Europeanization of Italian foreign policy, here operationalized as Italy's participation and support to a European formalized coalition including at least the majority of EU member states, has been key to Italian foreign policy, because it has allowed the country to play this niche role in a way that is consistent with its identity and strategic culture, and because it has increased Italy's structural opportunities and status. The possibility of politics of scale inherent to the European formalized coalition has progressively allowed the country to amplify its weight and initiate a more active foreign policy. This is all the more relevant in multilateral contexts, and in particular in the UN, not only because they are traditional forums for middle powers, but also because multilateralism is a declared feature in the identity of both the EU and Italy, and it has been a key component of the international liberal order promoted by the US after World War II with the support of its Western European allies. However, changes in domestic identity and security culture, in international systemic pressures and in the global norms that allow a country to claim status may all affect the effectiveness of this modality of status search. As the US-led hegemonic order has entered a crisis and crises in the EU recur, it is useful to assess whether variations in the Italian membership of the European formalized coalition have occurred.

In the UN context, looking at Europeanization as the creation of a political coalition would be in line with a consistent field of research looking at voting patterns of states in the UNGA (Alker 1964; Alker and Russett 1965; Kim and Russett 1996; Voeten 2000), and it is particularly pertinent because coalition politics heavily structures UN hierarchies of standing (Pouliot 2016: 4) and more in general UN diplomatic life (Laatikainen 2017). However, it also presents methodological problems. The first has to do with the operationalization of the European formalized coalition. The term European refers to an area wider than the EU and Europeanization has also been explored outside the EU (Börzel and Risse 2012). It has also long been acknowledged that in the UNGA candidate members and associated members regularly vote like the EU bloc (Johansson-Nogués 2004), making the EU bloc more consistent and influential within the UNGA. However, because here the interest is in understanding how Italian foreign policy may be influenced by EU dynamics, the focus will be on EU member states. Given the characteristics of a Europeanized foreign policy identified by Hill and Wong (2011: 211) and the characteristics of the political coalition formed by EU states already described in the first chapter, the European formalized coalition at the UN will present itself as a subset of states representing at least a majority of the EU membership that has developed a negotiated convergence of interests and strategies that allows them to present themselves as a single unit that persists over time and despite the absence of enforcing mechanisms, even when some members of the unit have little stake in the outcome. The expectation is not that of a granitic bloc, because coalition members can occasionally defect and even the ideal-typical Europeanized state is entitled to defect, according to the definition of Hill and Wong (2011: 211). Maintaining the European formalized coalition in a forum like the UN is particularly challenging, because here sovereignty is crucial, states belong to multiple groups presenting contrasting inputs and requests, and the variety of issues in the agenda may include issues of great relevance for EU member states or their closer allies. The European formalized coalition at the UN therefore creates whenever at least the majority of EU member states coalesce to adopt a single position. This operationalization is in line with existing literature, in that the creation of an EU majority has already been taken as a reference in studies on EU voting coherence in the UNGA (among others, Luif 2003; Laatikainen and Smith 2006a; Panke 2013 and 2017b; Burmester and Jankowski 2018).

Consistent with its status as a middle power, and with its frequent description in literature as bridge or coalition builder or facilitator, the role that Italy is here expected to play at the UN within the European formalized coalition is the one of coalition facilitator, which at the UN is assumed to confer a higher status (Pouliot 2016: 4). While the three terms are interchangeable in this context, the term facilitator has been preferred to coalition builder, because definitions of coalition builders normally tend to focus on the initiation of the coalition, so on leadership (Maull 2008; Ravenhill 1998). Here the focus intends to be broader and longer at the same time: broader, because it will go beyond the initiation phase of the coalition; longer, because the focus will not be on single episodes but on the capability to perform that specific role on a long-term basis. Indeed, in the life of a political coalition it is not only the negotiation of a common position that is important. Maintaining cohesion and preventing defections is probably more important (Karns and Mingst 2013: 147). This means that the entire life of the coalition before its disappearance is relevant, from initiation to maintenance, from enlargement to empowerment. As a facilitator, Italy is expected to contribute to the creation and maintenance of a European political coalition, and therefore to be a regular component of the European formalized coalition, especially when EU member states are divided. Accordingly, if Italy plays the role of facilitator, it should act together with the European formalized coalition more than it does separately, and acting separately from the European formalized coalition should be a residual behavior. Moreover, it should stick with the European formalized coalition even when EU member states are divided to maintain cohesion and strengthen the attractiveness of the coalition.

It is here argued that the Europeanization of Italian foreign policy implies the inclination to adapt foreign policy actions to be part of the European formalized coalition. This would have to manifest itself in the Italian prevalent and regular choice for acting with the majority of EU member states, not defecting from common positions, when they do exist, and being part of the EU majority group when a common EU position could not be reached.

Because different institutional dynamics provided by the context change incentives and constraints for the creation of a coalition, it is important to differentiate between the General Assembly and the Security Council, the two main UN institutions. The UNGA is where most studies on voting behavior are based to analyze foreign policies, because it allows to explore the existence of variations over time, and this is traditionally used to assess the position of a state in relation to the main political groups and clashes in the international system (Alker 1964; Alker and Russett 1965; Kim and Russett 1996; Voeten 2000). Because in the General Assembly most resolutions are adopted by consensus, focusing on recorded votes only, that is the most conflictual ones, has become the standard way of analyzing voting behavior in the UNGA. This choice will be followed here as well. However, because here the interest is in identifying Italian foreign policy adaptation to the European formalized coalition and the Italian role as coalition facilitator, contrary to existing literature that focuses only on the last part of the decision-making process, that is votes on resolutions, it is here proposed to look at all recorded votes. That is, to include votes also on operative paragraphs and procedures, on which EU member states might be encouraged to vote differently from the European formalized coalition to express their preferences while knowing that this will not affect the final outcome, and therefore the final vote on the resolution, normally used to assess the cohesion of EU member states. These votes can at times be extremely important to understand divisions within the EU (Luif 2003).

Another issue in the analysis of voting behavior in the UNGA concerns how to treat absence. Literature is divided on this, because some delegations are so small that they simply cannot cover all the sessions and committees, so their absence may not be strategic but due to lack of resources (Voeten 2013). However, here it has been preferred to focus on the existence of divisions, and therefore to regard "yes," "no," "abstention," and "absence" as four distinct positions, considering all of them as political decisions. This choice has been made considering that no EU member state mission to the UN is so small that it cannot afford the presence of a national representative and that at times EU member states were absent only for specific votes but were present both before and after the missed votes. This rather seems a position adopted in order not to displease other states by choosing sides.

Abstention is another difficult position to assess (Voeten 2013). However, because here the interest is toward Italian membership of the European formalized coalition or distance from it, following Luif (2003) the Italian distance from the EU majority will be weighted attributing a weight of 1 to full disagreement, and a weight of 0.5 to partial disagreement, and abstention when the EU majority votes "yes" or "no" will be treated as an intermediate position, so as a partial disagreement, and vice versa.

A critical issue is how to consider vote changes. This may happen because of a lack of timely and clear indications from the ministry of foreign affairs.

However, it is often the case that states indicate later how they intended to vote and communicate it to whoever is presiding to include the correction in the official records. Here the choice has been to consider the corrections included in the official records, because they are in line with the final position the state has adopted or was willing to adopt. This allows to reduce the potential bias due to the influence of autonomous choices made by diplomats in New York and to give more importance to the decisions made in the capitals.

Following the previously mentioned choices, a database has been built including all recorded votes, that is votes not just on resolutions, but also on operative paragraphs and procedures, since the 59th (2004–2005) until the 71st (2016/2017) regular sessions of the General Assembly,[7] drawing data from the website of the General Assembly[8] and from the UN website UNBISNET.[9]

In the UNGA the Europeanization of Italian foreign policy, that is Italy's inclination to adapt its foreign policy to be part of the European formalized coalition, will be assessed by looking at the Italian distance from the EU majority in its voting behavior. In all cases of EU split votes, the position of Italy will be assessed in relation to the majority group (i.e., the group in which the majority of EU member states was present). When no majority group is discernible, the case will be discarded. Next to the number of cases in which Italy distanced itself from the EU majority, the distance will be weighted, to calculate whether there was partial or full disagreement. Cases of absentee will be treated as partial disagreement.

In the UNGA, should Italian foreign policy be Europeanized, we would have to expect Italy being part of the EU majority group in voting as its predominant strategy. Had Italy de-Europeanized its foreign policy, we would have to expect an increase in the distance of Italy from the EU majority group in voting and an increase in the number of full disagreements.

Given the role of Italy as ally of the US, to see whether the tensions expected in the current phase of the US-led hegemonic order are affecting allegiances and therefore weakening the strength of the dominant coalition, Italian voting cohesion with the EU will be compared with Italian voting cohesion with the US and the BRIC group. Should Italian foreign policy be subject to the structural changes expected in the current phase by hegemonic theories, its voting cohesion with the US may be initially low and with irregularities, but its trend should be increasing over time.

However, looking at voting behavior only could hide the overlapping of occasional preferences, so it is here proposed that next to it the analysis of sponsoring behavior should be included as a more reliable indicator of coalitional behavior. In the UNGA the sponsoring of draft resolutions can be done by a single state, so there is no immediate incentive in building a supporting coalition, but it has become customary practice to involve other countries to show that the resolution has wide support, often adding them to the original sponsors. This support is an essential element in coalitional activities. Accordingly, a dataset has been built collecting all Italian-sponsored draft resolutions in the General Assembly from the 55th (2000/2001) until the 71st (2016/2017) session from the *Index to Proceedings of the General Assembly* regarding all the sessions concerned.[10] Collected data included the resolutions sponsored in the six committees. This choice raises the threshold because it increases the potential differences between Italy and the other EU members in that the creation of a European formalized coalition would be expected in the plenary, where the final vote is taken, while less pressure to co-sponsor would exist in the committees, which represent a still intermediate phase. Because the aim here is to analyze Italian coalitional behavior, all draft resolutions proposed were included, so even proposals successively revised or withdrawn were included, because they provide information on coalitional activity. These choices insert a bias against the Europeanization of Italian foreign policy, because it is often the case that a proposal is revised to allow the inclusion of more EU members. However, they allow to better identify with whom Italy tends to organize its activities.

Looking at draft resolutions sponsored by Italy gives information on Italian support to the UN as an institution, but also on common preferences and political projects that Italy has promoted at the UN, and on its preferred coalition partners. Accordingly, data regarding the Italian sponsoring trend, its preference to sponsor draft resolutions alone/with non-EU member states or with a majority of EU member states have been collected. Among EU member states, the countries more often sponsoring with Italy have been identified. To see whether this was done as a support maintenance activity and whether the expected volatility of coalitions in the current phase of crisis of the US-led hegemonic order has taken place, Italian co-sponsoring with the EU, the US, and the BRIC countries has been compared.

Had Italian foreign policy de-Europeanized, a regular prevalence of Italian sponsoring alone or with a minority of EU states should be present. Should Italian foreign policy still be Europeanized, it would have to be expected that Italy regularly and prevalently prefers to sponsor draft resolutions with a majority of EU states.

Whether Italy builds on the European formalized coalition to perform system maintenance activities in support of the order and increase its status can be analyzed by looking at the number of draft resolutions promoted by Italy, because acting through the UN is a means of legitimizing the organization and promoting its initiatives. With whom Italy co-sponsors is particularly important, though, because system maintenance activities to increase status could receive recognition only if in agreement with the global leader. Indeed, if voting with the US has become a standard measure of preference alignment with the hegemon and the liberal international order (Pouliot 2016: 301; Voeten 2004), sponsoring with the US should be even more so. Should Italy play the role of supporter of the US-led hegemonic order, the number of draft resolutions promoted by Italy over time should not fall dramatically and Italy should tend to co-sponsor with the US more than with the BRIC countries.

Despite being most frequently used for analyzing countries' foreign policy behavior, the UNGA is not where the most important decisions take place and its resolutions are not binding. To have a clearer picture of Italian foreign policy behavior, it is here suggested that the most important forum where Italian behavior should be analyzed is the Security Council. It is here that the most important security issues are debated and that authoritative decisions are taken. However, due to the regular practice of adopting resolutions by consensus, it is more useful to look at sponsoring behavior to analyze variations in the foreign policy of a country (Monteleone 2015). A draft resolution does not need to be sponsored by more than one state to be processed and approved. However, it has become increasingly frequent over time to have other Security Council members and non-members to co-sponsor draft resolutions, in show of support and to signal the existence of a common political project. Sponsoring a draft resolution is a political act that indicates that the issue is politically relevant for the sponsor. It also indicates that the issue is a conflictual one, as non-controversial draft resolutions are normally presented "according to prior consultation," and therefore by the entire UNSC. Moreover, while draft resolutions presented "according to prior consultation" are normally automatically approved, sponsored draft resolutions may encounter opposition and be rejected. However, Security Council members that are more active in sponsoring can gain control of the agenda.

Analyzing sponsoring behavior in the Security Council, however, still presents methodological challenges because five members are permanent and ten rotate on a two-year mandate. Adapting the analysis provided in Monteleone (2015), it is here proposed that, if Italy is part of the European formalized coalition, it must co-sponsor its draft resolutions together with the same subgroup of Security Council members, which is the European subgroup, as its regular and predominant strategy in the analyzed period.

In order to test empirically with whom Italy tends to co-sponsor draft resolutions the most, a database with all draft resolutions sponsored by Italy in the period 2000–2017 has been built using as a source the UN website UNBIS-NET.[11] In this period, Italy held a seat in the Security Council in 2007–2008 and in 2017 for one year only of its split term with the Netherlands.

Had Italian foreign policy de-Europeanized, we would have to expect that in the analyzed period Italy has chosen as its top co-sponsors non-EU countries, or that it has increasingly co-sponsored mostly with non-EU countries. Should Italian foreign policy be Europeanized, we would have to expect Italy co-sponsoring prevalently and regularly with EU countries as its predominant strategy.

Because we also want to check whether Italy adapts its foreign policy in order to be part of the European formalized coalition as a system maintenance activity, it is also important to see how much Italy sponsors draft resolutions, that is how much it processes its political demands through the Security Council, and whether it does it predominantly with the US or with the rising powers. Should Italy act to support the US-led international hegemonic order, we would have to expect it to sponsor regularly or increasingly and to do so together more with the US than with Russia or China.

The quantitative analysis of voting and sponsoring behavior will be followed by a focus on specific issues of relevance for the Europeanization of Italian foreign policy to identify cases of convergence or divergence between Italy and the European formalized coalition and better understand Europeanization processes (downloading, uploading, and cross-loading) within both the UNGA and the Security Council. The analysis of specific cases will also help to distinguish between cases in which Italy exercised leadership in the coalition formation and cases in which it facilitated coalition maintenance.

NOTES

1. Information provided in the website of the Italian Permanent Mission to the UN, https://italyun.esteri.it/rappresentanza_onu/en/l_italia_e_l_onu (accessed on 30 July 2018).

2. Italian Permanent Mission to the UN https://italyun.esteri.it/rappresentanza_onu/en/l_italia_e_l_onu (accessed on 30 July 2018).

3. UN Security Council website http://www.un.org/en/sc/inc/list_eng_region.asp?region=we (accessed on 1 August 2018).

4. The other members are Argentina, Brazil, China, Colombia, France, Germany, India, Japan, Pakistan, Russia, UK, and US.

5. For the Congressional reports produced by the State Department since 1983, see https://www.state.gov/p/io/rls/rpt/index.htm (accessed on 2 August 2018).

6. This paragraph re-elaborates on Monteleone (2018).

7. It was not necessary to collect data on the previous period, because data going back to the 1990s can be found in Laatikainen and Smith (2006a: 11).

8. See http://www.un.org/en/sections/documents/general-assembly-resolutions/index.html (accessed on 23 December 2018).

9. See http://unbisnet.un.org/ (accessed on 23 December 2018). For instance, data from the 68th UNGA session were drawn from http://www.un.org/en/ga/68/resolutions.shtml (accessed on 26 November 2017) and the keyword search in UNBISNET was A/68/PV* (only PV documents relating to the 68th UNGA session were used).

10. Available at https://library.un.org/index-proceedings/general-assembly (accessed on 6 December 2018). A textual search of the word "Italy" has been performed and cases of sponsored draft resolutions were retained.

11. It can be accessed at http://unbisnet.un.org/ (accessed on 1 April 2018). The keyword search was done inserting under Title "draft resolution," under Author keyword "Italy," and under UN document symbol "s*."

Chapter Three

In the General Assembly

VOTING BEHAVIOR

The General Assembly is where coordination among EU member states is most evident and most studied. In the UNGA all UN member states are present and have equal right to vote, so formally it is the most equalizing institution (Panke 2013). Group politics (Laatikainen 2017) in this forum has traditionally been assimilated to party politics (Alker and Russett 1965) because of competition dynamics.

The regular plenary sessions of the UNGA normally start in September and end in December, unless it is necessary to hold new meetings. Works for the plenary are prepared in six committees (Disarmament and International Security; Economic and Financial; Social, Humanitarian & Cultural; Special Political & Decolonization; Administrative and Budgetary; and Legal). This makes it highly probable that resolutions will be approved by consensus in the plenary, limiting the number of recorded votes to more contested resolutions or parts of them. The UNGA can deal with any matter related to international affairs, since the dividing line between matters under UNGA competence and the ones under the Security Council competence has become increasingly blurred. However, its resolutions are non-binding, limiting the stakes for member states to invest in it heavily. This chapter will assess the Italian voting and sponsoring behavior in the UNGA focusing on the country's coalition facilitating capacities in relation to the European formalized coalition. It will also assess whether Italy facilitates the creation and maintenance of the European formalized coalition in support of the US-led hegemonic order and as a status-seeking strategy.

Looking for the Europeanization of an EU member state's foreign policy in the UNGA means searching for mostly the modes II, III, and IV identified by Hadfield, Manners and Whitman (2017a), because, although the EU has gained observer status and now coordinates meetings, only its member states can vote, and they need to negotiate external support to successfully influence UNGA decision making. The adaptation of EU member states' foreign policy to ensure consistency and effectiveness of the EU voice identified by Laatikainen and Smith (2006a: 9) as an indicator of Europeanization at the UN is an intergovernmental activity. Looking at the behavior of EU member states in the UNGA it is possible to search for the elements identified by Hill and Wong (2011: 211) as characterizing the ideal type Europeanized foreign policy: taking common EU positions as the country's major reference point, despite operating in other multilateral forums; not generally defecting from common positions; attempting to pursue national priorities principally (but not exclusively) through the means of collective EU action; and subscribing to "the values and principles expressed by the EU in its international activity, to the extent of becoming part of a shared image and identity, in the eyes of both other Europeans and outsiders."

Adapting Hill and Wong (2011: 211), it is here argued that in the UNGA the Europeanization of Italian foreign policy should translate into Italy's inclination to adjust its foreign policy actions to be part of the European formalized coalition. The Europeanization of Italy's foreign policy should thus lead the country to prevalently and regularly act with all the other EU member states, not defecting from common positions when they do exist, or at least be part of the EU majority group, when a common position cannot be reached.

In the UNGA, it is possible to systematically analyze variations in the Europeanization of Italian foreign policy over time. The literature on the voting behavior of EU member states in the UNGA has highlighted that in the 1990s the Italian cohesion with the other EU member states was particularly high. Laatikainen and Smith (2006a: 11) recorded very high levels of Italian voting with the EU majority in the UNGA in the period 1991–2003, regardless of the EU overall cohesion registered, indicating that Italy was regularly part of the EU majority (figure 3.1). However, while in the 1990s the Italian position could hardly be differentiated from the EU majority, starting from the 54th UNGA (1999–2000), both the Italian cohesion with the EU majority and the EU overall cohesion started declining.

Analyzing the issues debated in the UNGA and using a scale from 0 (minimal distance) to 100 (maximum distance), Luif (2003) pointed out that the distance between Italy and the EU majority in the UNGA during the 1990s and at the beginning of the 2000s on crucial issues such as the Middle East, security and disarmament, decolonization and human rights was minimal: Italy did belong to the existing EU majority regardless of the issue (table 3.1). Considering the distance from the EU majority, at the beginning of the 1990s

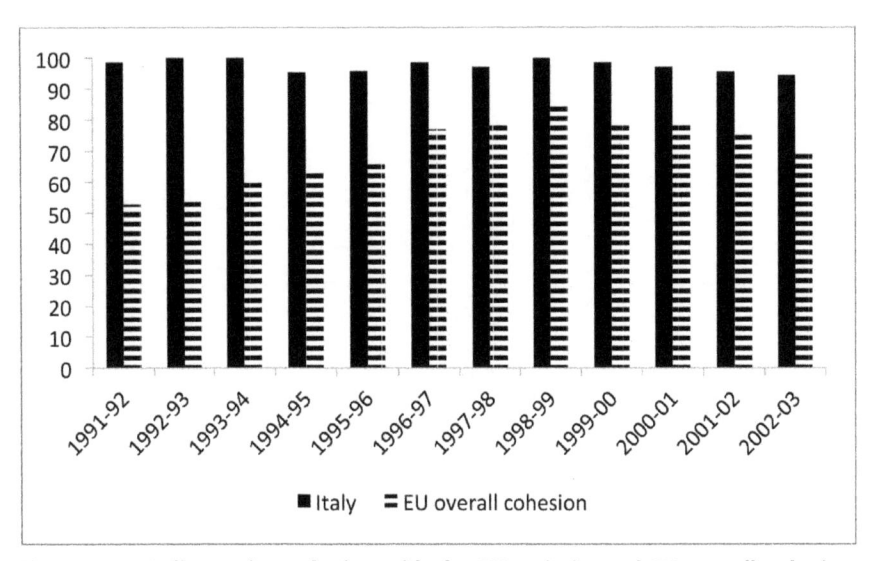

Figure 3.1. Italian voting cohesion with the EU majority and EU overall cohesion, UNGA roll-call votes (percentage), 1991–2003.
Source: Laatikainen and Smith (2006a: 11) (elaboration by the author).

Italy was regularly part of the inner core of the EU majority together with Germany, Belgium, Luxembourg, the Netherlands, and Portugal. In the second half of the 1990s Finland, Spain, Greece, Denmark, and Austria became regular coalition partners too. In the 1990s Italy was a more regular member of this coalition than in the 1980s. However, in 2000 the country started to slightly diverge from it, and in the early 2000s signs of a distance between Italy and the EU majority were registered (Luif 2003: 36).

The existing analyses on Italian voting behavior in the UNGA confirm the good record of Europeanization of Italian foreign policy also highlighted by Rosa (2003). However, they focus mostly on the 1990s and early 2000s, while more recent analyses have indicated a trend toward a de-Europeanization of Italian foreign policy (Brighi 2011; Dobrescu et al. 2017). In order to assess variations over time in the Europeanization of Italian foreign policy, it is here proposed to analyze the Italian voting behavior in the UNGA in the following period, that is, in the 2000s and 2010s. This period corresponds to a phase of crisis of the US-led hegemonic order and may therefore create incentives for old coalitions to reshuffle. For Italy, this might also mean a reduction in the returns of leveraging on the European formalized coalition to gain status.

The Europeanization of Italian foreign policy, that is Italy's inclination to adapt its foreign policy to be part of the European formalized coalition, in the UNGA can be operationalized as the distance of Italy from the EU majority group (i.e., the group in which the majority of EU member states was

Table 3.1. Distance of Italy from the EU majority in the UNGA on crucial issues, 1979–2002

Year	1979	1981	1983	1985	1987	1989	1990	1991	1992	1993	1994	1995	1996	1997	1998	1999	2000	2001	2002
Middle East	2	2	0	2	1	0	0	0	0	0	0	0	0	0	0	0	0	2	0
Security, disarmament	3	2	1	3	0	0	0	0	0	0	1	0	0	0	0	0	2	3	1
Decolonization												0	6	0	0	0	0	0	0
Human rights												0	0	0	0	3	4	4	3

Source: Luif (2003: 34–37) (elaboration by the author).

present) in voting behavior in the UNGA. In all cases of EU split votes, the position of Italy was assessed in relation to the EU majority group. When no EU majority group was discernible, the case was discarded. Besides identifying the number of cases in which Italy distanced itself from the majority, the distance was weighted, to calculate whether there was partial or full disagreement.[1]

Should Italian foreign policy be Europeanized, in all the years under consideration membership of the European formalized coalition in UNGA voting should be the predominant Italian strategy. That is, the number of Italian votes with the EU majority should be at least equal or more than 50 percent of the total number of Italian votes in the period under consideration and the trend should be constant or increasing over time. Had Italy de-Europeanized its foreign policy, we would have to expect an increase in the distance of Italy from the European formalized coalition in voting and the trend of Italian voting with the EU majority should be decreasing. That is, Italian votes with the EU majority should be less than 50 percent of the total number of Italian votes in the period under consideration, and the number of disagreements should be increasing over time.

The context is important too, and it is worth analyzing it to better assess Italian behavior. Recent analyses have highlighted that Europeanization at the UN may have been arrested because both the intergovernmental decision-making process and the external context discourage it (Smith 2017). Italian foreign policy therefore needs to be evaluated in the context of variations in EU member states voting. An increase in EU split votes would indeed create a greater incentive for Italy to free ride, and it would make it more difficult to facilitate the creation and maintenance of the European formalized coalition. On the other hand, it would make the Italian support to this coalition more valuable. A reduction in EU split votes, on the contrary, would reduce incentives to free ride, but it could also reduce the added value of the Italian contribution to the creation and maintenance of the European formalized coalition.

Looking at the EU context (figure 3.2), the percentage of EU split votes in the analyzed period is discontinuous, with disagreement among EU members ranging from 23 percent in the 66th UNGA (2011–2012) to 41 percent in the 70th UNGA (2015–2016). The downward trend in EU member states' voting cohesion already identified by Laatikainen and Smith (2006a: 11) at the beginning of the 2000s and depicted in figure 3.1 has therefore continued and worsened in the 2010s. EU member states still predominantly vote together (on at least 59 percent of the recorded votes in the analyzed period), confirming their presence as a stable political coalition. But the trend of EU split voting (represented in figure 3.2 by the dotted line) is increasing. The increase in EU split votes indicates a greater difficulty of EU member states in finding a

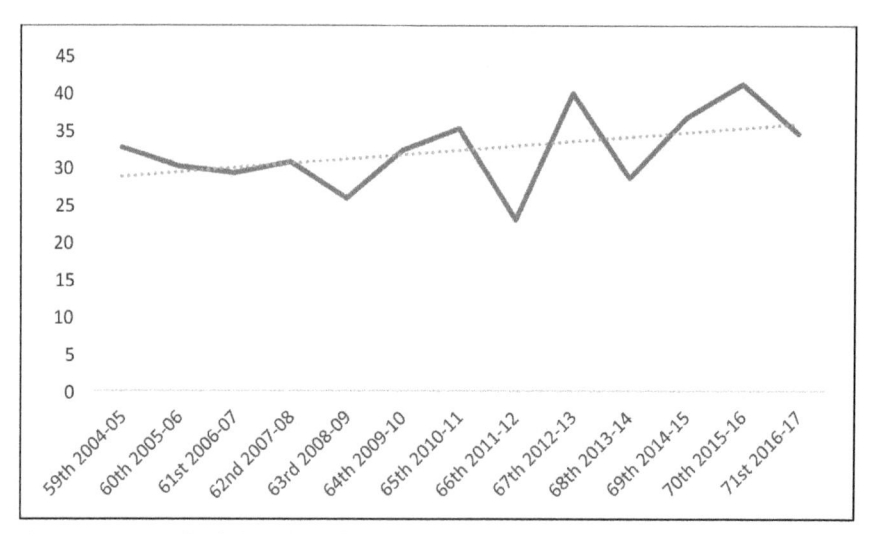

Figure 3.2. EU divided votes in the UNGA (percentage), 2004–2017.
Source: UNGA website and UNBISNET (elaboration by the author).

common position in the UNGA and reveals the existence of internal disagreements that may encourage defection.

Literature has highlighted that it is not infrequent that EU divisions are caused by the defection of one or two members (Kaufmann 1980; Burmester and Jankowski 2018). In the analyzed period too, it is rather frequent that EU split votes are caused by only one or two states defecting from the EU unanimity, very often France and the UK because of their special status in the Security Council. However, even considering the percentage of EU member states' quasi-unanimous votes, that is votes in which only one or two members defected from EU unanimity, on the total number of EU divided votes (figure 3.3), after the regrouping following the European crisis over the Iraq war in 2003 there has been a decrease in the capacity of EU member states to act cohesively and contain free riding. EU split votes are now caused by more member states' defections, and next to the UK and France a longer list of defectors has formed. So far EU member states still maintain cohesion and avoid important divisions and fragmentation, but the current context favors occasional free-riding and makes it more difficult to create a stable coalition. Another indication that EU voting cohesion has become more difficult is the rise, so far limited, in the 2010s of the number of cases in which an EU majority could not form at all because EU member states were deeply divided (table 3.2). This confirms that in the current context EU member states have greater incentives to free ride, while remaining members of the European formalized coalition is a deliberate choice.

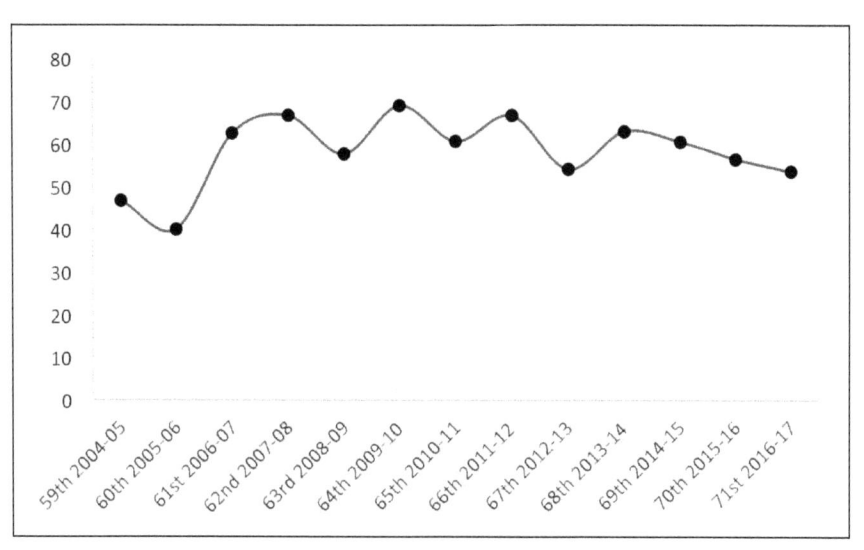

Figure 3.3. EU quasi unanimous votes in the UNGA (percentage), 2004–2017.
Source: UNGA website and UNBISNET (elaboration by the author).

It is within this context that the Italian voting behavior in the UNGA develops and that the Italian facilitating behavior in relation to the creation and maintenance of the European formalized coalition should be assessed (table 3.2). In all the years under consideration, whenever EU member states were divided, Italy voted with the EU majority in at least 80 percent of the cases. Italian voting with the EU majority reached a minimum of 80 percent during the 60th session (2005–2006) under the center-right Berlusconi government and a maximum of 100 percent during the 61st session (2006–2007) under the center-left Prodi government. It is noticeable that, compared with the Italian behavior registered by Laatikainen and Smith (2006a) in the 1990s, when Italian voting with the EU majority was regularly above 95 percent, Italian voting cohesion with the EU majority in the analyzed period is reduced (except for the 61st session). However, in the analyzed period the trend of Italian voting with the EU majority is constant and in all the years under consideration Italy was well above EU cohesion percentages, confirming the high Europeanization of its foreign policy and that Italy is actively behind the creation and maintenance of the European formalized coalition. In eight of the years under consideration the percentage of Italian voting with the EU majority was around 90 percent. Italian voting with the EU majority confirms claims in literature that center-right governments were more detached from the EU than center-left governments, and therefore more inclined to occasional free riding, but it does not confirm the de-Europeanization of Italian foreign policy under center-right governments presented in literature, if

Table 3.2. Italy and the European formalized coalition, 2004–2017

	59th 2004–2005	60th 2005–2006	61st 2006–2007	62nd 2007–2008	63rd 2008–2009	64th 2009–2010	65th 2010–2011	66th 2011–2012	67th 2012–2013	68th 2013–2014	69th 2014–2015	70th 2015–2016	71st 2016–2017
EU divided votes	30	30	32	30	26	29	33	24	37	27	38	39	43
Cases in which an EU majority did not form	1	0	1	0	0	0	1	0	2	0	1	1	2
I distance from EU majority (abs)	3	6	0	3	2	5	2	3	3	3	4	3	4
I with EU majority (abs)	26	24	31	27	24	24	30	21	32	24	33	35	37
I with EU majority (%)	90	80	100	90	92	83	94	88	91	89	89	92	90
EU cohesion (%)	67	71	71	69	74	68	65	77	60	72	63	59	66
EU majority (member states)	13	13	14	14	14	14	14	14	15	15	15	15	15
Prime Minister (main)	Berlusconi II	Berlusconi III	Prodi	Prodi	Berlusconi IV	Berlusconi IV	Berlusconi IV	Berlusconi/ Monti	Monti	Letta/ Renzi	Renzi	Renzi	Renzi/ Gentiloni

Source: UNGA website and UNBISNET (elaboration by the author).

not in relative terms. Indeed, Italian foreign policy remained predominantly Europeanized even under governments that were less inclined to follow the traditional guidelines of Italian foreign policy. Even in those years Italy acted in support of the creation and maintenance of the European formalized coalition in the UNGA. Variations in EU cohesion, however, may be related to the influence of systemic factors, particularly the weakening of the dominant coalition and, within it, the European formalized coalition, that is to be expected in the current phase of the hegemonic cycle and may lead to an increase of tensions among old-time coalition partners.

To understand whether Italy tends to facilitate the creation and maintenance of the European formalized coalition or acts to widen internal disagreements as suggested in literature (Brighi 2011), a specific focus was made on the Italian voting distance with the EU majority. The Italian voting distance from the EU majority was calculated as the percentage of votes that Italy cast differently from the EU majority in EU split votes when an EU majority formed (figure 3.4). In the second half of the 2000s the Italian voting distance from the EU majority varied, ranging from the 20 percent of different votes reached during the 60th session (2005–2006) to the maximum cohesion reached during the 61st session (2006–2007). Italian voting distance from the EU majority peaked twice, during the 60th (2005–2006) and 64th (2009–2010) sessions under center-right Berlusconi governments that were characterized by a more critical stance toward the EU and multilateral institutions. The minimum Italian voting

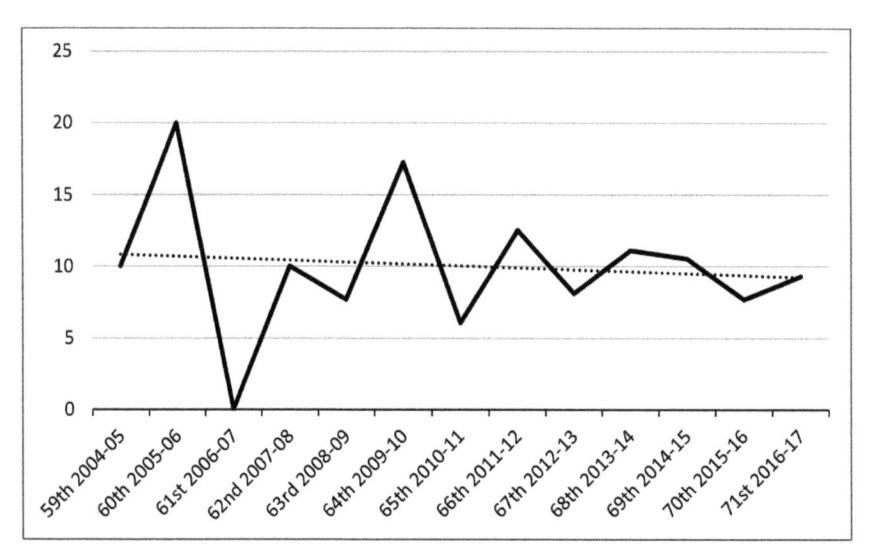

Figure 3.4. Italian voting distance from the European formalized coalition (percentage), 2004–2017.
Source: UNGA website and UNBISNET (elaboration by the author).

distance from the EU majority coincides with the center-left Prodi government, characterized by full support to the EU and multilateral institutions. Following periods of shorter Italian distance from the EU majority, the two peaks in Italian voting distance from the EU majority indicate a reduction in the degree of Europeanization or a relative de-Europeanization of Italian foreign policy. However, even then, acting with the European formalized coalition remained by far the prevalent strategy of Italy. Moreover, the last peak in the Italian distance from the EU majority was reached during the 64th session (2009–2010), but after that such a distance has progressively been reduced, and the trend line (the dotted line in the figure) is decreasing. The Italian voting distance from the EU majority in the analyzed period is limited and decreasing, indicating the Europeanization of Italian foreign policy.

In absolute numbers, the extent of the Italian choice to vote independently from the European formalized coalition is rather limited, the average being three dissenting votes per session, and does not reflect the increase in EU split votes (table 3.2). This means that Italy does not take the opportunity of wider intra-EU disagreements to free ride. On the contrary, it limits defections to occasional dissents on issues of importance to its foreign policy. Otherwise it tends to vote with the European formalized coalition and supports its formation and maintenance.

This interpretation is confirmed by the analysis of the Italian weighted distance from the EU majority (figure 3.5), in which a weight of 1 is attrib-

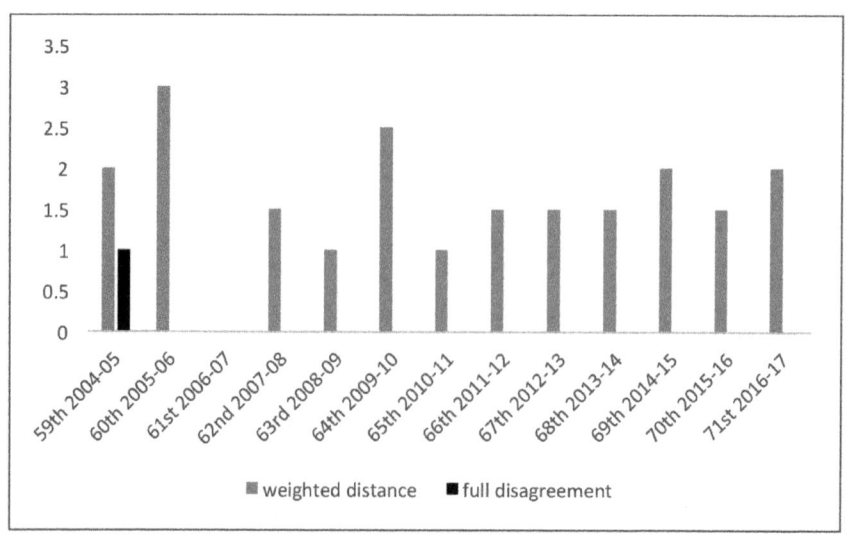

Figure 3.5. Italian weighted distance from the European formalized coalition, 2004–2017.
Source: UNGA website and UNBISNET (elaboration by the author).

uted to full disagreement and a weight of 0.5 to partial disagreement. Only one case of full disagreement was registered in the analyzed period, in 2005 on human cloning. In the rest of the votes, Italy has shown a more conciliatory approach, limiting itself to partial disagreement whenever it dissented from the European formalized coalition. This behavior is compatible with the ideal-typical Europeanized foreign policy behavior described by Hill and Wong (2011: 211) in that Italy predominantly takes the European formalized coalition as its reference point and supports it, defecting from it only in rare occasions. Acting together with the European formalized coalition is the normal Italian behavior, that confirms the Europeanization of its foreign policy.

Looking at the 41 votes in the analyzed period on which Italy expressed a dissenting voice, voting with the EU minority, 12 votes were cast on human rights and development issues and 18 votes were expressed on disarmament and nuclear weapons. Italy acted in complete isolation seven times: 5 times on environmental issues (absences concentrated in the 60th UNGA), once on Western Sahara (absence in the 60th UNGA) and once in the case of the resolution "Follow-up to nuclear disarmament obligations agreed to at the 1995, 2000 and 2010 Review Conferences of the Parties to the Treaty on the Non-Proliferation of Nuclear Weapons" in the 70th UNGA. In the case of nuclear disarmament, while the other 27 EU member states and the US voted against the resolution, Italy abstained. Voting in isolation from its traditional partners suggests the importance of the issue of nuclear disarmament for the country.

Except for the previously mentioned seven votes in isolation, all expressing partial disagreements and not an upfront confrontation, in the analyzed period even when in the minority Italy tended to act with other EU member states, within minority coalitions ranging from four to thirteen members. The countries more regularly in EU minority coalitions of which Italy was also a member are Portugal (21 times), Luxembourg (15), and Slovenia (15). Of the big EU member states, Germany (13 times) is the one that participated the most in EU minority coalitions of which Italy was also a member. These countries are the ones that Italy relies on and provides support to the most even when a European formalized coalition fails to form. Most importantly, they are also among the EU states in the upper quartile of voting cohesion with Italy in all votes and all years under consideration, which reveals with which EU states Italy tends to create coalitions. Slovenia was in the upper quartile of voting cohesion with Italy for 12 years, Germany and Luxembourg for nine, Portugal for eight together with Denmark and Slovakia. On the contrary, among the EU states in the lower quartile of voting cohesion with Italy in all votes and all years under consideration, which indicates the countries that are most distant from Italy and less likely voting coalition partners, the UK was present for all the 13 years under consideration, France and Malta for

Table 3.3. Top and bottom co-voters of Italy, 2004–2017

Top co-voters	Average voting cohesion percentage (weighted)	Bottom co-voters	Average voting cohesion percentage (weighted)
Slovenia	91	United Kingdom	42
Luxembourg	90	France	48
Germany	88	Cyprus	71
Portugal	88	Malta	71
Slovakia	88	Sweden	77
Belgium	87	Ireland	79
Denmark	87	Austria	80
Spain	87	Croatia	81
		Latvia	81

Source: UNGA website and UNBISNET (elaboration by the author).

12, Cyprus for 11, Spain for ten and Ireland for seven. The analysis of the weighted average voting cohesion percentage (table 3.3) confirms that Italy regularly votes with the above-indicated group of states.[2] Slovenia, Luxembourg, Germany, Portugal, Slovakia, Belgium, Denmark, and Spain voted with Italy in at least 87 percent of the EU divided votes in the analyzed period, while the UK and France were the most distant EU member states.

Because Italy tends to vote predominantly with the European formalized coalition, these differences should not be overamplified, as distances in absolute numbers can be small. However, this coalitional voting behavior indicates that among the other big EU member states, Italy is closer to Germany than to France or the UK. This picture partly coincides with the one emerging out of Luif's analysis (2003) on the EU member states Italy was regularly creating the EU majority with at the beginning of the 1990s, suggesting that coalitional patterns with some EU states may have strengthened over time. The Italian coalitional voting behavior also reveals that the country does not fit the traditional North-South division, since its coalitions tend to include Southern and Northern, Eastern, and Western, old and new EU members, while other members expected to be traditional allies (especially among Southern countries and founding members), can be rather distant from Italy. This diversity strengthens the idea traditionally self-portrayed of Italy as a bridge between countries belonging to different areas and therefore as a coalition facilitator.

To take into account changes at the international system level, the Italian voting cohesion with the European formalized coalition was compared with the Italian voting cohesion with the US and with the BRIC countries in the analyzed period (figure 3.6).[3] This comparison provides us information on whether Italy is now more attracted by non-European actors than by European actors, an indication of de-Europeanization. Also, this comparison allows us to better explore Italy's role in the international system. Italian sup-

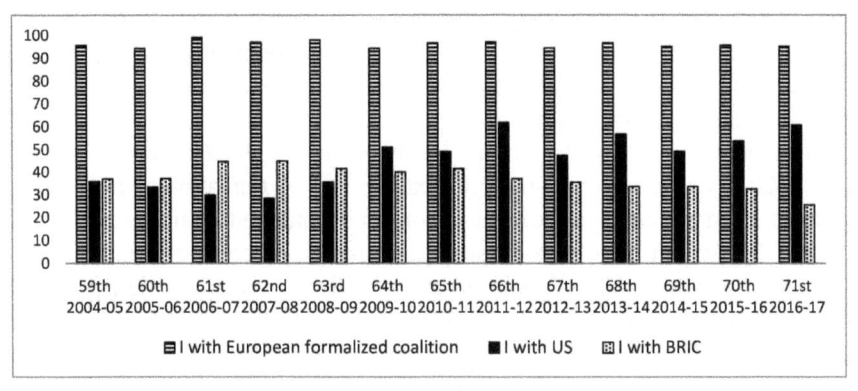

Figure 3.6. Italian voting cohesion with the European formalized coalition, the US, and the BRIC countries (percentage), 2004–2017.
Source: UNGA website and UNBISNET (elaboration by the author).

port for the UN is here supposed to be strongly linked to its role in system maintenance. Should Italy still play its role as supporter of the organization of the international system promoted by the US, its voting cohesion with the US should be higher than its voting cohesion with the BRIC countries.

Italy votes more cohesively with the European formalized coalition than with other potential poles of attraction, like the US or the group of BRIC countries, excluding a potential source of de-Europeanization. As for the Italian role in system maintenance, from the 59th (2004–2005) until the 63rd (2008–2009) session Italy voted with the BRIC group roughly as much or even more than it voted with the US. Starting from the 64th session (2009–2010), however, Italy voted more cohesively with the US than with the BRIC countries and did so by wider and wider margins. However, the BRIC countries started regular meetings of their foreign ministers only in 2006, and they began their annual summits in 2009. Moreover, they started making their presence felt as a potential group once the financial crisis started and a re-discussion of global governance institutions took place. It is therefore noticeable that once the BRIC countries began appearing as a potential competitive political coalition challenging the authority of the US as a global leader, Italy's voting cohesion with the US sharply increased, while its voting cohesion with the BRIC countries decreased. This behavior conforms to expectations of hegemonic theories for the current phase in that the strength and cohesion of the old dominant coalition are low, but once potential challengers arise the core members of the dominant coalition strengthen their bonds to face them. Moreover, once a potential challenger appears, it becomes clear that the Italian belonging to the European formalized coalition is not against the US, but in support of the US. That is, although EU unanimity reduces, and the context is less favorable to the creation of the European formalized coalition, from the 64th session the majority of Italian votes are cast together with both the US and the EU majority, so Italy contributes to strengthening the bonds between the dominant coalition members.

The analysis of Italian voting behavior in the UNGA in the period 2004–2017 has revealed a slight decrease in the participation of Italy to the creation and maintenance of the European formalized coalition compared to the 1990s, but also that, despite the presence of context variations that make the creation of this coalition more difficult, Italian foreign policy is still highly Europeanized and, when differences emerge, they tend not to be exasperated. In this respect, Italian foreign policy seems to correspond to the picture of the ideal-typical Europeanized foreign policy depicted by Hill and Wong (2011: 211). The analysis of Italian voting behavior also reveals the important growth in voting cohesion with the US, traditionally quite isolated in the UNGA, and a progressive reduction in the Italian voting cohesion with the BRIC countries. Considering that the BRIC countries have emerged as a potential competitive coalition in the late 2000s and have made of increasing their cooperation at the UN one of their programmatic points, this variation confirms the Italian closeness to the US and Italy's role of support to the existing organization of the international system.

However, looking at voting behavior only could hide the overlapping of occasional preferences, so next to it the analysis of Italian sponsoring behavior is needed to gather more accurate elements for the analysis of Italian foreign policy, allowing to look at the ascendant phase of a resolution and therefore at the active contribution of the country in a situation in which fewer incentives to coalesce are present.

SPONSORING BEHAVIOR

In the UNGA any UN member state can sponsor a draft resolution and there is no immediate incentive in building up a supporting coalition, but it has become widespread practice to do so to show that the proposed draft resolution has wide backing. It is also common that the draft resolution is revised to include additional sponsoring states to the original ones. This support is an essential element in coalitional activities. Contrary to voting behavior, sponsoring behavior is not yet considered an indicator of EU cohesion, so it is not regularly monitored and no pressure exists on EU member states to co-sponsor their draft resolutions together, unless they are considered signature EU resolutions, typically initiated and promoted by the EU and reflecting the EU identity, values, and interests. Sponsoring activities reflect better than voting the willingness of a state to support the creation and maintenance of a political coalition and allow to better identify regular coalitional partners and issues of relevance for the sponsoring state. Accordingly, Italian sponsoring behavior in the UNGA will be here analyzed to assess variations in Italian foreign policy.

Draft resolutions sponsored by Italy in the UNGA give information on Italian support to the UN as an institution, but also on preferences and political projects that Italy has promoted at the UN. Data regarding the Italian sponsoring trend, its preference to sponsor draft resolutions alone/with non-EU member states or with the majority of EU member states have been collected for the period 2000–2017. Among EU member states, the countries more often sponsoring draft resolutions with Italy have been identified to better understand with which EU member states Italy tends to be in a coalition. Had Italian foreign policy de-Europeanized, a regular prevalence of Italian sponsoring alone or with a minority of EU states would have to be present. On the contrary, should Italian foreign policy still be Europeanized, Italy should regularly and prevalently prefer to sponsor draft resolutions with at least the majority of EU states.

To see whether Italy sponsored draft resolutions in the UNGA as a support maintenance activity to increase its status, Italian co-sponsoring with the US and the BRIC countries has been compared. Should Italy perform support maintenance activities, the number of draft resolutions promoted by Italy over time should remain constant or increase, and Italy should tend to co-sponsor with the US more than with the BRIC countries.

As for the Europeanization of Italian foreign policy as reflected in the country's sponsoring activity, in all the years under consideration the Italian strongly predominant strategy was to regularly sponsor draft resolutions with the majority or unanimity of EU member states and therefore with the European formalized coalition (figure 3.7). Sponsoring alone or only with non-EU states was an occasional and exceptional activity, at times representing an honor conceded on issues on which the country exercises leadership (in the Italian case, this may happen on cooperation in crime prevention and criminal justice). In the analyzed period, sponsoring with a minority only of EU member states was between 8 percent and 21 percent of the Italian sponsoring activity.[4] On the contrary, Italian sponsoring with at least a majority of EU member states was regularly around 80 percent (the minimum was 76 percent in the 69th session, the maximum was 92 percent in the 55th and 57th sessions), confirming the Europeanization of Italian foreign policy. It is also important to take into account variations in the number of draft resolutions sponsored with all EU member states (a subgroup of the previous category). Despite a large drop in the Italian sponsoring activity with all EU member

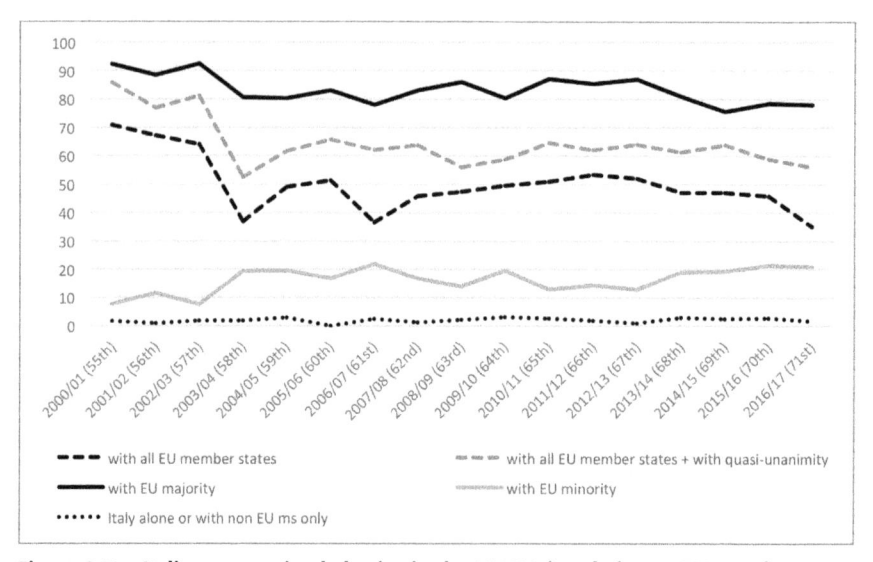

Figure 3.7. Italian sponsoring behavior in the UNGA in relation to EU member states (percentage), 2016–2017.
Source: Index to Proceedings of the General Assembly, 55th–71st UNGA sessions (elaboration by the author).

states in the 58th, 61st, and 71st sessions, the prevalent Italian behavior is sponsoring with the EU majority, not acting alone or with other UN partners. To be clear, a limited rise in actions with a minority of EU member states is present and sponsoring with a majority of EU member states is slightly declining over time, both indicating a relative de-Europeanization. But if we were to include draft resolutions that were sponsored by almost all EU member states (minus one or two members),[5] it would appear evident that in all the years under consideration Italy sponsored at least 50 percent of its resolutions (the minimum was 52 percent in the 58th session) with all or almost all EU member states. Variations in the Italian sponsoring behavior therefore seem to be related to unsuccessful attempts to build European support on political initiatives of interest to Italy and to a drop in EU cohesion already evident in the analysis of voting behavior. In all the years under consideration, Italy acted with the European formalized coalition as its predominant strategy despite the lack of constraints to do so and considered other options as subordinate. This behavior is remarkable because little incentive exists to create a sponsoring coalition. Nevertheless, this is a regular pattern exhibited in the UNGA that highlights the Italian role as coalition facilitator.

Italian sponsoring activities are not uniformly distributed in the UNGA forums (table 3.4). They are concentrated in the plenary and in the first and third committees. The plenary deals with all UNGA issues. It is the forum in which contested draft resolutions are decided. The first committee deals

Table 3.4. Distribution of Italian sponsoring activity

	55th 2000–2001	58th 2003–2004	61st 2006–2007	64th 2009–2010	67th 2012–2013	69th 2014–2015	71st 2016–2017
Plenary	45	33	27	28	34	45	36
I–Disarmament and International Security	13	15	18	13	14	20	24
II–Economic and Financial	6	5	9	8	4	6	9
III–Social Humanitarian and Cultural	44	41	22	41	41	41	38
IV–Special Political and Decolonization	4	5	2	3	3	4	4
V–Administrative and Budgetary	0	0	0	0	0	0	0
VI–Legal	5	4	4	4	4	3	3

Source: *Index to Proceedings of the General Assembly*, 55th–71st UNGA sessions (elaboration by the author).

with political and security matters, but it is specialized in disarmament and related international security items, including nuclear weapons. The third committee devotes most of its time to human rights questions, but it has traditionally included issues related to world social development (Kaufmann 1980). The concentration of Italian sponsoring activities in these committees reflects the Italian interest in these issues already observed when looking at Italian voting behavior. On the issues discussed in these forums, Italy initiates its own actions through the sponsoring of draft resolutions and tries to build support for its initiatives from the other EU members or supports the initiatives of other EU members in the ascending phase to influence them. On these issues Italy is therefore not only a coalition supporting member, but it can be capable of leadership.

Some EU member states figure with more regularity as sponsoring partners of Italy (table 3.5). To be clear, the weighted average cohesion percentage of sponsoring with Italy[6] of the most distant EU state, Latvia, is remarkable and well above the majority (71%), showing that acting together has become a habit for EU states and confirming that they form a stable political coalition. However, there is a group of countries to which Italy is much closer, with co-sponsoring percentages of 90 percent or above. In the analyzed period, Italy regularly acted together with them either because it supported them in their initiatives or because it was supported in its own initiatives. Interestingly, the group of states closer to Italy in the sponsoring activity is not the same as the group closer to Italy in the voting activity, but in this case less pressure was put to coalesce. The creation of a regular sponsoring coalition is not the result of the occasional overlapping of preferences, but it is the result of an intentional action to initiate together a process

Table 3.5. Top and bottom co-sponsors of Italy. Average cohesion percentage of EU member states sponsoring with Italy in 55th–71st UNGA sessions

Top co-sponsors	Average cohesion percentage (weighted)	Bottom co-sponsors	Average cohesion percentage (weighted)
Portugal	94	Malta	71
Austria	92	Latvia	71
Spain	92	Estonia	74
Greece	91	Czech Republic	75
Luxembourg	91	Slovakia	76
Finland	90	Bulgaria	77
Germany	90	Lithuania	78
Belgium	88	Hungary	79
France	88	Romania	80
Ireland	88	Poland	80
		Cyprus	80

Source: *Index to Proceedings of the General Assembly*, 55th–71st UNGA sessions (elaboration by the author).

eventually leading to the approval of a resolution. Sponsoring behavior is therefore a better indicator than voting behavior of closeness between the political position of two states. The sponsoring behavior adopted by EU member states in the analyzed period confirms the closeness between Italy and Germany, Luxembourg and Portugal already seen in voting behavior. The distance present in voting behavior between Italy and France is not confirmed, and even the UK is less distant. Among the big EU states, Italy is closer in its sponsoring behavior to Spain and Germany and more distant from the UK and Poland. France is in the middle, with 88 percent of co-sponsoring. Italy is therefore mostly attracted by Germany (or the France-German engine, when it is active), supporting its initiatives or asking its support for Italian initiatives. Otherwise the Italian support net is made of Mediterranean and small EU countries. In its sponsoring activity Italy is less capable of being in a coalition with Eastern European countries (except for Slovenia) and, despite its geographical closeness, with Malta.

Combining the results of Italian voting and sponsoring activity in the UNGA and selecting EU states with at least 85 percent in both voting and sponsoring cohesion with Italy (table 3.6), that is the EU countries partnering with Italy in most of its activities, it emerges that the ten countries more regularly acting in partnership with Italy are Portugal, Spain, Greece, Luxembourg, Finland, Germany, Belgium, the Netherlands, Denmark, and Slovenia. This can be considered the core of the Italian EU support network in the UNGA, the one that Italy regularly builds on and uses as a leverage, but also the one Italy regularly provides support to, and confirms the closeness to Germany and Spain, but also the reliance on Mediterranean and small EU countries already identified in relation to the Italian sponsoring activity.

Table 3.6. Italian core EU support network in the UNGA

EU states voting (2004–2017) and sponsoring (2000–2017) in the UNGA with Italy with percentages equal or above 85 percent

Belgium	Luxembourg
Denmark	Netherlands
Finland	Portugal
Germany	Slovenia
Greece	Spain

Source: UNGA website, UNBISNET and *Index to Proceedings of the General Assembly*, 55th–71st UNGA sessions (elaboration by the author).

The number of draft resolutions presented by Italy at the UN, here considered an indicator of Italian support maintenance activities to the institutions of the international system, progressively reduced in the first analyzed years and suffered a setback between 2006 and 2008, but it rose again in the following years (figure 3.8). No meaningful domestic influence can be identified in this trend, at least not in the expected direction according to existing literature. Although limited, the most important reduction in the number of draft resolutions presented by Italy took place during the 61st and 62nd sessions, when the Italian government was run by a center-left coalition led by Prodi, considered a staunch supporter of multilateralism and multilateral institutions. On the contrary, of the five peaks in Italian sponsoring activity, two (in the 60th and 65th sessions) took place under center-right governments led by Berlusconi, traditionally considered a more moderate supporter

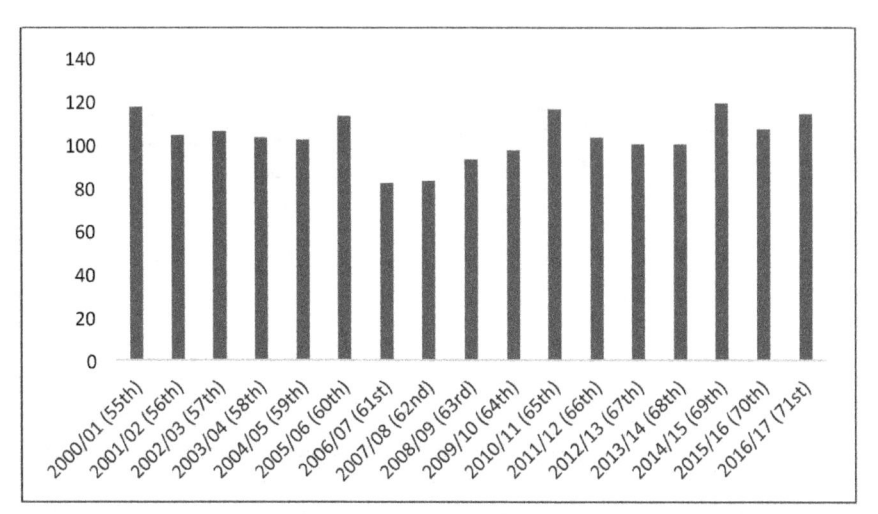

Figure 3.8. Draft resolutions presented by Italy in the 55th–71st UNGA sessions (absolute numbers).

Source: *Index to Proceedings of the General Assembly*, 55th–71st UNGA sessions (elaboration by the author).

of multilateralism and multilateral institutions. The other three took place under the governments led by Amato (55th session), Renzi (69th session), and Gentiloni (71st session). Changes at the international system level can help to explain these variations. The Italian sponsoring activity at the UN seems to reflect the disentanglement of the US from the UN under the first Bush administration, and then a reengagement under the Obama administration. In this respect, variations in the US interest toward the UN may help to explain variations in the Italian support to the main institution of the US-led hegemonic order and confirm that the support provided by Italy to the main institution of the US-led international hegemonic order is strictly related to support to the US-led hegemonic order. This support can also be considered a status seeking activity. But supporting the institution as a status seeking activity when the hegemon is not appreciative of the effort provides limited returns, reducing incentives to engage. Once the hegemon's support for the institution increases, also the Italian engagement toward the institution to provide system maintenance and therefore gain status increases.

The comparison of the Italian sponsoring activity with the US and with the BRIC countries, both as a group and individually (figure 3.9), reveals that in all the years considered Italy sponsored more with the US than with the BRIC countries as a group. Italian sponsoring with the US has important ups and downs, strongly declining until the 62nd UNGA session and then rising steeply until the 66th UNGA session when it declined again slightly,

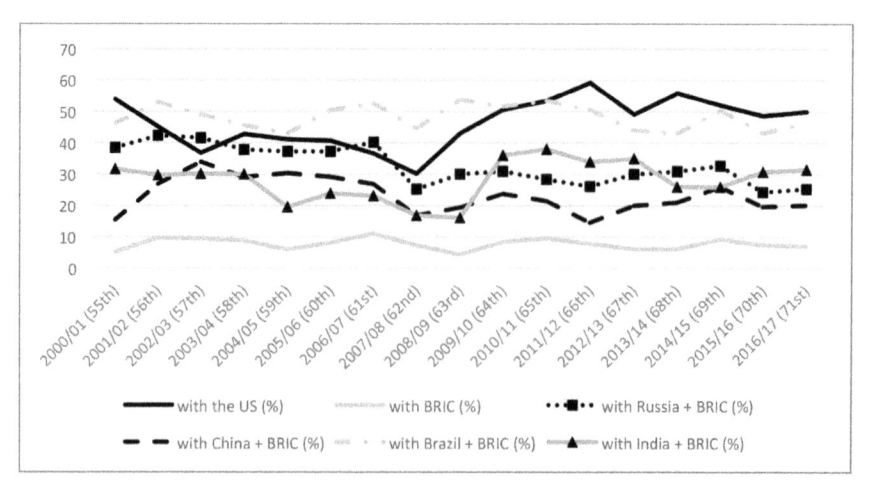

Figure 3.9. Italian co-sponsoring with the US and the BRIC countries in the 55th–71st UNGA sessions (percentage).
Source: *Index to Proceedings of the General Assembly*, 55th–71st UNGA sessions (elaboration by the author).

although remaining around or above 50 percent. The initial important drop in co-sponsoring activity with the US coincides with the Berlusconi government, which strongly pressed for strengthening the Atlantic pillar of Italian foreign policy and established a personal relationship with US President Bush. If domestic factors do not seem to be relevant, once again these variations more probably reflect the disengagement and reengagement with the UN of the second Bush and Obama administrations. They also reflect the effects of the paradox of hegemony described by Cronin (2001): as long as no competitor is on the horizon, the hegemon can play the role of great power, so it can disentangle from the main institutions it contributed to creating. But the rise of China and Russia and the increased coordination among the BRIC countries also at the UN made it more important for the US to reengage and for its coalition partners to increase their cohesion. It is therefore interesting to see that, although the BRIC as a group emerged only in the late 2000s, in the analyzed period there was no significant variation in Italian sponsoring with the BRIC group, which remained a marginal activity always around or below 10 percent, but there was a great increase in the Italian sponsoring activity with the US once the BRIC group emerged as such.

Considering that the Italian close relationship with Russia has been taken as an indicator of de-Europeanization of Italian foreign policy and that China is currently reputed to be the most probable future potential competitor of the US for global leadership, the sponsoring activity that Italy performed with each BRIC member was calculated on top of the one in which they participated as a group (figure 3.9). Only in the 57th and 61st sessions Italy sponsored with Russia slightly more than it did with the US. Otherwise, Italy sponsored with the US more than it did with Russia and China. In the analyzed period, the Italian sponsoring trend with the US is on the rise, being regularly around or above 50 percent since the 64th session, while the sponsoring trend with Russia is decreasing. This is interesting because Russia has traditionally been a strategic partner for Italy, with governments of both center-right and center-left trying to keep close relations. The Italian sponsoring with China has always been limited, between 20 percent and 30 percent of Italian sponsoring activities, and in all the years under consideration it has always been below the Italian sponsoring with the US. The trend is decreasing. Likewise, Italian sponsoring with the BRIC countries as a group in the analyzed period remained a marginal activity (the maximum value was 11 percent during the 61st session). India in all the analyzed years was consistently below the US, but Italy increased its sponsoring with India between the 64th and the 67th UNGA session. Brazil is the only country of the group above or equal to the US in sponsoring with Italy until the 65th session, when the Italian sponsoring with Brazil declined. Brazil is also the country traditionally closer to European states in the BRIC group. The Italian sponsoring activity in the UNGA confirms that Italian activities at the UN are influenced by variations at the systemic level and reflect the Italian role as ally of the US trying to perform system maintenance activities. Confirming expectations of hegemonic theories regarding the current phase, the Italian relationship with the US as a member of the dominant coalition is initially weak, but once potential challengers arise, Italy as a core member of the dominant coalition contributes to strengthening the bonds.

This result is confirmed when comparing the Italian sponsoring with the US, the BRIC as a group, Russia, China, and two big EU member states, one close to Italy (Germany), the other more distant and traditionally considered close to the US (the UK) (figure 3.10). In the analyzed period, Italy regularly sponsored most of its draft resolutions with the European countries, no matter how distant. Except for the 57th and 61st sessions it always preferred the US over potential alternatives.[7] When Brazil, Russia, China, and India acted together, this did not attract Italy. Even adding sponsoring with individual BRIC countries to sponsoring with the BRIC countries as a group, Russia and China remained non-credible attractors for Italy. The strategic friendship Italy has with Russia and its capability of pushing Italy to defect from the European formalized coalition has been taken as an indicator of de-Europeanization. However, in all the analyzed sessions, Russia was not an alternative to the European formalized coalition, confirming the Europeanization of Italian foreign policy and that the Italian coalition with EU members acts in support of and not in opposition to the US, allowing Italy to perform system maintenance activities that can be used to increase its status.

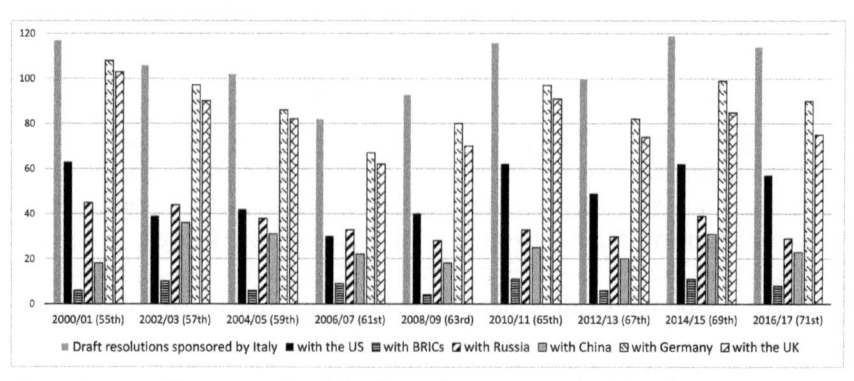

Figure 3.10. Italian sponsoring behavior and co-sponsors in the 55th–71st UNGA sessions (absolute numbers).

Source: Index to Proceedings of the General Assembly, 55th–71st UNGA sessions (elaboration by the author).

Focus on Indicative Issues

To understand whether and how variations in the Europeanization of Italian foreign policy have occurred it is also useful to focus on specific issues of relevance to Italy and its national interests (disarmament) and to the EU and its identity (human rights). Italian voting and sponsoring behavior in relation to the other EU member states will therefore be analyzed on two issues considered important for the Europeanization of foreign policy to identify cases of convergence and divergence with the majority position of EU member states. Focusing on specific issues over time will also allow to better define the processes of Europeanization at play.

Human Rights

Human rights and Europeanization have been strongly associated because of the longstanding commitment of the EU to prioritize the promotion of human rights at the UN (Smith 2017; Council of the European Union 2017) and because of the self-representation of the EU as a normative power. Literature has focused on the case of the abolition of death penalty to explain how the EU may best be conceived as a normative power Europe (Manners 2002). Interestingly, this is a case in which Italy acted "with passion and without much political circumspection" (Salleo and Pirozzi 2008: 105), claiming success for it, to the point that this could also be considered a case of Italian uploading. Exploring the Italian coalitional behavior in relation to human rights issues will therefore help to explore not only whether variations in the Europeanization of Italian foreign policy have occurred, but also how, and it will help to trace processes of Europeanization in the Italian case.

Italian foreign policy on human rights issues does not always converge with the position of the other EU member states. It has been noted that differences between Northern EU member states, that tend to prefer vigorous actions, and Southern EU member states, that prefer to engage with third countries and avoid prioritizing human rights, exist and tend to result in a number of inconsistencies (Smith 2015). However, Italy is particularly sensitive to the issue of human rights.

Italian voting behavior on human rights issues confirms that Italy acts predominantly with the European formalized coalition and therefore the Europeanization of Italian foreign policy in this area (table 3.7).[8] This is an area where EU unanimity is remarkably high. In the analyzed period, when EU member states did not act cohesively, Italy voted with the EU majority more than with an EU minority. Italy never voted alone on human rights issues.

Table 3.7. Italy and the European formalized coalition on human rights issues, voting behavior (absolute numbers), 2004–2017

	59th 2004–2005	60th 2005–2006	61st 2006–2007	62nd 2007–2008	63rd 2008–2009	64th 2009–2010	65th 2010–2011	66th 2011–2012	67th 2012–2013	68th 2013–2014	69th 2014–2015	70th 2015–2016	71st 2016–2017
Total	28	24	23	23	22	16	16	15	13	13	14	18	16
With all EU member states	25	22	22	22	21	12	13	12	11	11	12	13	11
With EU majority	1	2	1	1	1	1	3	1	1	1	1	4	3
With EU minority	2	0	0	0	0	3	0	1	1	1	1	1	2
Alone	0	0	0	0	0	0	0	0	0	0	0	0	0

Source: UNGA website and UNBISNET (elaboration by the author).

Some elements of divergence are present, though. In the 64th session Italy voted with a minority of EU member states on three occasions (once on "The human right to water and sanitation" resolution; and twice on decisions related to the resolution "Global efforts for the total elimination of racism, racial discrimination, xenophobia and related intolerance and the comprehensive implementation of and follow-up to the Durban Declaration and Programme of Action"). And since the 66th session it voted with the EU minority on one resolution per session (two in the 71st session). In the 66th session Italy voted with the EU minority on the resolution on the "Inadmissibility of certain practices that fuel racism." Since the 67th session, Italy regularly voted with a minority of EU member states on the "Right to development resolution." In the 71st session it added a minority vote on the "Declaration on the right to peace." On none of these votes Italy expressed full disagreement, but only a partial disagreement.

The "Right to development" resolution—traditionally sponsored by the Non-Aligned Movement and intersecting the human rights and development spheres—remains the most evident case of Italian dissent and lack of willingness to adapt to the European formalized coalition in the analyzed period. While it cannot be ruled out that this behavior was opportunistic and necessary to increase the Italian electoral base in the UNGA in view of the election to the Security Council for the period 2017–2018, it has to be noted that development has been an important issue for Italy since the first years of the Italian participation to UN works (Tosi 2010; Carbone 2011). Attention to development increased in the foreign policy agenda of the Renzi and Gentiloni governments, also in relation to the politically salient migration issue. Despite remaining at much lower levels than in the 2000s, in 2015 and 2016 the Italian development budget doubled compared to the period 2012–2014 when it had been much reduced because of the economic crisis.[9] On the "Right to development" resolution the Italian dissent with the rest of the EU countries has been widening over time. This is the only case in which Italy stood firm in a minority position, not adjusting to the EU majority. The resolution is a longstanding one in the UNGA and, because variations in voting behavior from one year to another on the same resolution are politically important, it is also a case that allows assessing more thoroughly variations in the Europeanization of Italian foreign policy.

In the analyzed period voting on the "Right to development" resolution has registered great variations in the position of EU members (in the 59th session they quasi-unanimously voted against, in the 60th they unanimously voted in favor, in the 61st and 62nd they unanimously voted against, and in the 64th they unanimously voted in favor, until the prevailing position became abstaining). These variations indicate that the issue is highly contested. Italy followed the EU majority until the 66th session, but it started voting in favor of the resolution in the 67th session with a group of eleven EU member states (Austria, Cyprus, France, Greece, Ireland, Italy, Luxembourg, Malta, Portugal, Slovenia, and Spain), that reduced to six members (Cyprus, Greece, Italy, Luxembourg, Malta, and Portugal) in the 70th session and to four members (Italy, Cyprus, Luxembourg, and Portugal) in the 71st session. Voting with a decreasing EU minority coalition and accepting the consequent progressive isolation on this issue represents a deviant behavior for Italy. This behavior indicates that the issue is high on the Italian agenda but also confirms that on issues that it considers important, Italy follows its line, it does not change its foreign policy to adjust to the EU majority. This is not in contradiction with the ideal-typical model of Europeanized foreign policy described by Hill and Wong (2011: 211), that allows occasional defections on important issues. However, since the 67th session, on this issue and resolution Italy has started to consistently adopt this behavior.[10]

If the "Right to development" resolution is a case of diverging Italian behavior from the EU majority, in the analyzed period other recurring resolutions on human rights issues on which recorded votes were taken show the Italian willingness to be part of the European formalized coalition, taking common EU positions as a major reference point and subscribing positively to the values and principles expressed by the EU in its international activity. The first is the "Rights of the child" resolution. This resolution was presented every year, and, in some years, related recorded votes were taken. As already mentioned, the recurring recorded vote is an indication that the issue is contested in the UNGA. However, on the 16 votes taken in the analyzed period, Italy always voted with all EU member states. Votes on the resolution "Human rights and unilateral coercive measures" were recorded every year, and also in this case Italy always voted together with all the other EU member states. Another recurring resolution is the one on "Extrajudicial, summary or arbitrary executions." On the 14 recorded votes on the resolution and related decisions in the analyzed period, Italy always voted cohesively with all EU member states. A partially recurring resolution is the one on "The right to food" present from the 59th until the 63rd session. In this case too the EU member states always managed to act cohesively. Likewise, full EU member states' voting cohesion was present in votes on resolutions on specific countries such as the Democratic Republic of Congo, Turkmenistan, Iran, Uzbekistan, North Korea, Myanmar, Belarus, Syria, Crimea, some of them considered EU-sponsored resolutions. Out of the 46 votes cast in the analyzed period, EU member states voted by majority twice (in the 70th and 71st sessions when voting on Syria, Greece defected). Otherwise they always voted unanimously. Similar cohesion can be found on the recurring resolution "Globalization and its impact on the full enjoyment of all human rights," on which EU member states regularly voted unanimously until the 70th session, when Greece started defecting. In the analyzed period, Italy always voted with the European formalized coalition and never defected from the common position adopted.

Other resolutions were not presented every year but are still particularly important and can provide information on the processes of Europeanization of Italian foreign policy. Among them, the one on the "Moratorium on the use of the death penalty." On this resolution recorded votes were taken six times in the analyzed period, and EU member states always voted cohesively. This resolution is important for three reasons: because it is a case used to explain why the EU should be considered a normative power (Manners 2002), because Italy showed leadership in the creation of the supporting coalition for this resolution and is therefore a clear case of uploading, and because Italy acting on its own had already tried before to pass this resolution but it had failed (Kissack 2017). Italy was the norm entrepreneur, it spent its political capital and managed to gain support from the other EU members, some of which were quite reluctant to move from a stricter abolitionist language, and the EU eventually became instrumental in drafting the resolution and having it approved in the UNGA in 2007, something that Italy had failed to achieve on its own previously (Kissack 2008 and 2012). Once the resolution was approved, it was the EU that took full leadership on this initiative (Iakovidis 2017). This resolution is therefore a clear case of politics of scale, in which Italy managed to gain leadership and be successful at the UN on an issue of great relevance for the country and the domestic political coalition of the time thanks to the support from the other EU states.

In the UNGA the pendulum effect and negotiated convergence typical of cross-loading could also be seen at play. In the case of the resolution "Global efforts for the total elimination of racism, racial discrimination, xenophobia and related intolerance and the comprehensive implementation of and follow-up to the Durban Declaration and Programme of Action," in the 64th session Italy defected twice with a minority of EU member states, but in the 65th session it voted with the majority of EU member states, since the coalition of seven members Italy had voted with during the 64th session doubled to 14. In the 66th session Italy voted with all EU member states again, but while in the previous years it had voted against, in this session it abstained, showing the willingness to adapt its foreign policy to the position of the EU majority. From then on, EU member states stopped voting cohesively, but Italy always voted with the EU majority. Another instance of recurring resolutions in which cross-loading was evident is the group of resolutions on the "Inadmissibility of certain practices that fuel racism." Breaking with its previous voting pattern, in the 66th session Italy voted with an EU minority group, but the following year it reverted its position to vote cohesively with all the other EU member states, adapting its foreign policy to be part of and support the European formalized coalition, showing the negotiated convergence and pendulum effects that typically indicate cross-loading.

Combining information on Italian voting behavior with information on Italian sponsoring behavior helps to better understand some of the Italian choices made and provides useful information on whether Italy exercised leadership and managed to gain support for its initiatives from the other EU member states or whether it just contributed to maintaining the European formalized coalition together. The analysis of the cases in which Italy voted with a minority of EU member states indicates how relevant those issues actually were for Italy, since in some cases Italy had initiated the decision-making process and sponsored the related draft resolutions. In the case of the vote with an EU minority group on cloning in the 59th session, Italy sponsored the draft resolution "International convention against human cloning" in the sixth committee together with Ireland and Portugal and it sponsored alone the draft resolution "International convention against reproductive cloning of human beings," evident sign of the relevance of the issue for the country. Although with an EU minority group of ten states, Italy voted on the "United Nations Declaration on Human Cloning" with a larger European group than the sponsoring one (besides Ireland and Portugal, the group enlarged to Austria, Germany, Hungary, Malta, Poland, Slovakia, and Slovenia).

When Italy voted cohesively with all the other EU member states, it was often a co-sponsor of some of the recurring draft resolutions. In the 59th session, this was the case of the resolutions on the rights of the child, on human rights in specific countries, on extrajudicial, summary or arbitrary executions, and on the elimination of religious intolerance. In other cases, Italy was a co-sponsor with a group of EU member states, but then all EU member states voted cohesively in favor, therefore enlarging the supporting coalition at the moment of voting. The evolution in sponsoring of some recurring resolutions provides further information on the capacity of Italy to act with the European formalized coalition. The recurring draft resolution "Right to food"—particularly relevant for Italy because of the presence of the FAO in Rome—is a case of widening of the supporting coalition. In the 56th session Italy sponsored it with Germany, Greece, Ireland, Portugal, and Spain. In the 57th session, Austria, Finland, and France joined. In the 58th session, Cyprus and Slovenia joined, but Spain, dropped. In the 59th and 60th sessions the draft resolution was sponsored by 13 EU member states, reduced to 12 in the 62nd session. The 63rd session saw an increase to 13 EU states. In the 64th and 65th sessions the European formalized coalition grew to 17 states but reduced to 16 in the successive session. Since the 67th session the coalition grew to 20 members, then 23 in the 68th session and 25 in the 69th, to reduce to 24 EU members in the 70th session and 21 EU members in the 71st session. That is, the sponsoring coalition of EU states on this draft resolution grew over time from the initial group of six members to a group of 25, strengthening a proposal that was important for Italy, but the high level of support reached was hard to maintain.

The analysis of the sponsoring of the recurring draft resolution on "The girl child" over time allows for the analysis of another aspect of the Europeanization of Italian foreign policy. This draft resolution is one on which EU member states regularly voted together considering it consonant with EU values. From the 55th until the 60th session EU member states sponsored this draft resolution unanimously. Starting from the 62nd session, however, it proved more difficult for EU member states to provide unanimous support. In the 62nd session Poland defected, in the 68th session four countries defected, in the 70th session ten countries defected. Italy, however, always sponsored the resolution with the majority of EU member states and supported the maintenance of the European formalized coalition.

Although not directly related to human rights issues, the third committee also regularly hosted the draft resolution "Strengthening of the United Nations Crime Prevention and Criminal Justice Programme, in particular its technical cooperation capacity," one of the few draft resolutions in which Italy could be found sponsoring alone in the analyzed period and therefore worth examining. In the long evolution of this recurring draft resolution Italy played a leading role in widening support. It is not infrequent for draft resolutions to be initially presented by a limited number of sponsors and then revised to include more sponsors and gain wider acceptance. In the period under consideration, this draft resolution almost always gained sponsorship from all EU member states, but in the 56th session this was preceded by a proposal by Austria, Greece, Italy, and Spain, in the 62nd session by a sponsoring group composed of Austria, Cyprus, Czech Republic, Estonia, Germany, Ireland, Italy, Luxembourg, Netherlands, Poland, Romania, Spain, UK, in the 65th session by Italy and seven EU member states, in the 67th session by Italy, the Czech Republic and Denmark, in the 68th session by Italy and a group of seven EU states, in the 69th by Italy and Croatia, in the 70th session by Italy and other 15 countries, in the 71st session by Italy, Austria and Bulgaria, in the 61st, 63rd, 64th, 65th sessions by a proposal by Italy only. In all cases Italy was in the initial proponent group and, in all cases, the group enlarged and adapted its original proposal to gain support from the wide majority or unanimity of EU member states.

Overall, the analysis of the Italian behavior on human rights issues shows the prevalence of support to the EU common positions, the upholding of EU values, a convergent and adaptive—but not passive—behavior (except for the "Right to development" resolution) and the capacity to build on the European formalized coalition to amplify Italian initiatives.

Disarmament and Nuclear Issues

Disarmament and nuclear issues are particularly sensitive for EU member states. This is an issue area recognized as a priority by the EU and on which the EU has recently decided to coordinate more at the UN (Council of the European Union 2017). But it is also an issue area in which wide disagreements exist within the EU, because member states have different interests and are deeply divided on the issue (Galariotis and Gianniou 2017: 70; Dee 2017).

The nuclear issue points to some contradictions in the Italian strategic culture. As widely reconstructed by Nuti (1993a, 2007, 2011b, and 2017), the obsession with status in a country that had the technical possibilities to become a nuclear power and was coming out of the peace treaty as a losing power, made gaining nuclear status something that was on the mind of Italian decision makers in the aftermath of World War II, but a national choice was always excluded. During the 1950s Italy requested American units equipped with nuclear-capable rocketry and since then it strongly relied on the nuclear protection from the US and on a multilateral nuclear protection within NATO, allowing the US to install its nuclear weapons on the Italian territory under a dual-key arrangement: nuclear weapons are owned and controlled by the US, but they can only be used with Italian agreement and authorization (Ronzitti 2008; Nuti 1993b). Because of the Italian security culture, the fear of protests convinced Italian decision makers to present decisions on nuclear matters and American military bases as part of the political routine, avoiding the involvement of the Parliament or the wider public (Nuti 2011b). But the nuclear issue has traditionally been a sensitive one in Italy, not just in its military component or because of the strong pacifist movement. The civilian use too has been considered with hostility, leading Italians to overwhelmingly vote against nuclear plants within the Italian territory in 1987 and then again in 2011.

On security and disarmament issues Luif (2003: 35) reports that since 1987 Italy was regularly part of the EU majority, with no distance recorded from the EU majority until 1999. Only Belgium and Luxembourg reported better scores, while the Netherlands had the same distance and Germany was slightly more distant, indicating that on this issue these countries were regularly coalescing. Some distance appeared in the following years (2000, 2001, and 2002), indicating that a slight divergence between Italy and the rest of the EU group with which Italy had regularly formed a coalition was taking place.

In the analyzed period, on disarmament and nuclear issues Italy voted with an EU minority coalition 17 times and once it voted alone (table 3.8). This

Table 3.8. Italy and the European formalized coalition on disarmament and nuclear issues, voting behavior (absolute numbers), 2004–2017

	59th 2004–2005	60th 2005–2006	61st 2006–2007	62nd 2007–2008	63rd 2008–2009	64th 2009–2010	65th 2010–2011	66th 2011–2012	67th 2012–2013	68th 2013–2014	69th 2014–2015	70th 2015–2016	71st 2016–2017
With all EU member states	12	25	30	14	32	24	24	35	19	35	28	20	43
With EU majority	15	14	17	17	11	11	14	9	21	11	17	21	17
With EU minority	0	0	0	3	2	0	1	2	2	2	2	1	2
Alone	0	0	0	0	0	0	0	0	0	0	0	1	0
No EU majority	1	0	0	0	0	0	1	0	1	0	1	1	2
Total	28	39	47	34	45	35	40	46	43	48	48	44	64

Source: UNGA website and UNBISNET (elaboration by the author).

is the area in which the widest disagreement between Italy and the other EU member states can be found, and it is also an area in which Italy is not shy when it comes to disagreeing. The only vote Italy cast alone in the analyzed period was in the 70th session on the resolution "Follow-up to nuclear disarmament obligations agreed to at the 1995, 2000 and 2010 Review Conferences of the Parties to the Treaty on the Non-Proliferation of Nuclear Weapons," on which all the other EU member states voted against (like the US) and Italy abstained in isolation. Although numbers are small, starting from the 62nd session there are signs of a diverging trend, since on a limited number of decisions Italy voted with an EU minority or alone, while previously it had only voted together with the European formalized coalition.

It would be wrong to say that in this area Italian foreign policy is not Europeanized. Not only also in this area Italy predominantly voted with the European formalized coalition, but it also voted cohesively when resolutions important for the EU were present. For instance, on the 21 decisions related to the "Arms trade treaty," of particular concern for the EU, Italy always voted cohesively with all the other EU member states. Likewise, on the 13 resolutions in the analyzed period on "Promotion of multilateralism in the area of disarmament and non-proliferation" that should be of interest to the EU, EU member states were always divided, but Italy always voted with the European formalized coalition. Considering that on this resolution it had voted differently from the EU majority in the 57th session (Luif 2003: 68), this suggests that Italy adjusted its position to come into line with the European formalized coalition.

However, some elements of divergence emerge too, and they are helpful to understand the Europeanization processes of Italian foreign policy in this area. Looking at the single decisions a few interesting elements are present. The first one concerns the single vote cast by Italy in full isolation on the resolution "Follow-up to disarmament obligations agreed to at the 1995, 2000 and 2010 Review Conferences of the Parties to the Treaty on the Non-Proliferation of Nuclear Weapons." Italy abstained in the 70th session when not only all the other 27 EU member states but also the US, an important actor for Italy on the issue, voted against. The resolution is a recurring one and in the analyzed period before the vote in isolation Italy had already voted cohesively with all the other EU member states nine times and with the EU majority twice. Moreover, in the same session on the sixth preambular of the same resolution Italy voted with the EU majority. This is the only vote cast by Italy in isolation in the analyzed period that was not corrected subsequently by the Italian delegation. This is an interesting element, because Italy had already been isolated on disarmament and nuclear issues in previous sessions, but it had always corrected its vote later. For instance, during the 65th session it was the only EU member to vote against the operative paragraph 15 of the draft resolution on nuclear disarmament, but it subsequently communicated that it had intended to vote in favor, that is with the EU majority, what normally indicates that directions initially received by the capital were reversed to join the European formalized coalition and the US. Likewise, Italy was the only absent EU member state during the 65th session in decisions on the resolutions "Implementation of the Convention on the Prohibition of the Use, Stockpiling, Production and Transfer of Anti-personnel Mines and on Their Destruction," "Conventional arms control at the regional and subregional levels," "Prevention of an arms race in outer space" and "Conclusion of effective international arrangements to assure non-nuclear-weapon States against the use or threat of use of nuclear weapons." But it subsequently indicated that it wanted to vote as the European formalized coalition had done, reversing its position, and adjusting its foreign policy.

In the same session, though, on the operative paragraph 2 of the draft resolution "Conventional arms control at the regional and subregional levels" Italy had initially abstained to subsequently indicate that it wanted to vote with the EU minority, in a sign that accommodation with the EU majority on this issue could not be achieved. Likewise, on the 21 decisions on "The risk of nuclear proliferation in the Middle East" in the analyzed period, Italy had traditionally voted with the European formalized coalition, be it all EU member states or the EU majority. However, during the 71st session it voted with an EU minority of 13 states comprising all EU big member states, suggesting the difficulty for EU member states to accommodate and reach a common position.

Among recurring resolutions, the Italian divergence with the European formalized coalition is present on the resolution "Effects of the use of armaments and ammunitions containing depleted uranium." The resolution was presented six times in the analyzed period and EU member states were always split into three groups, while four times an EU majority could not be formed, indicating great disagreements on this resolution among them. The only two times in which the majority could be formed, Italy voted with the EU minority together with Germany, Austria, Cyprus, and Ireland. During the 62nd session Italy voted with a small coalition of five states, that enlarged to eight during the 63rd session, to 12 during the 65th session and to 13 during the 69th session. Starting from the 69th session, however, Germany changed its vote to abstention and Italy remained the only big EU member state of the coalition.

Divergence is also present on the recurrent resolution on "Conventional arms control at the regional and subregional levels." Out of the 21 decisions in the analyzed period, Italy voted with all EU member states until the 65th session, when it began voting with all EU member states on the resolution, but with an EU minority on the operative paragraph 2 of the resolution. This voting pattern was repeated in the following sessions, suggesting divergence on the specific issue of the operative paragraph.

On disarmament and nuclear issues too, it is useful to analyze Italian sponsoring behavior and, when possible, to connect it with Italian voting behavior to better understand whether Italy was among the initiators of the resolutions. Italian sponsoring of the resolution "Conventional arms control at the regional and subregional levels" reveals a case of uploading. In the 55th session Italy was a sponsor of this resolution with Germany and Spain. They were joined by the Netherlands for one year during the 58th session. However, Germany abandoned the small group in the 63rd session and Spain abandoned it in the 64th, leaving Italy to sponsor alone with non-EU member states only until the end of the analyzed period. All the EU member states voted the resolution unanimously until the 64th session, but once Italy started sponsoring alone it had more trouble getting the other EU member states to support it. Not so much the entire resolution, but specific aspects of it. In this case, Italy was regularly relegated to vote with an EU minority. On diverging aspects with the other EU members, though, Italy converged with the US.

Italy sponsored alone with non-EU member states also the draft resolutions on the "Report of the Disarmament Commission" in the 57th session and "A path to the total elimination of nuclear weapons," but both were later approved unanimously by all EU member states.

In this area, these are the only draft resolutions that Italy sponsored alone in the first committee. Resolutions sponsored by Italy with a minority of EU member states are confined to the first part of the analyzed period. In the 57th session, Italy co-sponsored with eight other EU members (including France, Germany, and the UK) the draft resolution "Compliance with arms limitation and disarmament and non-proliferation agreements" that was approved without a vote. In the 58th session it sponsored with the Czech Republic the Report of the Disarmament Commission that was approved without a vote. In the 59th session it sponsored again the draft resolution "A path to the total elimination of nuclear weapons," this time with a group of five EU member states (including Belgium, Luxembourg, Netherlands, and Spain). In the 60th session it sponsored the draft resolution "Renewed determination towards the total elimination of nuclear weapons" in a group of seven EU member states (including Belgium, Germany, Lithuania, Luxembourg, Netherlands, and Spain), and the draft resolution "Prevention of the illicit transfer and unauthorized access to and use of man-portable air defence systems" with Latvia and Malta. In the 61st session it sponsored the draft resolution "Renewed determination towards the total elimination of nuclear weapons" within a group of 13 states (Austria, Belgium, Bulgaria, Cyprus, Czech Republic, Finland, Germany, Italy,

Lithuania, Luxembourg, Netherlands, Slovenia, Spain). In the 64th session it co-sponsored the "Report of the Disarmament Commission" with the Netherlands and Poland. In the 65th session it sponsored the "United Nations study on disarmament and non-proliferation education" with 12 other EU states (Austria, Belgium, Estonia, Germany, Greece, Hungary, Luxembourg, Netherlands, Poland, Spain, Sweden, UK) and the "Report of the Disarmament Commission" with Bulgaria, Greece, Hungary, Italy, Spain. Starting from the 66th session, however, Italy only sponsored with a majority or with all EU member states.

It is remarkable that, even on the issue on which it defected the most, Italy not only sponsored the vast majority of its draft resolutions with the European formalized coalition, but over time it converged with the other EU member states and started sponsoring almost all of its draft resolution with a vast majority of EU member states, when not with all the other EU member states.

NOTES

1. The terms European formalized coalition and EU majority will be used interchangeably.

2. Weighted to take into account the different EU membership period of the states under consideration.

3. Only votes in which the BRIC countries voted alike were considered.

4. Data includes voting alone or with non-EU states only.

5. This is a subgroup of the votes cast by Italy with the EU majority.

6. Calculated by multiplying the sum of the absolute number of draft resolutions co-sponsored with Italy for 100 and dividing it for the absolute number of draft resolutions sponsored by Italy in the analyzed period. If a state became member of the EU later than the 55th session, only the years in which it was an EU member were considered.

7. The same analysis was performed for all the years under consideration but could not be shown for reasons of clarity. It is confirmed that the 57th and 61st are the only two exceptions in the entire analyzed period.

8. Only votes referring exclusively to human rights issues were considered. This means that, although pertaining to human rights, votes on issues bordering between human rights and Middle East issues were not included, because different dynamics, typical of the political competition on the Middle East, might influence the result. Likewise, for the resolutions on the promotion of a democratic and equitable international order. To be clear, on all the votes on bordering issues excluded, EU member states acted unanimously, so adding them would only further strengthen the Europeanization of Italian foreign policy on this issue.

9. See OECD Data, Distribution of Net ODA, https://data.oecd.org/oda/distribution-of-net-oda.htm (accessed on 17 August 2018).

10. This strengthens suggested hypotheses on a more limited Europeanization of Italian development policy (Carbone and Quartapelle 2016).

Chapter Four

In the Security Council

FACILITATING THE EUROPEAN FORMALIZED COALITION

Scholars have mostly focused on states' behavior in the UNGA to detect their foreign policy preferences. However, the UNGA is not a very authoritative forum and it is not where the most important UN decisions take place. This may affect incentives and constraints for states to coalesce within that forum. The UN Security Council (UNSC) is a more representative forum of ongoing dynamics at the international system level. It is in the UNSC that the most important security issues are debated, and UN authoritative decisions are taken. It is therefore in the UNSC that coalition dynamics may better reflect incentives and constraints present also at the international system level.

To have a clearer picture of Italian foreign policy behavior, it is thus necessary to analyze Italian behavior also in the UNSC.

In relation to the Europeanization of foreign policy, the UNSC represents a much harder test than the UNGA, because not only cooperation among EU member states in this forum is traditionally much more limited, but EU member states are also very jealous of their national prerogatives, and they need to be careful not to interfere with the works of the Security Council. Italian convergence and divergence with the other EU member states sitting in the UNSC will be analyzed, and its behavior as a European formalized coalition member will be explored. In this forum it will also be possible to better assess whether the ongoing crisis of the US-led hegemonic order is affecting Italy's role as a member of the dominant coalition and whether Italy facilitates the creation and maintenance of the European formalized coalition as a system maintenance activity and therefore as a support strategy to the hegemonic order or in opposition to it.

Following the analysis from the previous chapter, also in the UNSC it should be expected that, in case of Europeanized foreign policy, Italy should act predominantly with the majority of EU member states, but because of the composition and working habits of the institution, the European formalized coalition will rotate around France and the UK. Moreover, considering that acting with the European formalized coalition at the UN increases its status, because it allows the country greater weight and influence, evidence that this is done together with the US more than with the BRIC group countries, and particularly Russia and China, should be found too. However, the UNSC is quite different from the UNGA, so a few specifications are needed to gain a long-term perspective of the Italian behavior in this organ.

The UNSC is the organ that according to the UN Charter has the primary responsibility for the maintenance of international peace and security, and it is the only organ whose decisions under Chapter VII of the UN Charter are binding for all UN member states. However, because of its composition, decision-making process and working habits, it is difficult to systematically analyze the behavior of Italy within the UNSC using voting records. In the UNSC five members are permanent (P5) and ten rotate on a two-year mandate, five of them substituted every year and not eligible for immediate reelection (Rule 144 of the Rules of Procedure of the General Assembly). The five permanent members are the US, Russia,[1] China, France, and the UK. Permanent membership gives them the possibility of relying on an institutional memory not available to nonpermanent members, who normally spend some time to catch up and get acquainted but remain at a disadvantage. Consequently, permanent members control the agenda setting of the UNSC and oversee the drafting of most of the resolutions.

Strictly related is the decision-making process.[2] A resolution is approved with an affirmative vote of nine UNSC members, but the five permanent members have veto power. This means that UNSC members have different voting power (Hosli et al. 2011; Junn 1983; Winter 1996). As pointed out by Coleman (1973 and 1986), because of difference in voting power, nonpermanent members have an incentive to build coalitions with permanent members, because this would allow them to gain voting power. On the contrary, permanent members have absolute power to prevent action, so when they are against a resolution, coalition building is not attractive for them. The voting power difference lowers the incentive of permanent members to coalesce and limits variations in voting patterns. This is particularly relevant in the case of EU member states, because although the EU presence in the UNSC is based on two permanent members and at least two nonpermanent members, France and the UK have a low incentive to coalesce. This makes the formation and maintenance of the European formalized coalition much harder than in the UNGA.

However, it has also been shown that once a coalition in the UNSC forms, its existence can influence how states vote, because if it is known that most members will vote for a resolution, it is to be expected that a further member will vote for it (O'Neill 1996: 221). It has therefore been suggested that the high probability that a specific group of states will vote together changes the distribution of voting power because, in exchange for solidarity and long-term influence, members vote based on loyalty to the coalition rather than on preferences on the issue at stake (O'Neill 1996: 236).

Furthermore, veto power use has become increasingly costly from a political point of view due to widespread opposition of non-veto holders, who perceive it as an outdated privilege. It has therefore become an increasingly recurring practice to propose widely shared or politically significant draft resolutions in the knowledge that they would be stopped by a veto. This has repeatedly happened in the case of the US on the Israeli-Palestinian conflict and in the case of Russia on the Syrian conflict. While in the past the threat of a permanent member to use its veto power was a very effective tool that discouraged the presentation of a draft proposal that risked being vetoed, more recently instances in which a threat of a veto has deterred potential sponsors from approaching the UNSC with a draft resolution have become rare (Gharekhan 2006). The purpose of this behavior is to shame the veto user, to force it to publicly justify its vote. When a significant majority exists in the UNSC in favor of a draft resolution, it becomes more difficult for a permanent member to justify the use of its veto power, because no one wants to be seen as holding up the consensus (Gharekhan 2006: 41; Hulton 2004: 238). As a result, permanent members have now reduced their veto power usage to situations when they perceive their vital national interests to be at stake, while they prefer to abstain or be absent on other issues, allowing draft resolutions to be voted for and approved. The two European permanent members have stopped using their veto power since the end of the Cold War and have supported the proposal of a code of conduct for UNSC members in case of genocide, crimes against humanity and war crimes, with France supporting the idea that permanent members should restraint their veto power usage in case of mass atrocity.[3] However, veto power has been repeatedly used also recently, with Russia and China making increasing use of it.

Some working practices are relevant too. The first is the habit of deciding by consensus, that restricts the number of decisions on which a vote is taken to a very limited number and to highly contested cases, making it more difficult to use voting behavior to detect the existence of the European formalized coalition in the UNSC and to analyze the behavior of its members over a long period. The rise of decisions by consensus is strictly linked to another relevant UNSC practice: informal consultations. Informal consultations have no legal standing, they take place behind closed doors, and no official information is released. They have rapidly grown, and it is within this forum that the real UNSC decisions are taken. Moreover, the P5 and the P3 (the US, the UK, and France) have the habit of holding their own separate informal consultations (Garekhan 2006; Smith 2006). This further reduces the possibility of tracing variations in the position of UNSC members.

Looking at the Italian voting behavior when Italy was a UNSC member in the analyzed period (in 2007, 2008, and 2017) confirms these difficulties (tables 4.1, 4.2, and 4.3). The tables include the agenda item and draft resolution on which the vote was taken and present the voting coincidence between Italy, all the EU members sitting in the UNSC[4] and the US, Russia, and China. The presence of Italy in the UNSC is discontinuous, and the second term is limited to one year by the Italian choice to split the term with the Netherlands. The number of recorded votes is also extremely limited. However, on all the recorded decisions the Italian vote coincided with the vote of all the European states sitting in the UNSC, so the European formalized coalition was regularly present, and Italy was part of it.

Widening the analysis to the US, only on two occasions the votes of Italy and the US did not coincide: in 2008 on Sudan, on a draft resolution sponsored by the UK, when Italy voted in favor and the US abstained in relation to the language used; and in 2017 on a draft resolution sponsored by Egypt that would have called upon all states to refrain from establishing diplomatic missions in Jerusalem following the US administration announcement, when Italy voted in favor and the US used its veto power. The latter case is an interesting one. It concerned an issue on which the US has repeatedly used its veto power and on which distances between the US and the rest of the UN

Table 4.1. Italian voting coincidence with EU states and permanent members, 2007

Topic and draft resolution	Belgium	Slovakia	France	UK	US	Russia	China
Myanmar S/2007/14	Y	Y	Y	Y	Y	N (N)	N(N)
Middle East situation S/2007/315	Y	Y	Y	Y	Y	N(A)	N(A)
Iraq S/2007/390	Y	Y	Y	Y	Y	N(A)	Y
International Tribunal–Yugoslavia S/2007/541	Y	Y	Y	Y	Y	N (A)	Y
Afghanistan S/2007/548	Y	Y	Y	Y	Y	N(A)	Y

Source: UNSC meeting records, http://www.un.org/en/sc/meetings/records/2007.shtml (accessed on 20 August 2018) (elaboration by the author).

Table 4.2. Italian voting coincidence with EU stats and permanent members, 2008

Topic and draft resolution	Belgium	Croatia	France	UK	US	Russia	China
Non-proliferation—Iran S/2008/141	Y	Y	Y	Y	Y	Y	Y
Peace and security—Africa (Zimbabwe) S/2008/447	Y	Y	Y	Y	Y	N (N)	N (N)
Sudan S/2008/506	Y	Y	Y	Y	N (A)	Y	Y
Middle East situation, including the Palestinian question S/2008/787	Y	Y	Y	Y	Y	Y	Y

Source: UNSC meeting records, http://www.un.org/en/sc/meetings/records/2008.shtml (accessed on 20 August 2018) (elaboration by the author).

membership, including European states, have long been known. However, it is also one of the cases in which the US was "taking names" (Hansler 2017; Kolinovsky 2017) and "watching those votes" (Landler 2017). The stakes for voting differently from the US were therefore high, and an abstention not to displease the US could have been possible. Indeed, once the same text was

Table 4.3. Italian voting coincidence with EU states and permanent members, 2017

Topic and draft resolution	Sweden	France	UK	US	Russia	China
The situation in the Middle East S/2017/172	Y	Y	Y	Y	N (N)	N (N)
The situation in the Middle East S/2017/315	Y	Y	Y	Y	N (N)	N (A)
The situation in the Middle East S/2017/884	Y	Y	Y	Y	N (N)	N (A)
The situation in the Middle East S/2017/962	Y	Y	Y	Y	N (N)	N (A)
The situation in the Middle East S/2017/968	Y	Y	Y	Y	N (Y)	N (Y)
The situation in Somalia S/2017/945	Y	Y	Y	Y	N (A)	N (A)
The situation in the Middle East S/2017/970	Y	Y	Y	Y	N (N)	N (A)
The situation in the Middle East, including the Palestinian question S/2017/1060	Y	Y	Y	N (N)	Y	Y

Source: UNSC meeting records, http://www.un.org/en/sc/meetings/records/2017.shtml (accessed on 20 August 2018) (elaboration by the author).

presented in the UNGA, in an emergency special session, Croatia, the Czech Republic, Hungary, Latvia, Poland, and Romania defected from the European formalized coalition, abstaining while the other 22 EU members voted in favor (United Nations General Assembly 2017a). However, the EU member states sitting in the UNSC coordinated and decided to adopt a common position in line with previous European positions on the issue. And all of them, Italy included, maintained it. In the statement following the vote, France and Sweden explicitly recalled the common position adopted by the EU member states in the UNSC and remarked the unity (United Nations Security Council 2017a). All of this goes in the direction of strengthening the hypothesis that Italian foreign policy is still Europeanized.

For Italy the relationship with the US is important too, though. Contrary to France and Sweden, in the statement following the vote on Jerusalem Italy remarked that it continued to see a crucial role to be played by the US in the intensification of efforts to reach peace in the Middle East, emphasizing the importance of its relationship with the US (United Nations Security Council 2017a). Another element that is evident from Italian voting behavior in the UNSC is the distance with Russia and China compared to the one with the US. While Italy in the analyzed period regularly voted with the US, with the two exceptions already described, it never voted like Russia in 2007 and 2017 (with the exception of the resolution on Jerusalem), and more and more it disagreed with China. On the majority, of recorded votes in the analyzed period Italy voted differently from China, but this became particularly evident in 2017. To be clear, in the UNSC when a permanent member abstains, this allows a resolution to pass. However, from the political point of view it still signals a distance, although more limited than if the veto were to be cast. Interestingly, despite the strategic partnership that Italy has with Russia, in its voting behavior Italy is more distant from Russia than it is from China.

However, the limitations of the analysis of voting behavior in the UNSC make these observations of limited value. Following Monteleone (2015), it is here proposed that to systematically analyze variations in the Europeanization of Italian foreign policy and in the strategic use made of it at the international system level, we should rather look at the Italian sponsoring behavior, and eventually combine it with voting behavior.[5]

Sponsoring a draft resolution is a political act that indicates the political relevance of the issue for the sponsor (the state originally proposing the agenda item usually leads the drafting process). Non-controversial draft resolutions are normally presented following the formula "according to prior consultation," so sponsored resolutions typically indicate the potential presence of a political conflict. Sponsored draft resolutions need not be sponsored by more than one UNSC member, so co-sponsoring is a way of signaling political support. From a political point of view, sponsoring is an act of association and approval of the entire content of the draft resolution. Due to UNSC dynamics, there is a difference between sponsoring by UNSC members and nonmembers, that makes sponsoring by the former group politically more relevant. UNSC members make efforts to act by consensus and show unity. UNSC unity is considered a value that should be preserved and when the UNSC divides it is rather common that during meetings reciprocal accusations regarding defections and perceived provocations are launched. UNSC members act as gatekeepers, limiting the number of draft proposals that could be perceived as useless provocations by one of the other UNSC members and especially the P5, and advancing proposals that have real chances of being processed by the UNSC in that specific composition. From a procedural point of view, draft resolutions can be proposed by any UNSC member, but also by UN members that are not UNSC members. In the latter case, though, the draft resolution can be put to the vote only at the request of a UNSC member (Bailey and Daws 1998: 221). This leaves the control of the agenda in the hands of UNSC members. UNSC members that are more active in sponsoring gain greater control of the agenda. However, while draft resolutions that are presented according to prior consultation are normally automatically approved, sponsored draft resolutions may more easily encounter opposition and be rejected.

Sponsoring of UNSC draft resolutions has been growing enormously since the 2000s, while the presentation of draft resolutions according to prior consultations has been drastically reduced (Monteleone 2015: 62). By investigating the sponsoring of draft resolutions and the states that oppose them, we can gain a more reliable picture of variations in a state's foreign policy and its coalitional activities than that gained by investigating states' voting behavior alone. For the sake of analyzing Italian behavior systematically over an extended period, also draft resolutions sponsored by Italy as a non-UNSC member will be here considered. However, due to the UNSC dynamics, only the co-sponsors of Italy sitting in the UNSC will be considered. To be clear, analyzing sponsoring behavior inserts a bias toward permanent members, so in the case of EU member states, the Italian sponsoring with France and the UK is more relevant than the Italian sponsoring with the other European UNSC nonpermanent members, and only the behavior in relation to France and the UK can be systematically evaluated over time. This presents problems in relation to the limited interest so far shown by the two countries in representing the EU position (Hill 2006; Tardy and Zaum 2016) and to the distance already registered in voting in the UNGA in the previous chapter that indicates that France and the UK are more distant than Italy from the European formalized coalition. But it has the advantage of allowing the analysis of variations over time within a forum where ongoing changes at the international system level are most likely to be reflected.

Had Italian foreign policy de-Europeanized, we would have to expect that in the analyzed period Italy regularly and prevalently chose as its top co-sponsors the non-EU countries sitting in the UNSC, or that it increasingly sponsored mostly with non-EU countries. Should Italian foreign policy be Europeanized, we would have to expect that in the analyzed period Italy sponsored prevalently and regularly with the EU countries sitting in the UNSC as its predominant strategy.

In order to check whether Italy adapts its foreign policy in order to be part of the European formalized coalition as a system maintenance activity, it is also important to see how much Italy sponsors draft resolutions, that is how much it processes its political demands through the UNSC, and whether it does it predominantly with the US or with the so-called rising powers. In case Italy acted to support the US-led international hegemonic order, in the analyzed period it should have sponsored regularly or increasingly, and it should have done so together more with the US than with Russia or China.

As for Italy's co-sponsors in the UNSC, Italy regularly sponsored with the US, France, and the UK, and more in general with the other EU member states sitting in the UNSC as its regular and predominant strategy (table 4.4). While during the first years under consideration (2000, 2002, and 2004) this effect was somehow hidden by the extremely limited number of draft resolutions sponsored by Italy, once Italian sponsoring increased it became more evident. In the years when Italy sponsored more than three draft resolutions, looking at the top scores (bold numbers) of co-sponsors, the P3 were always among the countries registering the top three scores. This is not to say that Italy acted with all the EU members sitting in the UNSC in the same way, as differences exist. Starting with the permanent members, in the analyzed period Italy sponsored 97 draft resolutions with France and 92 with the UK.

Due to the UNSC composition, it is not appropriate to compare the Italian sponsoring with the two EU permanent members of the UNSC with the Italian sponsoring with the other EU members that were seating in the analyzed period as nonpermanent members. Looking at the EU states that in the analyzed period were UNSC nonpermanent members, however, interesting minor variations emerge in relation to some countries. In 2009 Italy sponsored eight draft resolutions with the UK and France, but six with Austria, that was out of the top three scores; in 2014 Italy sponsored 11 draft resolutions with France, the UK, and the nonpermanent member Luxembourg, but eight with the nonpermanent member Lithuania that was out of the top three scores. And differences in various years emerge on the number of draft resolutions sponsored with the other EU member states. This is somewhat understandable given the

Table 4.4. Co-sponsors of Italy in the UNSC (UNSC members only)

2000	2002	2004	2007	2008	2009	2010
2 Canada	1 Bulgaria	1 France	6 Belgium	**16 US**	9 US	3 France
2 France	1 France	1 Germany	6 France	15 UK	8 France	3 US
2 Netherlands	1 Germany	1 Romania	6 UK	14 Belgium	8 UK	2 Austria
2 UK	1 Ireland	1 Russia	6 US	14 Croatia	7 Turkey	2 Turkey
2 US	1 Norway	1 Spain	5 Slovakia	14 France	7 Croatia	2 UK
1 Russia	1 Russia	1 UK	3 Panama	6 Costa Rica	6 Austria	1 Bosnia
	1 UK	1 US	3 Peru,	6 Russia	5 Burkina Faso	1 Brazil
			2 Congo	5 Panama	4 Costa Rica	1 Gabon
			1 Russia	3 Burkina Faso	4 Japan	1 Japan
				3 China	4 Mexico	1 Lebanon
				2 South Africa	2 Uganda	1 Mexico
					2 Russia	1 Nigeria
						1 Russia

2011	2012	2013	2014	2015	2016	**2017**
5 France	5 France	3 France	11 France	10 France	11 France	17 France
4 Germany	5 Germany	3 UK	11 Luxemb.	10 Spain	11 Spain	17 Japan
4 Nigeria	4 UK	3 US	11 UK	10 UK	11 UK	16 UK
4 Portugal	4 US	2 Luxemb.	10 Australia	9 US	10 US	15 Sweden
4 US	3 Portugal	1 Argentina	10 R. Korea	9 Lithuania	9 Japan	15 Ukraine
3 Gabon	1 Azerbaijan	1 Australia	10 US	8 Malaysia	9 Ukraine	15 US
3 Russia	1 India	1 Azerbaijan	9 Jordan	8 New Zealand	8 Malaysia	9 Uruguay
3 UK	1 Morocco	1 R. Korea	8 Lithuania	6 Jordan	8 New Zealand	9 Senegal
2 India	1 Russia	1 Russia	7 Chile	5 Angola	8 Senegal	8 Ethiopia
2 Lebanon	1 South Africa		7 Rwanda	5 Chile	7 Uruguay	7 Kazakhst.
1 Bosnia			6 Chad	4 Nigeria	6 Angola	2 Russia
1 Colombia			5 Argentina	3 Chad	4 Egypt	2 Bolivia
			5 Nigeria	3 Venezuela	2 Venezuela	1 China
			3 Russia	2 Russia		1 Egypt
			2 China	1 China		

Note: In bold the years in which Italy was sitting in the UNSC and, when the total number of Italian-sponsored resolutions is above three, the first three scores.

Source: UNBISNET (elaboration by the author).

workings of the UNSC and the preeminence of the permanent members. But it also indicates that EU member states do not necessarily act cohesively when sponsoring draft resolutions in the UNSC. This makes it even more relevant that Italian top co-sponsors in the analyzed period are EU members and suggests that Italy reaches out to facilitate the maintenance of the European formalized coalition, strengthening indications that Italian foreign policy is still Europeanized. Only in 2008 and 2009 Italy sponsored with a non-EU member more than with European States. In both cases it was with the US.

The other relevant top co-sponsor of Italy is indeed the US, that in the analyzed period co-sponsored with Italy 84 draft resolutions. Next to France and the UK, the US was among the top three co-sponsors in all the years considered except for 2002 and, as already seen, in 2008 and 2009 it co-sponsored Italian draft resolutions even more than the European P3 members. Many states traditionally considered close allies of the US and members of the Atlantic pluralistic security community (Adler and Barnett 1998), like Canada, Australia, New Zealand, South Korea, and Turkey figure among the non-European states sitting in the UNSC with whom Italy sponsors most of its draft resolutions. Russia occupied a top sponsoring position in 2011 only, when Italy sponsored with it three draft resolutions. China never did. Moreover, with the increase in Italian sponsoring in the 2010s, Russia and China tended to be progressively more distant and at the bottom of the list of co-sponsors of Italy. This confirms that Italy acts firmly within the dominant coalition that, although currently mutating, is still dominant in the UNSC (Monteleone 2015). In this respect, Italy's support to the European formalized coalition next to the US should be interpreted as playing as a member in good standing of the dominant coalition providing system maintenance and therefore backing the existing organization of the international system.

As for support to the UN, in the analyzed period Italy sponsored only occasionally draft resolutions until it held a UNSC seat in 2007 (table 4.5). This

Table 4.5. UNSC draft resolutions sponsored by Italy (absolute numbers), 2000–2017

	2000	2001	2002	2003	2004	2005	2006	**2007**	**2008**
Draft resolutions sponsored by Italy	2	0	1	0	1	0	0	7	16

	2009	2010	2011	2012	2013	2014	2015	2016	**2017**
Draft resolutions sponsored by Italy	9	3	5	5	3	11	10	11	19

Note: In bold the years in which Italy was sitting in the UNSC.
Source: UNBISNET (elaboration by the author).

is in line with the more limited sponsoring activity by UNSC members until the second half of the 2000s and with the more limited responsibilities attributed to UNSC nonpermanent members until then. Once Italy became a nonpermanent member and the context started being more conducive to a greater use of sponsored resolutions, the country became more active in sponsoring even when it was not sitting in the UNSC. The trend of Italian sponsoring is an increasing one, suggesting that in the analyzed period Italy tried to influence the UNSC agenda and to process political demands through the UN, and indicating support to the main institution of the organization of the international system.

All the four draft resolutions sponsored between 2000 and 2004 concerned the former Yugoslavia, an area of immediate interest and geographical contiguity for Italy. Draft resolutions sponsored by Italy afterward, on the contrary, widely expanded the areas and issues of concern for Italy.

Considering sponsors that are not UNSC members introduces some methodological problems due to the UNSC dynamics previously described. UNSC members are more active in sponsoring and, due to the highly closed nature of UNSC works, non-UNSC members tend to be associated with sponsoring only when involved by UNSC members and when the context allows it. Accordingly, a strong bias toward EU members that were UNSC members is to be expected. On the other hand, looking at all the co-sponsors of Italian draft resolutions gives an idea of the countries Italy works with the most and of variations over time.

In the analyzed period, the number of countries with which Italy sponsored its draft resolutions increased over time, and it became increasingly frequent that Italy sponsored draft resolutions with all EU members or at least with the majority of EU member states, that is, with the European formalized coalition. In the analyzed period Italy sponsored its first draft resolutions with all EU members in 2008 on acts of sexual violence against civilians in armed conflicts and in 2009 on sexual violence against women and children in situations of armed conflict. But the number of draft resolutions sponsored by all EU members including Italy expanded in absolute numbers (4 in 2014, 3 in 2015, 7 in 2016, 1 in 2017) and in terms of issues. Moreover, it was rather frequent that Italy co-sponsored draft resolutions sponsored by almost all EU members, with only one or two EU members defecting (six times in 2017 only), and by a majority of EU members. Looking at the EU members Italy sponsored with the most (table 4.6), confirms the expected bias toward EU members that were also UNSC members. Besides the permanent members, the EU states that sponsored the most with Italy were the ones that had the possibility to sit in the UNSC (in the case of Germany and Spain twice) in the analyzed period. However, it is also possible to observe that Italy was closer

Table 4.6. EU member states' co-sponsoring of Italian draft resolutions (including non-UNSC members), 2000–2017

Number of draft resolutions co-sponsored	EU member state	Number of draft resolutions co-sponsored	EU member state	Number of draft resolutions co-sponsored	EU member state
97	France	48	Denmark	42	Estonia
92	United Kingdom	48	Portugal	42	Romania
68	Belgium	45	Lithuania	42	Slovenia
63	Germany	45	Slovakia	41	Cyprus
60	Croatia	44	Austria	40	Ireland
60	Spain	44	Finland	39	Hungary
52	Netherlands	44	Greece	39	Poland
51	Sweden	42	Bulgaria	38	Latvia
50	Luxembourg	42	Czech Republic	32	Malta

Note: No distinction was made between actual and prospective EU members.
Source: UNBISNET (elaboration by the author).

to the EU founding members, with whom it co-sponsored 50 percent or more of its resolutions, than to the Eastern European ones and in general to the newer members (except for Croatia). This strengthens indications that Italy tends to work in closer coordination with the original European members of the dominant coalition.

Combining information on sponsoring and voting behavior, 15 of the draft resolutions sponsored by Italy in the analyzed period translated into UNSC divisive votes. This is not a marginal number, considering that the UNSC tends to work based on consensus. Italian-sponsored draft resolutions in the analyzed period were never vetoed by the UK or France, but this is not surprising because the two countries have never used their veto power since the end of the Cold War. The two countries never abstained either on draft resolutions sponsored by Italy, confirming closeness with the Italian proposals. The only draft resolution sponsored by Italy that was vetoed by the US was draft resolution S/2002/712 on the extension of the UN mission in Bosnia that involved the risk of putting US personnel under the jurisdiction of the International Criminal Court in 2002. The draft resolution was sponsored by Bulgaria, France, Germany, Ireland, Italy, Norway, Russia, and the UK.[6] The issue of the International Criminal Court was particularly important for the EU, that strongly promoted it despite opposition from the US, Russia, and China. In the analyzed period, the US never abstained on Italian-sponsored draft resolutions.

As for Russia, in the analyzed period it vetoed seven draft resolutions sponsored by Italy and it abstained on four of them. China vetoed three draft resolutions sponsored by Italy and it abstained on eight of them. Most importantly, there is a progression that indicates an increasing distance between Italy, Russia, and China in the analyzed period. Russian vetoes on Italian-sponsored draft resolutions were cast in 2014 (2), 2015 (1), 2016 (1), and 2017 (3). Chinese vetoes were cast in 2014 (1), 2015 (1), and 2017 (1).

The analysis of the Italian behavior in the UNSC confirms that Italy regularly and prevalently acts in this forum as a member of the European formalized coalition. EU members are its top co-sponsors, and intra-European disagreements are overcome because the stakes are high. Most importantly, in this forum it is evident the role of Italy as a member of the dominant coalition and ally of the US. Italy is remarkably close to the P3, that is to the stable core members of the dominant coalition within the UNSC. Indeed, the P3 are its regular top co-sponsors. Minor signs of disagreements were registered in the early 2000s, when according to hegemonic theories the cohesion and strength of the dominant coalition could be expected to be weaker. But once Russia and China started exercising their role as veto players, Italy strengthened its bonds with the other core members of the dominant coalition and increased its distance with the two potential challengers. All of this reinforces indications that the Europeanization of Italian foreign policy is not in conflict with its support to the US and the US-led order but aims at strengthening it.

ITALY AS A EUROPEAN MEMBER OF THE SECURITY COUNCIL AND THE 2017 "SPLIT TERM"

Voting and sponsoring provide broad information on Italian coalitional behavior in the UNSC, but to better understand Italian convergence or divergence with the European formalized coalition in this forum it is useful to explore more in-depth some significant cases. The case of the 2017 "split term" represents a case of convergence worth exploring because splitting UNSC terms is rather exceptional. The 2017 split term also gives the opportunity to further explore Italian behavior in the UNSC and identify issues of interest to Italy on which it managed to collect European support. Finally, it allows to better understand how Italy interprets its role as a member of the European formalized coalition when it sits in the UNSC.

With the 1963 UNSC expansion it was decided that the ten elected members should be distributed on a regional basis (five for African and Asian countries, one for Eastern European countries, two for Latin American and Caribbean countries, two for Western European and Other countries), but formally they are elected in the UNGA and the General Assembly should pay "due regard [. . .] to the contribution of Members of the United Nations to the maintenance of international peace and security and to the other purposes of the Organization, and also to equitable geographical distribution" (Rule 143 of the Rules of Procedure of the General Assembly). While in the past rotation within regional groups tended to prevail over other criteria and elections to select nonpermanent members were often decided in advance, over time candidate members have started going through competitive elections and have therefore needed to pay attention to positions expressed in their "regional constituency" (Malone 2000; Hurd 2007). Given that EU members are divided into different UN regional groups, a variable number can seat in the UNSC. However, the largest number is normally provided by the Western European and Others Group (WEOG), whose selection practices have always been particularly competitive and whose members have started announcing their candidacies further and further in advance (Malone 2000: 4–5).

Italy is the EU member state with the most UNSC mandates as a nonpermanent member. This does not grant an easy election to the country, as the failed candidature for the 2001–2002 mandate reminds. However, it is a remarkable achievement that Italy has tried to turn into a European one associating it with its reform proposal of the UNSC. Salleo and Pirozzi (2008) describe the Italian experience as a UNSC member in 2007–2008. Italy was elected with Belgium and both countries wanted to give a European dimension to their UNSC mandate. However, while Belgium adopted a more pragmatic approach, Italy adopted an activist stance (Drieskens 2009). For the Italian Ministry of Foreign Affairs (Ministero degli affari esteri 2007) this should have been an opportunity "to strengthen Europe's role on the international stage, with a view to developing and honing those mechanisms for consultation and coordination already existing between the countries of the European Union but whose potential has not yet been fully exploited." Most importantly, there was awareness that the Italian "top priority—European integration—can bring added value to our efforts to further qualify our presence on the Security Council" and of "Italy's choice of banking on European integration" as a strategy to deal with a complex world scenario (Ministero degli affari esteri 2007). Italy encouraged cooperation between the UN and the EU, made of coordination within the EU on UNSC issues one of its priorities and aimed at the "European value" of its UNSC seat (Ministero degli affari esteri 2007). Italy campaigned to make its UNSC seat an EU one, with the commitment to favor the harmonization of the different EU member states' positions and the emergence of an EU profile. The Italian proposal to integrate a representative of the EU Presidency or of the High Representative for CFSP into the Italian delegation was opposed especially by France and the UK. Nonetheless, Italy called for more effective coordination mechanisms among EU members in the UNSC, tried to bring attention on the European positions in its interventions in the UNSC and made of its delegation a focal point for contacts with the other EU countries, the EU Presidency, and the EU Council Secretariat (Salleo and Pirozzi 2008: 106–107). According to Pirozzi (2009: 66), during Italy's mandate the representation and role of the EU in the UNSC improved significantly, as the positions and decisions of the General Affairs and External Relations Council gained visibility, the High Representative had the possibility to intervene and the Joint Statement on UN-EU Cooperation was renewed.

Initially by accident more than intentionally, the European value was present also during the Italian 2017 UNSC mandate. Italy competed for one of the two WEOG seats for the 2017–2018 mandate against Sweden and the Netherlands. Sweden was immediately elected with 134 votes. The Netherlands received 125 votes and Italy 113, so none of them was elected. At the second round of voting, the two countries started closing their gap: the Netherlands received 99 votes and Italy 92. At the third round of voting, the only competition remaining was the one between the two European countries: the Netherlands received 96 votes and Italy 94. At the fourth round of voting, the Netherlands received 96 votes and Italy 95. At the fifth round of voting both countries received 95 votes (United Nations 2016). At this point a compromise solution was agreed to split the term: Italy would have served in 2017 and the Netherlands in 2018. The solution was not an orthodox one, as it was a practice followed very few times between the late 1950s and the mid-1960s, and it caused concern in some countries, notably Russia and Egypt (Security Council Report 2017: 2).

The split term solution came immediately after the vote on Brexit. Speaking at the UNGA, the then Italian foreign minister Gentiloni declared that the two states "wanted to send a message of unity between two European countries" and that they would have cooperated during the two years (United Nations General Assembly 2017b). This was stressed again by Gentiloni's successor, who during his first UNSC meeting in January 2017 confirmed that Italy was sharing its mandate with the Netherlands "in the best spirit of European unity and solidarity" (United Nations Security Council 2017b). In relation to the split term solution, although not denying that it was a second-best solution for the country, Gentiloni further stressed the connection between the adopted solution and the Italian long-term vision of an EU seat: "In a moment when Europe seems to be breaking up, this agreement counter the notion of further divisions" (Baldini 2016). That this was a "European" solution was further remarked by the then Italian ambassador Cardi in the UNGA on 30 June 2016, when Italy was elected with 179 votes. Cardi underlined that the Dutch and

Italian ambassadors had "worked for this objective in a spirit of cooperation between two European Union members at a moment in which the cohesion of the Union is of great importance" (United Nations General Assembly 2016).

While the solution was quite an original one, it was clear that the term was split, rather than shared. However, beyond the frequent niceties of the two delegations toward each other, including unusual statements of reciprocal support,[7] elements of cooperation between them were present in terms of staff exchanges, information sharing and organization of joint events and meetings, but also of identification of priority issues (Government of the Netherlands 2016). This cooperation survived the Italian UNSC mandate, as suggested by the Joint Stake out on Gaza of 15 May 2018 in which all the EU member states sitting in the UNSC or prospective UNSC members participated and Italy was involved too in the framework of the split term with the Netherlands.

The European spirit was remarked several times during the Italian mandate, but it was particularly evident on 9 May 2017, when during a UNSC meeting on UN-EU cooperation the Italian representative remarked that Italy was "committed to making a constructive contribution to strengthening the European voice at the United Nations and in the Security Council together with European partners" and "The decision to split our term in the Council with another founding member of the EU, the Netherlands, is shaped by our shared European values" (Rappresentanza Permanente 2017).

In its first speech at the UNSC, the then Italian foreign minister Alfano also stressed that the first priority of Italy during its mandate would have been a comprehensive UN reform. This is in line with the longstanding Italian and more recently European call for UN reform and translated into support for the UN reform project promoted by UN Secretary General Guterres aimed at streamlining the UN agencies and increasing cooperation with regional organizations among which the EU.

As for priorities during the Italian mandate, a focus on areas of concern for Italy was evident, starting from the Mediterranean area and Libya to refugees and human trafficking in conflict situations, particularly important in relation to the migration crisis that had invested the country. On the issue of human trafficking in armed conflicts, Italy wrote the concept note (United Nations Security Council 2017c), promoted a draft resolution (S/2017/973 sponsored by all EU member states with the exception of the Czech Republic and the UK) and an open debate under the agenda item "Maintenance of international peace and security: trafficking in persons in conflict situations." This led to the unanimous adoption of resolution 2388 (2017).

Together with France, Italy was also behind the insertion of the protection of cultural heritage in the UNSC agenda, focusing on the destruction and trafficking of cultural heritage by terrorist groups and in situations of armed conflict. Based on the Italian experience with the world's first special unit to protect cultural heritage in emergency situations, the Carabinieri Command for the Protection of Cultural Heritage, this initiative led to the sponsoring of draft resolution S/2017/242 (sponsored by all EU member states except for Portugal) that was adopted unanimously as resolution 2347 (2017).

In line with its experience as a major contributor to UN peacekeeping, Italy also focused on UN peacekeeping and its reform, sponsoring alone draft resolution S/2017/926 on including policing as an integral part of the mandates of UN peacekeeping operations and special missions. The draft resolution was unanimously adopted as resolution 2382 (2017). It also introduced the issue of the environmental impact of UN peacekeeping operations.

During the Italian Presidency of the UNSC Italy chose as priorities Africa, the Mediterranean area and the Sahel, and multidimensional challenges to security. During its mandate Italy therefore tried to bring to the fore areas and issues strictly related to its security perceptions and needs. And it often did it with the support of most EU member states: out of the 19 draft resolutions sponsored by Italy in 2017, ten were co-sponsored by at least a majority of EU member states (including non-UNSC members). That is, although UNSC dynamics do not favor it, during its UNSC mandate Italy promoted most of its initiatives with the support of the European formalized coalition. It is interesting to note, though, that this coalition was most often made by all EU members minus a very limited number of defecting states, indicating the difficulty of getting support from all EU members and for the EU to act cohesively in the UNSC.

THE REFORM OF THE SECURITY COUNCIL

The split term offered the opportunity to explore the Italian convergence with the European formalized coalition and the European support for Italian initiatives. To better understand the Europeanization of Italian foreign policy it is also useful to explore a case of divergence between the Italian position and the European one: the reform of the Security Council. The case offers a particularly interesting vantage point to analyze the Europeanization of Italian foreign policy in the perspective of this work, because "Nowhere else do states debate as explicitly on the international pecking order and the principles by which a privileged few are granted special status and powers" (Pouliot 2016: 154).

While the EU has managed to present a united front on most of the significant issues of UN reform (Smadja 2006), EU member states hold widely divergent views on UNSC reform and belong to competing groups, showing the limits of EU cohesion. Since the 1990s Italian governments of all political composition and the Italian diplomatic network have considered the fight on UNSC reform an out of the ordinary Italian national interest, leading to one of the most intense mobilizations the country has ever been capable of (Menzione 2017).

The issue of UNSC reform is strictly linked to the long-term evolution toward more inclusive security governance institutions built around democratic principles and representativeness (Pouliot and Thérien 2015). The UNSC architecture was established at the end of World War II and gave responsibility and privilege to the five permanent members, reflecting the power distribution of the time. The rapid growth of UN members led to the first revision of the original UNSC architecture and to the expansion of nonpermanent seats in 1963. With the end of the Cold War, a new debate arose, focusing on the widely perceived unrepresentativeness of the UNSC. The permanent members and their privileges came under scrutiny. In a UN in which the North-South divisions became a defining cleavage (Kim and Russett 1996), the overrepresentation of Northern industrial countries became an issue. Particularly evident was the disconnect between the two European countries, the UK and France, and the post–Cold War power distribution, but when the debate started, Russia and China were not in a strong position either.

Calls for UNSC reform were not unprecedented. Already during the Cold War, the growth of the Non-aligned movement (NAM) had led to unsuccessful attempts. The end of the Cold War provided some states a window of opportunity to redefine the world order and claim an upgrade in status. This tied well with the newly found Italian assertiveness and attention to the national interest. Calls for UN reform to increase its effectiveness were a leitmotif of the Italian presence at the UN already during the Cold War. UNSC reform, however, was in a league of its own. Menzione (2017: 11) recalls an interesting anecdote in this regard: a meeting in an unspecified year, presumably toward the end of the Cold War, in which the German foreign minister Genscher was called by the Italian foreign minister Andreotti and their Japanese colleague in the UN Delegates Lounge and asked by Andreotti whether, given their economic growth and political clout, it was not the time for the three powers defeated in World War II to claim a UNSC permanent seat to better reflect the realities of the international order of the time. The anecdote is interesting because it reminds of the importance that status has for Italy, but also because it reveals that the country was planning to pursue it through the UN and its activities.

This self-perception was not matched by perceptions of Italy held by the wider international community, so Italy remained leader of a blocking minority. The case, however, reveals not only the importance that status has for Italy, but also that, when an Italian national interest perceived as vital is at stake and the country is unable to gather support from its European partners, its first option, Italy can create alternative coalitions. Interestingly, this happens on an issue that sees the country as "one of the strongest advocates in Europe of a common EU representation in the Security Council in the long run" (Drieskens et al. 2007: 423), showing that, even when intra-European disagreements lead to alternative coalitions on specific issues, the European dimension remains part of the national interest. Although the major events regarding the Italian position on UNSC reform took place in the 1990s, they will be briefly traced to better understand current positions, focusing on Italian coalitional capacities and intra-European divisions.

In the 1990s the debate on UNSC reform gathered momentum. On 25 September 1990 at the 6th UNGA plenary session Italian foreign minister De Michelis forcefully expressed the Italian point of view that the UN had to be reformed and that, given the progress made in the European integration process, it was important to adapt the UN to give a more visible role to the EU (Tosi 2010: 404). On 27 September 1991 the same foreign minister, talking about UNSC reform, expressed the position that both permanent and nonpermanent members (but without veto power) should have increased, but permanent members should have been selected according to objective criteria (Tosi 2010: 414). This position was repeated on 24 September 1992 by the Italian foreign minister Colombo during the 10th UNGA plenary session, Colombo introduced the issue of the European representation in the UNSC stating that Italy aspired to a seat, "unless institutional developments in the European Union will not allow at some point the creation of a European seat in the Security Council" (Tosi 2010: 420).

Thanks to Indian activism, the issue of UNSC reform eventually entered the UN agenda in December 1992 and the UN Secretary General invited UN member states to provide comments on possible revisions of the UNSC. Lacking a common approach, the views submitted by EU member states varied considerably (Tsakaloyannis and Bourantonis 1997: 204). From the cautious approach of France and the UK, to the proposal of the Netherlands and Belgium emphasizing the role of regional groupings, from the Irish proposal to enlarge UNSC permanent membership taking into account effectiveness and representativeness to the Spanish proposal of new categories allowing more frequent presence of certain member states, from the Greek proposal to represent major regions of the world but without damaging effectiveness to Luxembourg's and Portugal's emphasis on not reforming at the expense of nonpermanent members, from the proposal of Denmark careful not to damage UNSC's effectiveness to the German expression of gratification for having been identified as a natural candidate for UNSC permanent membership and commitment to assume the relative responsibilities (United Nations General Assembly 1993a and 1993b). Of the twelve EU members, only Belgium, Portugal, Spain and Italy explicitly included a European dimension in their proposal, be it as in the case of Spain as a readiness to keep the views of the other EU member states "very much in mind" (United Nations General Assembly 1993a), or in the other cases as an issue that might arise in the future.

The Italian proposal identified three categories of seats: permanent seats with veto right, ten seats to be assigned to a group of twenty states that contribute the most to the goals of the UN and that would rotate in couples, actually becoming semi-permanent, and a third category of seats to be assigned to all the other states organized in regional constituencies on a geographical basis. The proposal considered potential new developments and, having clearly in mind the European situation, stated that "the day on which the European Union comes into being with a strong political identity on its own, the problem will arise regarding the position it will be given in the Security Council" (United Nations General Assembly 1993a). The proposal closed with a subordinate request: "Should it be decided to increase the number of permanent members, Italy feels entitled to be one of them, on the basis of its record as one of the major contributors to the United Nations and to the peace-keeping operations decided on by the Security Council" (United Nations General Assembly 1993a). The Italian proposal was running counter to the solution that seemed to emerge as the preferred one at the time, a quick fix that interpreted UNSC reform as the inclusion of Germany and Japan in reason of their economic strength. The quick fix solution was rebuked by Italy, at the time economically stronger than two of the permanent members, a top contributor to the UN budget, and a bigger contributor than Germany and Japan to UN peacekeeping operations. The country contested that the two countries had a global role superior to the Italian one (Fulci 1999–2000: 9). The quick fix solution was preferred by France and the UK, but for Italy it would have meant the creation of a new directoire from which the country would have been excluded for decades, so it was an unacceptable solution worth fighting against.

The Open-Ended Working Group on Equitable Representation on and Increase in the Membership of the Security Council was established. As remarked by the Italian ambassador Fulci (1999–2000: 8), the protagonist of the Italian battle at the UN at the time, the working group was charged with reaching a "general agreement" on the issue of UNSC reform, expression largely interpreted as less than consensus and more than two-thirds of the UNGA. In February 1995, the NAM group formulated the "2+3" formula that conditioned support to Germany and Japan as permanent members to the accession to the same status of at least three developing countries (Pouliot 2016:

155). This proposal too was problematic for Italy, because it risked reducing the relevance of the country for a very long period. Following debates within the group, on 15 May 1995 Italy presented a revised proposal for UNSC enlargement. The new proposal imagined only two categories, permanent and nonpermanent members, but no change in the permanent category: only 8–10 new nonpermanent seats should have been added. For each of the new nonpermanent seats, three states would be rotating, so that their presence would be more frequent. Objective criteria should have been at the basis of the selection of more frequently rotating nonpermanent seats, and the group of more frequently rotating countries should have been subject to periodic revisions and regular elections, but immediate reelection was barred. The objective criteria proposed were: the contribution to the purposes and activities of the organization, equitable geographic distribution, contribution to peacekeeping operations, and participation to voluntary funds.[8] In the new proposal the European integration project was no longer mentioned and the competition with Germany was evident. Given the impossibility for Italy to become a permanent member, it was important to bar Germany from becoming one, what would have reduced the Italian status and precluded the country's future access to a higher status.

As Menzione (2017: 40) points out, Italy further elaborated the proposal in June 1996 in an informal non-paper calling for higher contributions (7.5%) to UN peacekeeping operations from more frequently rotating countries and for a threshold of 25 percent of permanent members' contributions. This proposal was further redefined in 1997 and pointed in the direction of reducing UN dependence on permanent members. However, France and the UK kept supporting the quick fix (and later the 2+3) solution, seeing it as the lesser of two evils (Blavoukos and Bourantonis 2011: 736).

In 1997 the 2+3 formula was adopted as the basis of discussion in the so-called Razali Plan, that included fixed permanent seats for Germany and Japan, rotating permanent seats for the three main developing countries in Asia, Africa, and Latin America, and four new nonpermanent seats to all the geographic groups except the Western Group. As remarked by ambassador Fulci (1999), the main Italian protagonist, this proposal was even worse for Italy, because it would have introduced a sort of caste system and it would have made it impossible for Italy to ever seat in the UNSC again. Probably knowing that the proposal did not have the support of two-thirds of the members of the UNGA, Razali proposed that a framework proposal be approved by two-thirds of the UNGA members present and voting. The lack of support from European states and the vital national interest attributed to the issue motivated Italy to assume leadership of a group of countries (mostly middle powers) sharing similar interests and to create the "Coffee Club," an informal network of states (among which Spain) opposed to any increase in the number of permanent seats and advocating UNSC enlargement to nonpermanent seats only. In the words of ambassador Fulci (1999: 13), who created it, this was an unprecedented de facto alliance of approximately fifty members bringing together industrialized countries that did not want to be marginalized and developing countries that aspired to greater visibility, and that could potentially reach out to the Non-Aligned Movement group. Italy therefore created a minority bloc of 50–60 states that made the proposed UNSC reform impossible. A procedural battle ensued, won by Italy, that led Razali to declare that the Italian ambassador Fulci had won (Menzione 2017: 63). In 1998 a Belgian proposal (United Nations General Assembly 1998a) supported by France, the UK, the US, sixteen Western countries, five Eastern European countries, and one Non-Aligned Movement country to openly support Germany and Japan clashed with the Coffee Club proposal (United Nations General Assembly 1998b), at this point supported by China and Russia (Fulci 1999: 14). The Belgian proposal collected the support of ten EU member states out of fifteen, so the minority position of Italy, backed only by Spain, in the EU was evident.[9] The draft resolution proposed by the Coffee Club was unanimously adopted as resolution 53/30 and granted that any decision on UNSC reform should be taken by two-thirds of UNGA members. This represented an important political victory for Italy, that had led a coalition of a minority of states capable of blocking a decision that would have severely damaged the country.

Following the 1997–1998 procedural battle, in 2003 the UN Secretary General decided to task the High-level Panel on Threats, Challenges and Change to examine the issue of UNSC reform. While the Panel came out with two models, this initiative led groups to present their own proposals. However, a deadlock followed. Debates resumed with the 2008 UNGA decision to start an intergovernmental negotiation (IGN), and a text-based phase initiated in 2009 (Pouliot 2016: 156–157) and is still ongoing.

Several groups have emerged in the battle over UNSC reform over the years (Menzione 2017: 101–106; Pouliot 2016: 161–168). In 1999 the G4 (Japan, Germany, India, and Brazil) was created. It supported six new permanent seats and promised restraint on the use of the veto power. In 2005 the Uniting for Consensus (UfC) group was created, made of Argentina, Canada, Colombia, South Korea, Costa Rica, Malta, Mexico, Pakistan, San Marino, Spain, Turkey, and Italy as a focal point. It included China and Indonesia as observers. The group opposed the creation of new permanent seats. In 2007 the L-69 group was created, made of 40 developing states from Latin America, Asia and Africa and including Brazil and India, South Africa, and Nigeria. In 2013 it was the turn of the Accountability Coherence and Transparency (ACT) group coordinated by Switzerland and including the Nordic countries, New Zealand and Costa Rica and focusing on the effectiveness and management of the UNSC rather than on its enlargement. Furthermore, the group of Arabic countries and the African group have emerged. The composition and support for the groups underline once again the Italian distance from the European formalized coalition on the issue of UNSC reform and the direct competition between Italy and Germany. The G4 has support from 75 members (Pouliot 2016: 164), including France, the UK, and the majority of EU member states (Blavoukos and Bourantonis 2011: 736). The only EU members openly supporting the UfC are Italy, Spain, and Malta.

The evolution in the position of the other EU member states is important as well. As noted by Blavoukos and Bourantonis (2011: 737), if in the initial stage of the UNSC reform debate some small and medium EU states in light of the Italian proposal on the EU seat had remained ambivalent, once the proposal was shelved, they started supporting the permanent seat for Germany. In the second stage most of them supported the Razali plan, and therefore indirectly Germany. In the third stage, that is after 2004, France, the UK, Belgium, Denmark, the Czech Republic, Greece, Latvia, Poland, and Portugal supported the G4 plan through co-sponsoring and Finland, Sweden, Slovakia, Bulgaria, Lithuania, Romania, Estonia, Luxembourg, and Slovenia expressed indirect support. The Netherlands and Cyprus were more ambivalent but seemed to oppose the G4 plan. In its opposition to the G4, Italy was openly supported only by Spain and Malta. But in relation to UNSC reform a cluster of middle powers and EU neutrals, with positions that do not coincide with the German one and try to guarantee the role of small states, and a cluster of EU newcomers, trying to ensure one additional seat to their regional grouping, are also present (Blavoukos and Bourantonis 2011: 732), further diversifying positions within the EU and making support for the German seat fragile.

In a situation of extreme rigidity, but also of greater difficulty to hold the position, the UfC kept focusing on requests for a more democratic, representative, transparent, effective, and accountable UNSC, but made a change in its proposals. In 2009 Italy presented with Colombia a new proposal for a "transitional model" introducing the creation of longer-term seats (three- to five-year seats with no possibility of immediate reelection or two-year seats with the possibility of up to two immediate reelections), instead of permanent ones. The proposal also introduced new working methods to enhance transparency, access, and participation of nonmembers in the works of the UNSC. In 2014 the possibility of immediate reelection was also included, in what has been considered an "intermediate approach."[10] The new longer seats would not be attributed to single states, but to regional groups, confirming the Italian attention toward the regional dimension.[11] The new proposal, which could provide for a pragmatic intermediate solution, managed to attract interest from other countries, including the UK and France[12] (Pouliot 2016: 173). However, France still "pushes for the expansion of the Security Council by supporting the accession to a permanent seat of Germany, Brazil, India, Japan, an Arab country, as well as a greater presence of African countries"[13] and so does the UK,[14] confirming their traditional positions.

While their interest in UNSC reform is particularistic, both camps (the German-led one and the Italian-led one) invoke the European interest in their rhetoric. However, after the initial unsuccessful Italian proposal for an embryonic European seat, and despite the repeated Italian calls also in recent years for strengthening the representation of the EU in the Security Council,[15] the EU is of little relevance in the UNSC reform debate (Blavoukos and Bourantonis 2011: 731–732). The case of UNSC reform corroborates the Italian coalition facilitating capacities, but it also indicates that, on issues that Italy deems of vital national interest, if attempts at gathering support from the EU states fail, the country can diverge and even clash with the European formalized coalition, looking for support elsewhere. It also indicates that the regional dimension remains an important one for the country.

The case confirms the importance that status seeking has for the country. Italy invested all its diplomatic resources in the battle not to be marginalized and successfully managed to create a blocking minority. The issue of UNSC reform has something to reveal also about Italy as a member of the dominant coalition, because although the US never openly expressed itself against the Italian effort, it more explicitly sided with Germany. On the one hand, this exposes the role that Italy has as a junior partner in the dominant coalition. On the other hand, it exposes that in order to really count and be influential within the dominant coalition Italy needs to leverage on the support of the European formalized coalition. Finally, the issue of UNSC reform indicates that, in a context of weaker cohesion of the dominant coalition, Italy did not hesitate to search for support from China and Russia, strategically useful in that context. But once the stalemate dragged on and the two countries started being considered potential challengers, Italy reached out to its traditional coalition members with a more pragmatic intermediate proposal.

PROCESSES OF EUROPEANIZATION

Most of the issues on which Italy sponsored draft resolutions in the UNSC in the analyzed period strongly resonate with the EU agenda. To better understand the processes of Europeanization of Italian foreign policy in the UNSC, two cases considered close to Italian national interests, Somalia and human trafficking from Libya, and one typically representing European values and identity, human rights, will be analyzed.

Somalia was an Italian colony and Italy was present militarily in the country in the early 1990s once a civil war broke out, within the framework of UN peace operations that failed to bring peace to Somalia. Due to their historical ties, the Italian interest for the country has always been relatively high and Italy has often tried to insert the issue onto the EU agenda. The EU was highly active after the UN operation UNISOM failed, sending a special envoy, and creating the Somalia Aid Coordination Body, leading organism for providing humanitarian aid to the country. But the persistent state of failure of Somalia created a favorable context for piracy operations whose increase in the second half of the 2000s was noticed by the international community.

Italy was active in calling attention on Somalia also during its UNSC mandate in 2007, as evident from its statements. It held a debate under the Italian UNSC presidency, reminding that Somalia is a strong Italian priority, and it supported the operation of the African Union politically and financially. But the technical meetings to plan how to best intervene were organized by the UK (United Nations Security Council 2007).[16]

In the analyzed period Italy sponsored its first draft resolution (S/2008/351) on Somalia, and specifically on piracy off the costs of Somalia, in 2008, while holding a nonpermanent seat. The draft resolution received support from the two EU permanent members, but also from Belgium, the other EU member holding a nonpermanent seat at the time. Greece, Denmark, the Netherlands, and Spain, none of which was a UNSC member at the time, also offered support. A similar pattern was followed with draft resolution S/2008/633, on which Italy in the UNSC meeting that approved it commended France for "having spared no effort in building consensus around the decision" (United Nations Security Council 2008a), and with draft resolution S/2008/748, that also received Portugal's support. The interest toward the issue and the Italian involvement comes out clearly in Italian statements during UNSC meetings (see, for instance, United Nations Security Council 2008b, in which, besides calling for specific measures in relation to already approved UNSC resolutions, Italy indicates the Italian military contribution and political support also to NATO and EU operations under the UN aegis). This seems to indicate the uploading of an issue of interest to Italy: the reliance on the EU network of support and the possibility of mobilizing the EU helped the country to promote the issue higher onto the UNSC agenda.

To be clear, the threat was perceived as global and because of that many countries whose trade was disrupted were involved, so Italy did not always figure upfront. There were 11 draft resolutions approved in 2008 on Somalia. Five draft resolutions were sponsored by the UK alone, the penholder in this case, and two were drafted according to prior consultations. Of the remaining four, Italy was a sponsor of three. In the case of draft resolution S/2008/789, the only one that Italy did not co-sponsor, Italy was later involved in the Contact Group on Piracy Off the Coast of Somalia that was created with resolution 1851 (2008) and assumed the leadership of the Working Group on Disrupting Pirate Networks Ashore.[17] Italy unsuccessfully tried to go beyond the issue of piracy and to call attention to the need to stabilize Somalia. However, it contributed to the building up and maintenance of European support and to the involvement of the EU on the issue. Although limited, European support was effective. The possibility of an EU operation made it possible a wider interest of the UNSC for the case.

Once Italy stepped down from the UNSC seat, it sponsored other resolutions on piracy in Somalia. In 2009 it sponsored draft resolution S/2009/607. The draft resolution obtained support from the two EU permanent members, but not from Austria, the EU nonpermanent one. Austria voted in favor of the resolution, and its sponsorship was not needed, but its absence is interesting in symbolic terms and confirms that the interest for the Somali case was limited among EU members. However, Belgium, Bulgaria, Cyprus, Denmark, Germany, Greece, Luxembourg, the Netherlands, Portugal, Romania, Spain, and Sweden (none of which was holding a UNSC seat at the time) sponsored the draft resolution too, enlarging the group of original supporters to other EU members, most of which did not have a real interest in the issue. This was also the Italian-sponsored draft resolution on Somalia that attracted the highest support from EU member states.

The issue was taken up again in 2011 with draft resolution S/2011/228 and this time the list of sponsors was much shorter. The draft resolution was supported by one EU permanent member, France, but not by the UK; it was supported by the then nonpermanent EU member Portugal, but not by the other one, Germany. Furthermore, of the long list of EU states that had supported the previous draft resolutions, only Denmark and Spain remained. The situation slightly changed during the same year with draft resolution S/2011/650. The draft resolution was sponsored by all the EU members of the UNSC, permanent and nonpermanent, and Greece. But in 2012 the cosponsors of draft resolutions on Somalia sponsored by Italy became even less. While draft resolution S/2012/708 received the support of all the four EU UNSC members at the time (France, UK, Germany, and Portugal) and no other EU state, draft resolution S/2012/861 only enlisted among the supporters France, Germany and the non-UNSC member Spain. Italy sponsored a draft resolution on Somalia again in 2014 (S/2014/803 with all four European UNSC members and Croatia, Cyprus, Denmark, Netherlands, and Spain), and then again in 2017, in this case with all the European UNSC members but no external support.

Other UNSC resolutions on Somalia have been adopted without Italian sponsorship. The EU members of the UNSC regularly recalled the EU and its position on the issue or declared to be aligned with the EU position, and at times the head of the Delegation of the EU to the UN was invited to participate to the UNSC meetings (see, for instance, United Nations Security Council 2012). The uploading of the issue from the Italian national agenda to the European one was therefore successful, and attempts at keeping attention on the issue despite a limited interest from other EU member states were continuous. More limited was the Italian capacity to steer the decisions adopted by the UNSC.

The issue that Italy has probably tried to upload the most and Europeanize in recent times is the stabilization of Libya not only as a security challenge but also to curb the migration flow leaving from Libyan shores and reaching Italy through the Mediterranean Sea, a problem deeply felt by Italian public opinion. Italy has been involved—and has tried not to be excluded—in plans to stabilize the country, and draft resolution S/2014/629 that Italy sponsored with France, the UK, and Luxembourg (but not Lithuania) as European UNSC members was adopted unanimously as resolution 2174 (2014).

The most critical issue for Italy concerned dealing with the migration flow, tackling human smuggling and trafficking. This led Italy to strenuously promote action at the UN and search for support from the EU and EU states, particularly those sitting in the UNSC (among others, *La Repubblica* 2015; Rampini 2015; De Marchis 2015; D'Argenio 2015). The issue was indeed pushed also from the EU High Representative Mogherini in her statement in the UNSC in May 2015 (United Nations Security Council 2015). It took a while before the UNSC could act, also because some concerns had to be overcome, but eventually the UNSC approved of the initiative. The UK acted as the penholder and leading state, and all EU member states sponsored draft resolution S/2015/768 "On migrant smuggling and human trafficking into, through and from the Libyan territory and off the coast of Libya" that was approved as resolution 2240 (2015) with the abstention of Venezuela. This was an important resolution for Italy and a case of successful uploading not only to the European agenda but also to the UNSC one. The resolution was approved acting under Chapter VII and authorized EU forces already operating in the Mediterranean Sea (EUNAVFORMED Sophia was launched the same year under Italian command) to stop smugglers and seize their boats in the high seas, moving into the second phase of the European operation. The same dynamics led to the renewal and expansion of the mandate in the following years. All EU member states sponsored draft resolution S/2016/838 "On renewal for 12 months of the authorizations as set out in paras 7, 8, 9 and 10 of Security Council resolution 2240 (2015) concerning migrant smuggling and human trafficking into, through and from the Libyan territory and off the coast of Libya" adopted as resolution 2312 (2016) with Venezuela abstaining. All EU member states also sponsored draft resolution S/2017/827, again renewing the mandate for 12 months, adopted unanimously as resolution 2380 (2017). The last case is particularly important because this was one of the highest priorities of Italy in its 2017 UNSC mandate.

Resolutions 2240 (2015), 2312 (2016), and 2380 (2017) are clear cases of Europeanization and of Italian uploading. They are also evidence of the importance of European support for Italy to achieve its objectives in the UNSC. Once the issue was Europeanized, European states sitting in the UNSC acted as effective transmission belts, and the EU provided the much needed political, financial, and military resources that make it possible for the UNSC to approve action (Monteleone 2011).

The case of human rights too is instructive in relation to the Europeanization of Italian foreign policy, because of the importance attached by the EU to this issue and because it has been introduced somewhat recently in the UNSC agenda following the strong input from European states and the US, but its presence in the UNSC agenda is still highly contested from Russia and China. On human rights issues in the UNSC, Italy shows dynamics typical of downloading. In the analyzed period resolutions on the protection of civilians in armed conflicts, on women in armed conflicts and children in armed conflicts were approved. At the beginning of the analyzed period, although introducing a substantial change in the works of the UNSC, the relative draft resolutions were drafted according to prior consultations of the UNSC, indicating that they were non-conflictual issues.

Draft resolutions presented on "children and armed conflict" are repeated resolutions that started being presented in 1999 and were drafted according to prior consultations until 2009, when draft resolution S/2009/399 was sponsored by 46 states, among which 17 EU member states. Italy was a sponsor of that resolution and has kept sponsoring all the following draft resolutions every year.[18] In doing this, Italy acted with the majority of EU member states, although with important variations. In 2011 the relative draft resolution S/2011/425 was sponsored by all EU member states apart from Cyprus and the Netherlands. In 2012 (draft resolution S/2012/713) it was sponsored by 17 EU member states. In 2014 (draft resolution S/2014/149) it reached maximum EU cohesion, with all EU member states sponsoring it. But the following year this cohesion was lost, and Denmark and Malta defected from support to draft resolution S/2015/445. Italy, however, sponsored all the sponsored draft resolutions on the issue and did so regardless of the number of EU states supporting the thematic draft resolution.

As for the protection of civilians in armed conflicts, three draft resolutions on this topic have been presented: S/1999/981 in 1999, S/2000/335 in 2000, and S/2009/582 in 2009. Only the last one was sponsored by 41 states, among which 17 EU member states. Italy was one of them, also in this case acting with the EU majority.

Strictly related draft resolutions have been those focusing on sexual violence against civilians in armed conflicts. They started in 2008 with draft resolution S/2008/403 (on acts of sexual violence against civilians in armed conflicts), continued in 2009 with draft resolution S/2009/489 (on sexual violence against women and children in situations of armed conflict), then 2010 with draft resolution S/2010/641 (on sexual violence against women and children in situations of armed conflict) and finally in 2013 with draft resolution S/2013/368 (on sexual violence in armed conflict). Italy was always a sponsor together with the EU majority. At the beginning EU member states showed full EU cohesion, a testament to the importance of the issue for the EU identity and for the definition of its role as a normative power: not only EU states support those resolutions, but they want to be seen as doing it together. Not surprisingly, this issue area is taken as an indicator of Europeanization in literature. The same full EU cohesion was shown the following year with draft resolution S/2009/489 on the same topic, but three states (Cyprus, Latvia, and Poland) defected in 2010 and one (Malta) in 2013.

A final bloc of repeating draft resolutions concerns those on women, peace and security. Four of them have been presented since 2000, but the first one was presented according to prior consultations. In 2009 draft resolution S/2009/500 was presented, sponsored by Italy with a minority of EU states (five). The draft resolution was presented again in 2013 (draft resolution S/2013/614), this time by all EU member states except Cyprus, Ireland, Malta, Slovakia,[19] and then in 2015 (draft resolution S/2015/774) this time sponsored by all EU member states except Malta.

The Italian behavior on the issue of human rights in the UNSC is typical of downloading. Italy sponsored all the sponsored draft resolutions on the issue and did so regardless of the number of EU states supporting the proposal. But only one statement can be found on UNBISNET on children and armed conflict in the 1990s and one on women, peace and security in 2010, in the latter case by the Italian foreign minister Frattini, showing the higher importance of this specific issue for the country. In the case of resolutions on women, peace and security, Italy was among the first EU states to promote it, but the issue was immediately supported by the European formalized coalition. In the other cases, Italy regularly acted with the European formalized coalition and was present regardless of the number of EU states supporting the draft resolutions, but the interest was more in being part of the European formalized coalition and adhering to what is considered a European value than in defending a specific Italian interest. Human rights have recently entered the UNSC agenda under the strong input of European states and the US. Over time, Italy has internalized an important EU value that is high on the European political agenda, it has adhered to a common EU objective and has upheld the common EU position even in a forum in which it is difficult to do so.

The Somalian, Libyan, and human rights cases show different Europeanization processes—and degrees of success—of Italian foreign policy in the UNSC. Italy uploads issues in its close national interest to collect useful support (political, financial, personnel, etc.) to spend in the UNSC. But only when it strictly coordinates with an EU permanent member it also manages to steer the decision-making process. Italy has also downloaded the human rights issue. Actively supporting human rights resolutions, Italy also upholds EU core values in the UNSC and facilitates the maintenance and visibility of the European formalized coalition. The human rights issue, however, also shows that the process of building a permanent level of governance in the UNSC among EU members is difficult and subject to setbacks.

NOTES

1. The seat was previously held by the Soviet Union.
2. This section builds on and adapts Monteleone (2015).
3. Security Council Report, https://www.securitycouncilreport.org/un-security-council-working-methods/the-veto.php (accessed on 21 August 2018).
4. In 2008 Croatia, then a prospective EU member, is included because candidate members tend to associate themselves to EU positions.
5. An attempt in this direction was also made by Todd (1966).
6. Interestingly, this is one of the rare cases when, despite being a sponsor, a state (Bulgaria) abstained on the vote to avoid clashes with the US.
7. For instance, in September 2016—that is, before the mandate started—taking the floor at the Security Council open debate on the situation in Afghanistan, the Italian representative aligned Italy to the EU and supported "the statement by the Netherlands as part of our cooperation related to the upcoming split term in the Security Council" (ItalyUN.it 2016)
8. The Italian document is replicated in Menzione (2017: 149–157).
9. Sponsors of draft resolution A/53/L.42 were Australia, Austria, Belgium, Brazil, Bulgaria, Czech Republic, Denmark, Estonia, France, Germany, Hungary, Ireland, Japan, Luxembourg, Netherlands, Poland, Portugal, UK, US, and Uzbekistan. Sponsors of A/53/L.16/Rev.1 were Afghanistan, Argentina, Canada, Chad, China, Colombia, Democratic Republic of the Congo, Egypt, Equatorial Guinea, Fiji, Gambia, Indonesia, Iran (Islamic Republic of), Italy, Lebanon, Libyan Arab Jamahiriya, Malta, Mexico, New Zealand, Pakistan, Panama, Papua New Guinea, Qatar, Republic of Korea, Russian Federation, Samoa, San Marino, Sierra Leone, Singapore, Solomon Islands, Spain, Swaziland, Syrian Arab Republic, Turkey, and Zimbabwe.

10. Italian Permanent Mission to the UN, https://italyun.esteri.it/rappresentanza_onu/en/l_italia_e_l_onu/riforme (accessed on 1 September 2018).

11. See also Italian Ministry of Foreign Affairs, https://www.esteri.it/mae/it/politica_estera/organizzazioni_internazionali/onu/la_riforma.html (accessed on 2 September 2018).

12. See the 2010 UK/French position on reform of the UN Security Council, https://www.globalpolicy.org/images/pdfs/uk-french_position_on_unsc_reform.pdf (accessed on 2 September 2018).

13. French Delegation to the UN, https://onu.delegfrance.org/France-and-the-UN-Reform-8615 (accessed on 1 September 2018).

14. UK Government, https://www.gov.uk/government/speeches/security-council-reform-the-uk-supports-new-permanent-seats-for-brazil-germany-india-and-japan-alongside-permanent-african-representation (accessed on 1 September 2018).

15. See, for instance, the statement by the Italian permanent representative Sebastiano Cardi at the third informal meeting of the tenth round of the IGN, in which, after presenting the position of the UfC, he added, speaking in his national capacity: "My delegation would also be in favor of the strengthening the representation of the European Union in the Security Council. The EU is a political, institutional, economic and monetary reality. Everyone knows the role that the EU plays in the UN system, starting with the General Assembly. Many share the view that there is a wide gap between what the EU is already doing in various UN forums and what it could be doing in the Security Council. The European institutions and European public opinion are in favor of this aspiration and Italy has given voice to it for more than fifteen years. We think time has come to give it more serious consideration." Available at https://italyun.esteri.it/rappresentanza_onu/en/comunicazione/archivio-news/2014/04/2014-04-01-pr-cardi-sc-riforma.html (accessed on 2 September 2018).

16. In his statement in the UNSC on 17 December 2007 the Italian representative Spatafora closed by saying: "Somalia is a textbook case on the credibility of this Organization and its ability to make a difference on the ground. We cannot continue to pay lip service to doing more for Somalia and then do nothing. We need concrete—I repeat, concrete—steps forward, and we need to move from goodwill to action now" (United Nations Security Council 2007).

17. US State Department, https://www.state.gov/t/pm/rls/fs/2017/266864.htm (accessed on 2 September 2018).

18. This includes also draft resolution S/2018/667 presented in 2018.

19. But Ireland aligned itself with the statement made by the observer of the EU.

Chapter Five

The Challenge of Crises
Toward a De-Europeanization?

A CHANGING CONTEXT

The empirical analysis of Italian behavior in the UNGA and in the UNSC in the period 2000–2017 has shown that Italian foreign policy is Europeanized. In its foreign policy Italy acts predominantly with the European formalized coalition while acting independently is an exceptional behavior. This cooperative behavior is pursued consistently, across issues and over time, a necessary feature to identify cooperation as an observable implication of Europeanization (Moumoutzis 2011).

From the qualitative analysis, it emerged that in the Europeanization of Italian foreign policy both the logic of consequences and the logic of appropriateness were at play, as indicated by Börzel and Risse (2003: 74). Italy frequently built on the European formalized coalition and tried to upload its interests on the EU agenda because this offered additional resources to exert influence on decision-making processes and helped to achieve status, as it was evident in the UNSC on issues such as human trafficking from Libya. When it could not rely on the support of the European formalized coalition, Italy was less effective and could at best create blocking minorities, as it was evident in the case of the otherwise unsuccessful previous attempts at promoting the moratorium on death penalty and in the case of UNSC reform. Indeed, the EU changes the opportunity structure of Italy at the UN, a causal link needed to talk about Europeanization (Ladrech 2000: 190).

Italy acted together with the European formalized coalition also because over time it has redefined its identity, and acting with the other EU members is what is expected from the country, the socially accepted behavior. The "we-feeling" or idea of belonging to a community, played a significant role in Italian foreign policy and went beyond the "coordination reflex" long identified in the literature. Italy supported initiatives that may not have been specifically in its national interest but that are traditionally associated with the EU, as on human rights. And it regularly adapted its position not because of an evaluation of immediate costs and benefits, but because it had internalized those values and it wanted to be part of and support the existence of the European formalized coalition. At times the we-feeling could also be seen in the Italian adaptation to the position of the European formalized coalition on issues of importance for the country, as on disarmament and nuclear issues in the UNGA, where the initial divergence eventually made way to the Italian negotiated convergence on the European position.

However, de-Europeanization is always possible, and signs of a relative—but nonetheless present—de-Europeanization were detected in the UNGA. In the analyzed period Italy built on the European formalized coalition as a strategy to increase its status by providing system maintenance to the US-led hegemonic order. But changes at both the domestic and the international level may affect the effectiveness of this strategy and therefore the Italian preference for it. The present chapter will explore potential challenges to the Europeanization of Italian foreign policy at the domestic and international level focusing on crises that may alter incentives for Italy to continue to facilitate the maintenance of the European formalized coalition as its main strategy. Indeed, the "EU crises," that is the sequence produced by the Eurozone crisis, the migration crisis, and Brexit, may have directly or indirectly affected the Italian sense of belonging to a group, the we-feeling. The Eurozone crisis and the migration crisis shook the idea of European solidarity at the basis of the belonging to the group. Brexit broke any certainty about the very existence of that group. The EU crises also had an impact on the Italian domestic political system, as the rise of Eurosceptical parties less keen on considering the EU as the source of growth and stability and on reaching out to the traditional EU coalition partners has made evident. The EU crises may therefore have affected both the we-feeling and calculations about the possibility of building on the European support to promote Italian actions. It is thus useful to focus on the post-crisis period and analyze whether and how the Europeanization of Italian foreign policy may have been affected.

However, here it has been posited that the Italian membership of the European formalized coalition is related to the Italian role as a member of the US-led dominant coalition in a hegemonic system and to the Italian willingness to increase its status through the performance of system maintenance activities. So, it will also be explored whether and how some elements of the crisis of the international hegemonic order promoted by the US at the end of World War II with the support of its Western allies, and in particular the current US leadership, may alter incentives for Italy to act with the European formalized coalition.

THE IMPACT OF CRISES IN THE EU ON DOMESTIC POLITICS

The March 2018 national elections and the formation the following May of the first coalition government made of two declaredly Eurosceptical parties have been presented as *Italy's Revolt Against the EU* (Jones 2018). The coalition government made of the M5S and the League immediately signaled in a coalition agreement its intention to reform the country without considering the commitments with the EU agreed to by previous Italian governments. The EU was no longer seen as an external constraint whose acceptance could help modernize the country. On the contrary, it was deemed responsible for the low growth provoked by the imposition of austerity measures and the consequent incapability of the country to exit from the Eurozone crisis. As Jones (2018) notices, this attitude toward EU-imposed austerity measures is not totally unprecedented, because the Berlusconi government from 2008 until 2011 had already pushed back the idea that the external constraint was necessary and the Renzi government from 2014 to 2016 was assertive about lifting the European constraints on some of the issues now raised by the new government. What is different is that the new Italian government believes that the external constraint is not only unnecessary but also irrelevant. This represents a significant depart in Italian relations with the EU that might eventually affect one of the traditional pillars of Italian foreign policy by altering the opportunity structure for Italian domestic actors to act together with the European formalized coalition. This depart has been considered as the end point of crises in the EU, particularly the Eurozone and migration crises, that have provoked changes in the Italian political system comparable to the ones seen after the Cold War in the period 1992–1994 (Bull and Pasquino 2018).

Exploring the relationship between the crises and the Italian domestic system, Bull (2018) and Bull and Pasquino (2018) have pointed out that when the financial crisis started in the US in 2007, Italy was highly indebted and poorly competitive. The weaknesses of the Italian economy made the effects of the contagion to Europe, the beginning of the Eurozone crisis, more powerful and difficult to manage, making the effects of the crisis in Italy longer-lasting and more significant than in other affected states. But while at the beginning of the crisis it was member states and national institutions that had attempted to manage the crisis, in its second stage—the sovereign debt crisis—the EU started playing an important role, creating new institutions and processes that shifted responsibility for the crisis and for the incapacity to solve it at the EU level. This incapacity contributed to an increase in the level of Euroscepticism in Europe (Serricchio et al. 2013: 61). In Italy the Monti government embodied the austerity measures imposed by the EU and called for sacrifices in the name of Europe. But, as Lucarelli (2015: 52) notes, while this call for sacrifices could remind of a similar call made in the 1990s to join the euro, when Italy was "rescued" from Europe, what the EU is often called in Italy, this time the gap between expectations of eventual improvements of the economic situation and results increased the distance between Italians and the EU. Eurosceptics in Italy directed their fierce criticism at the troika and at Germany, believed to be ultimately responsible for the austerity measures adopted. Far from being a model to follow, an inherently benign external constraint, the EU became a burden (Bull 2018).

The debate on the euro became central in public debates, and in the main Italian newspapers the German position came under attack under the assumption that it showed lack of solidarity toward the affected countries, betraying the very idea behind European integration. Solidarity toward the other affected countries, and Greece in particular, became diffused. In the main Italian newspapers, the crisis was framed in national terms while the EU was depicted mostly as ineffective and confused or insignificant and incapable (Mazzoni and Barbieri 2014: 247). The crisis was a fertile ground for the explosion of tensions on the social dimension of integration, and particularly on welfare, resulting from the request of alignment of Eurozone states' public policies toward common goals. Ferrera (2016: chapter 1) has observed that these tensions originate in the late 1980s with the Single European Act and became even more evident after the adoption of the Maastricht treaty, but they cumulated over time to explode with the Eurozone crisis, when requests for social protection clashed with the austerity imposed by the membership of the Eurozone. This clash activated the conflict between an economic Europe versus a social Europe, but also the latent distributive conflict between rich and strong EU member states versus poor and weak EU member states. The cohesion at the basis of the we-feeling was therefore severely damaged.

Next to the economic crisis, the immigration crisis hit Italy particularly hard and combined with increasing effects (Barbulescu and Beaudonnet 2014). In Europe the growth in migration flows became robust after the Arab Spring and even more in 2015 as a consequence of the Syrian war. But the flow that invested Italy passed via the central Mediterranean route, with migrants predominantly originating from sub-Saharan countries, and it was more difficult to manage due to the extremely high instability and state fragility left by the French-led intervention in Libya, to which Italy reluctantly participated, and that became a source of intra-European tensions. Another important source of tensions was the contrast between the forceful Italian attempts to Europeanize the migration issue uploading it onto the EU agenda and the widespread perception that Italy, like Greece, had been left alone in the management of the migration crisis, given the reluctance of some European countries to share the burden and accept the limited redistribution of refugees agreed upon. Likewise, the different resources invested to stop the Eastern Mediterranean route and the central Mediterranean one created resentment. Most importantly, the management of the migration crisis by European leaders after 2011 evidenced serious faults, ranging from the delay in the formulation of a crisis management strategy to the lack of correct identification of the causes of the migration flow and the lack of agreement among European governments in the implementation phase once decisions were taken (Attinà 2016; see also Panebianco 2016). This is probably the issue that Italy has been trying to Europeanize the most in the recent past, identifying the EU as the right political forum in which migration should be addressed. It is also an issue on which Italy has been aggressively but unsuccessfully forcing European solidarity (Dobrescu et al. 2017: 94). Once again, the ineffectiveness of the EU answer and the lack of solidarity weakened the perception of cohesion at the basis of the we-feeling.

The two crises built onto each other and affected the idea of Europe as a myth (Diodato and Niglia 2017) and as a solution to national problems. The persistence of the financial and economic crisis radicalized anti-European ideological positions and affected the traditional Italian affective support for the EU: Europe was no longer a value, and it was no longer beneficial for Italy (Lucarelli 2015: 53). Public opinion polls have registered this disenchantment (figure 5.1). The positive EU image in Italy was already declining when the crisis broke out. But if until 2007 it remained above 50 percent

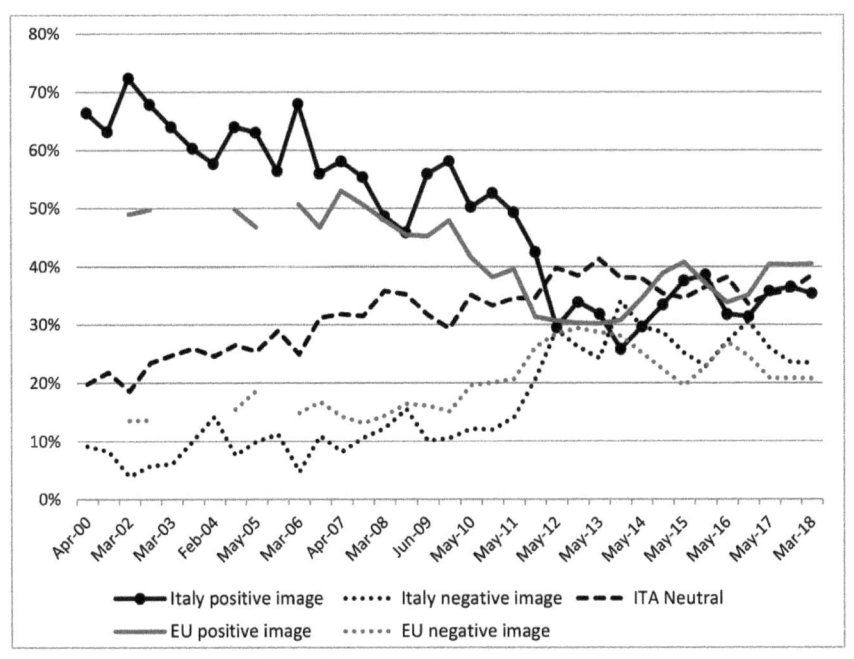

Figure 5.1.   EU image in Italy and European average, 2000–2018.[1]
Source: Eurobarometer (elaboration by the author).

and above the EU average, in 2008 it fell below 50 percent. It bounced back above 50 percent in 2009 and 2010 to then fall irreversibly below 50 percent and, since 2013, also below the EU average. The negative EU image in Italy dramatically rose and, starting from 2013 it became equal or above the EU average. In 2013 it even prevailed over the positive one. Most remarkably, a neutral EU image started growing in Italy, and since 2012 (except for 2015) it has prevailed over the other two options, confirming the disenchantment of Italian public opinion toward the EU (Lucarelli 2015). The exceptional support traditionally provided by Italy to the European integration project vanished in coincidence with the two European crises. Differences in numbers between the three public opinion groups (holding positive, negative, and neutral EU images) have reduced. Long gone the period of the European salvation myth, the negative EU image never prevailed over the positive one, but a more neutral stance has become the new normal in Italy in the 2010s.

The change of the EU image in Italy takes place in the context of a more general distrust in governing institutions. Looking at public opinion polls on the trust of Italians in the EU (figure 5.2), the impact of the crises emerges even more clearly: since 2011 distrust in the EU has regularly prevailed over trust in the EU. The drop in the trust of Italians in the EU in the period 2009–2012 is particularly remarkable: from 51 percent in 2009 to 22 percent in 2012. And since then the percentage of Italians trusting the EU has remained well below 40 percent, while from 2011 to 2018 (with a partial exception registered in 2015 and 2017) the percentage of Italians not trusting

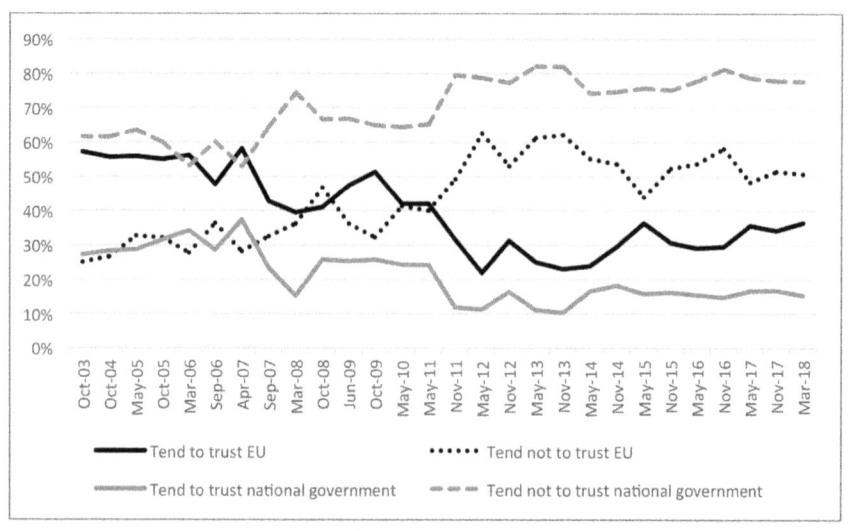

Figure 5.2. Trust in the EU and in the national government in Italy, 2003–2018.[2]
Source: Eurobarometer (elaboration by the author).

the EU has prevalently remained above 50 percent. After 2012, however, trust in the EU has increased and distrust in the EU has decreased. Trust in national governments is often considered a proxy for trust in the EU (Serricchio et al. 2013), but in the Italian case trust in the EU has always remained, even during the crisis years, well above trust in the national government. Moreover, since 2014 trust in the EU has increased more than trust in the national government and the gap between Italians not trusting the EU and Italians not trusting their national government has increased, suggesting that distrust in the EU has not crystallized yet and that for the Italian public opinion the EU remains a better governing space than the national government.

The previously described changes point toward an increasing Euroscepticism in Italy. The declining trend in support for European integration in Italy is not an isolated phenomenon and it is present also in other big and founding EU member states. A historical view shows rising support in the 1950s and 1960s based on affective and political considerations, that plateaued in the 1970s and 1980s, and dates the beginning of the continued path of long-term decline in the Italian support for the EU already in the late 1980s (Anderson and Hecht 2018; Isernia 2008). Euroscepticism predates the European crises and the economic dimension is not considered a good predictor of it (Serricchio et al. 2013). It is indeed with the Maastricht treaty that the EU salience increased, and public opposition was mobilized against it. But Euroscepticism has become more critical in European countries that were hit the hardest by the economic crisis and has become increasingly embedded in public opinions because the incapacity to adopt effective solutions has affected the EU's quest for legitimacy (Usherwood and Startin 2013; Serricchio et al. 2013; Conti et al. 2018).

In Italy the economic crisis had indirect effects on diffuse support for European integration by decreasing perceptions of the EU utility: the EU was no longer seen as a source of prosperity and economic growth. The crisis, however, did not weaken the Italian sense of belonging to Europe (Di Mauro 2014). Euroscepticism in Italy does not generate from principled opposition to Europe and to sovereignty delegation but seems to be based on a cost-benefit analysis, so Italians who became Eurosceptic did so based on the impact of EU institutions on their interests. Otherwise, Italians hold positive views about the integration process (Conti and Memoli 2015: 212).

The Eurozone crisis hit particularly hard in Southern EU member states. The Italian political system reacted unlike the other Southern European countries, channeling and institutionalizing the mounting resentment mostly through a new party, the M5S. The protest was transformed into electoral participation and parliamentary action that has eventually managed to turn into governmental action (Morlino and Raniolo 2017). The new party originated with a different goal, an anti-establishment one, but almost immediately it adopted a Eurosceptic tone, initially declaring support for an EU as a community and not for an EU as a banking, financial, or monetary union not representing weak economies such as those of Italy, Greece, Spain, and Portugal (Morlino and Raniolo 2017: 68) and later on calling for an Italian exit from the euro and vehemently criticizing EU institutions. Rather remarkable has also been the increase in Euroscepticism in right-wing formations, among which the (formerly Northern) League assumed a prominent position. The League criticized the EU for its negative impact on employment security and social harmony also in relation to immigration policies, another issue strongly affected by the economic crisis, and advanced requests to exit from the euro (Caiani and Conti 2014; Barbulescu and Beaudonnet 2014). Moreover, as in other European countries, the electoral success of Eurosceptic parties in Italy led mainstream parties too to be less supportive of European integration (Meijers 2017).

The 2013 national elections represented a watershed in domestic politics and in the Italian party system. The M5S became the first party but did not enter the coalition government. The change was confirmed in the 2018 national elections that led to the creation of an unprecedented coalition government made by two Eurosceptical parties, the M5S and the League. The Italian party system became tripolar and the electoral results showed the second highest volatility after elections in 1994, leading to a notable change in power relations and to a remarkable unpredictability (Chiaramonte and Emanuele 2018; Bull and Pasquino 2018; Valbruzzi and Vignati 2018). The 2018 national elections also emphasized the competition between, on the one hand, a periphery represented by the M5S, concentrated in the south of Italy and asking for social and economic protection, and by the League, concentrated in the north of Italy and asking for cultural protection and, on the other hand, the Democratic party and center-left parties in general in favor of European integration, the integration of migrants and an open society (Chiaramonte and Emanuele 2018: 150).

The crisis and the austerity measures, coupled with a strong centralization, led to a partial reshaping of previous cleavages (left-right and center-periphery) and to the growth and consolidation also in Italy of the pro- vs. anti-EU cleavage next to the establishment vs. anti-establishment one (Morlino and Raniolo 2017). It has been suggested that the results of the 2018 national elections show different modalities of politicization of the existing cleavages, with the more evident overlapping of the center-periphery and pro-anti-EU cleavages and the rotation of the conflict around broad ideas of center and periphery, and the repositioning of parties along these cleavages (Chiaramonte and Emanuele 2018; see also Giannetti et al. 2017). Most importantly, the cleavages have lost their traditionally structuring role as they can be found not just structuring competition between parties, but also present within ever weaker parties, increasing structural instability and the role of leaders (Morlino and Raniolo 2017: 113–114).

The 2018 elections confirmed the trends established in 2013. It remains to be seen whether the change will have a bigger impact in the future. However, it has been shown that, so far, the competition evident at the party level on the pro-anti-EU cleavage was not immediately translated at MPs level, leaving the consensus on the EU among party elites serving in public offices quite high (Charalambous et al. 2018). Analyses on Italian parliament members in 2014 indicated that, despite the economic crisis and the change in the characteristics of Italian elites, many of the trends observed before in the elites' attitudes toward Europe were continuing and confirmed the strong support for a single European foreign policy as the issue that should mostly be among EU competences (Conti 2017). Moreover, even the M5S, in an attempt at presenting itself as a potential governing force over time has moderated its anti-EU stances (Bressanelli and De Candia 2018) and has started an institutionalization process (Tronconi 2018). Indeed, in the 2018 elections, it was the League that campaigned more strongly against the EU, and in the coalition agreement between the League and the M5S the strong anti-EU positions of the League have been mitigated (Valbruzzi 2018).

The first months of the coalition government tell us of a widening of the conflict between Italy and the EU, and of attempts at redefining the traditional Italian allies within the EU. However, factors of stickiness and continuity remain, because the new leaders must refer to old experienced personnel and because policies are path dependent and influenced by the logic of bureaucratic behavior (Morlino and Raniolo 2017: 116). A few months into the legislature, the initial highly conflictual attitude toward the EU has left the way to a compromise on the respect of the budgetary rules, while talks of exiting from the euro have disappeared. But distances with the EU remain.

The registered decline of trust in the EU and the growing impression that Italian interests might differ from European ones might reduce the Italian willingness to work toward common European positions and prompt Italy to promote more assertive national stances. The Italian utilitarian view toward the EU is indeed a remarkable break with the more distant past when the choice for European integration was a choice for the Western camp, but also with the more recent past when affective and utilitarian support could live together (Conti and Memoli 2015: 218; Isernia 2008; Bellucci and Conti 2012). This Eurosceptical turn is also associated with a reduction in support for globalization and liberal economic values (Conti et al. 2018), that underlie the current international hegemonic order. It is therefore a change that may alter the Italian traditional foreign policy choices and trigger greater freedom of maneuver also in foreign policy. Indeed, Italian public opinion has become more divided on foreign policy choices, is more inward-looking and challenges the importance of traditional allies (Isernia 2017). Moreover, there is evidence of an inclination in Italian public opinion to act independently from alliances within the EU and to create a coalition of South European states to counterbalance German influence within the EU (DISPOC/LAPS and IAI 2017). It is therefore worth exploring whether the previously described changes have affected the Italian support for a common foreign policy among EU member states and the Italian choices of coalition partners.

Eurobarometer data on support for a common foreign policy among EU member states in the period 2000–2018 can give an indirect indication of variations in Italian public opinion support for the Europeanization of Italian foreign policy (figure 5.3). They can tell whether damage to the we-feeling due to the perceived lack of cohesion and solidarity and variations in the perceptions of EU utility for Italy has traveled to the foreign policy domain. In the analyzed period a stable majority (60 percent or above) of Italians has supported the idea of a common foreign policy among EU member states. But there is also decreasing support and a growing aversion. The declining trend predates the crises, but in 2007 for the first time Italian public opinion support toward a common foreign policy among EU member states was below the EU average support and since then, except in 2010, it remained substantially equal or below the EU average. On the contrary, Italian opposition to a common foreign

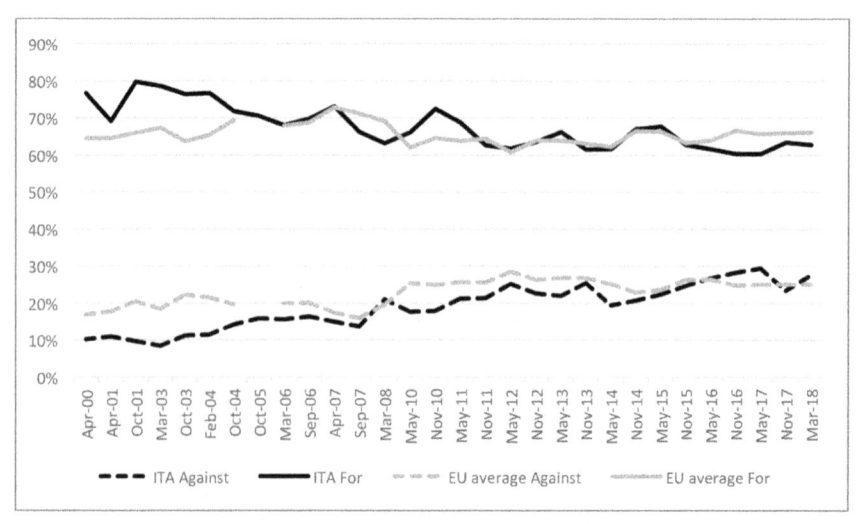

Figure 5.3. Italian and EU average public opinion support toward a common foreign policy among EU member states, 2000–2018.[3]

Source: Eurobarometer (elaboration by the author).

policy among EU member states increased from 15 percent in April 2007 to 29 percent in May 2017, when for the first time Italian public opinion was against a common foreign policy among EU member states more than the EU average.

Although the Eurobarometer confirms the support of Italian public opinion to a common foreign policy, there are also indications of a greater questioning of the traditional inclination to adapt Italian foreign policy to the European position and to create or support the European formalized coalition. For Italian public opinion the reduction of trust toward the EU and of the perceived benefits of EU membership may have touched upon crucial aspects of the sense of belonging to a community, leading Italian public opinion to see the EU not only as an opportunity but also as a problem.

Changes in public opinion, however, do not necessarily translate into actual foreign policy changes. In order to see whether the European crises and the related variations in public opinion have had any impact on Italian foreign policy behavior, it is useful to compare Italian foreign policy behavior before and after the first crisis, the Eurozone one, in the UNGA and in the UNSC.[4] In case the crisis had an impact on the Europeanization of Italian foreign policy, we should expect an increase in the Italian distance from the European formalized coalition after 2008, because de-Europeanizing implies greater freedom of maneuver and therefore reduced efforts at coordinating positions with the other EU member states. We should also expect variations in the traditional intra-EU alliances of Italy following the conflict lines of the two crises. That is, Italy should be closer to and create coalitions with Southern European members (Greece in particular) and should be more distant from the countries associated the most with the adoption of austerity measures at the EU level (Germany in particular).

In the UNGA in the period 2004–2017, taking the 63rd session (2008–2009) as a potential turning point, in which the crisis was felt in Italy, the Italian voting behavior does not show any major difference in the Italian distance from the European formalized coalition. Italy distanced itself from the EU majority on average 3 times per session before the 63rd session and 3.22 times per session after. A relative impact seems to be present in the percentage of Italian voting with the European formalized coalition. After the 63rd session the Italian voting cohesion with the EU majority dropped four times below 90 percent, otherwise it remained just above 90 percent. The 64th session is the one showing the most remarkable drop (83 percent). However, this cohesion drop was reabsorbed in the following sessions, so the effect was limited. Overall Italian voting behavior remained Europeanized, as Italy kept voting regularly and predominantly with the European formalized coalition.

A different picture emerges when considering Italian voting cohesion in the UNGA in relation to the countries that were involved the most or that

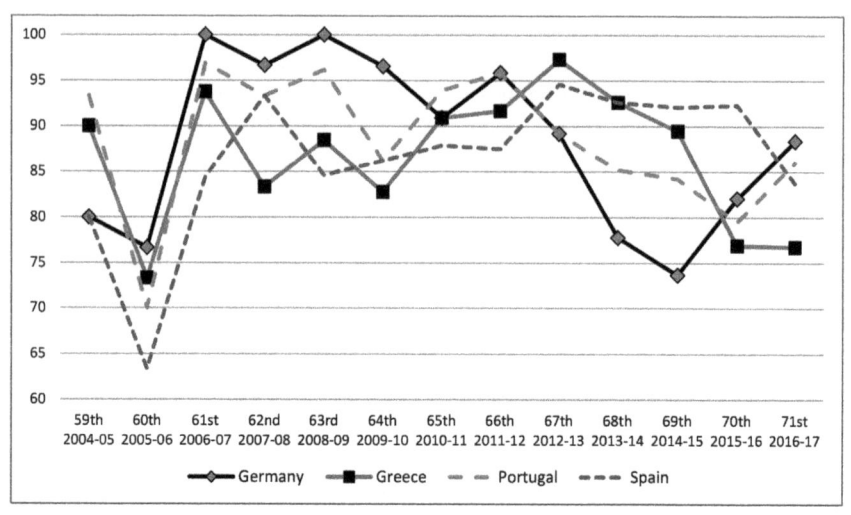

Figure 5.4. Italian voting cohesion in the UNGA with the countries most involved in the European crises (percentage), 2004–2017.
Source: UNGA website and UNBISNET (elaboration by the author).

were associated with conflicting positions in relation to the European crisis (figure 5.4). Had the crisis affected the coalitional behavior of Italy, this should have been reflected in an increased distance between Italy and Germany, the country most associated with the responsibility for the adoption of austerity measures, and in a reduced distance between Italy and the Southern European countries that were hit the most by the crisis, that is Greece above all, Spain and Portugal. A change does indeed emerge in the percentage of Italian voting cohesion with the four states in EU divided votes, although not immediately after the crisis hit. From the 60th until the 64th session, Italian voting cohesion with Germany was higher than Italian voting cohesion with the other Southern European states. Even considering all EU member states, in that period Germany was the EU member state Italy voted most cohesively with, reaching 100 percent cohesion in the 61st and 63rd sessions. This shows that they relied on each other's support for their political initiatives. But between the 66th and the 69th session the Italian voting cohesion with Germany dropped more than 20 percentage points and became lower than the Italian voting cohesion with the Southern European states. This suggests a greater convergence along the conflict lines of the crisis. Indeed, Italy started voting more cohesively with Greece and Spain after the crisis than it did before. The same cannot be said for Portugal, which is one of the countries that Italy regularly voted most cohesively with until the 67th session but not afterward. The distance with Germany becomes evident during the 68th and 69th sessions, when Germany fell within the group of most distant EU states from Italy. However, the trend was reversed after the 69th session and in the 71st session the Italian voting cohesion with Germany was higher than the one with the Southern European countries. It is also worth bearing in mind that the lowest percentage of voting cohesion scored with Germany is 73 percent, that means that even during the crisis Germany remained an important coalition partner for Italy.

Italian sponsoring behavior in the UNGA may better reflect the conflict originating from the crisis, because it is a more spontaneous and voluntary mechanism. However, Italian sponsoring behavior too is only modestly affected by the crisis. Since the 67th session (2012/13) a slight reduction in Italian sponsoring with the European formalized coalition and an increase in sponsoring with a minority of EU member states appear. From the 62nd to the 68th session there are countries that Italy sponsors with at least 90 percent of its draft resolutions: Slovenia (5 times), Luxembourg and Spain (3 times), and Austria, Belgium, Finland, Germany, Greece, Hungary, Portugal (once). But in the 69th, 70th, and 71st sessions Italian sponsoring behavior becomes more volatile in the choice of coalition partners, and none of the EU member states reaches 90 percent of co-sponsoring (in the 70th and 71st sessions the maximum cohesion reached was 85 percent).

Although it is not possible to establish a causal relationship between this reduction in sponsoring cohesion and the crisis, it is possible to see whether and how after the crisis variations in coalitional sponsoring behavior with the main actors of the conflict related to the crisis took place (figure 5.5). In the

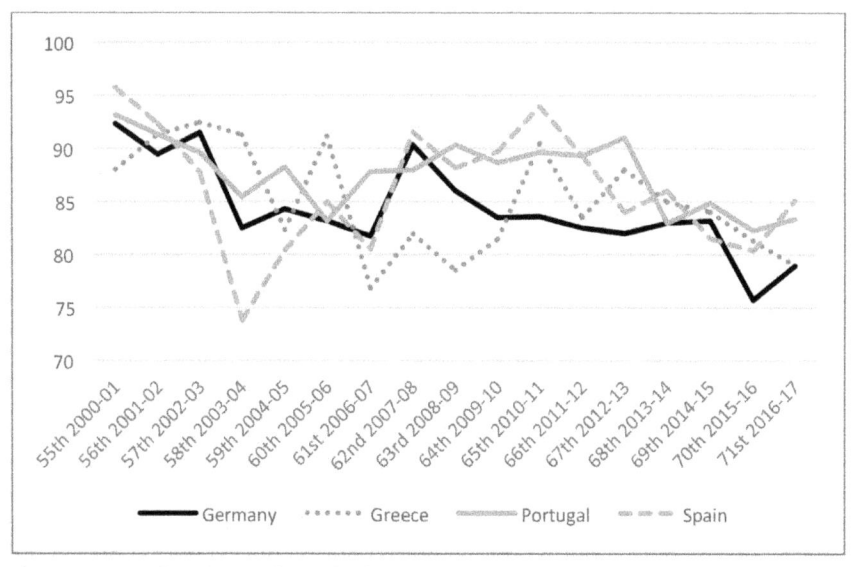

Figure 5.5. Italian sponsoring cohesion in the UNGA with the countries most involved in the European crises (percentage), 2000–2017.

Source: Index to Proceedings of the General Assembly, 55th–71st UNGA sessions (elaboration by the author).

analyzed period both Germany and the group of Southern European countries were good coalition partners of Italy, figuring among its top co-sponsors. When the crisis hit the most, Greece was more distant from Italy than the other countries. However, while before the economic crisis no specific trend could be identified, after the crisis Italy tended to sponsor with the other Southern European countries more than it did with Germany, and this trend became well established. This suggests a partial redefinition of the Italian coalitional behavior and a reduced reliance on Germany as an intra-EU coalition partner after the economic crisis. The downward trend in cooperation signals a greater political distance between the two countries. However, more than three-quarters of the draft resolutions sponsored by Italy after the crisis are co-sponsored by Germany, and in the 71st session an upward trend is visible, indicating that the cooperation is still strong and that the two countries still work together on their political initiatives.

The UNSC represents the highest threshold for analyzing variations in the Europeanization of Italian foreign policy, because it is the forum in which the most important issues are debated and decided upon. Due to its restricted composition and internal dynamics, a systematic comparison as the one presented for the UNGA is not possible. However, it is possible to see whether there have been variations in co-sponsoring with Italy before and after the crisis considering all co-sponsors, that is regardless of whether they were sitting in the UNSC at the time of sponsoring. It is worth reminding that because of UNSC dynamics, sponsoring is in practice strongly dependent on the willingness of UNSC members to involve other states, so the two EU permanent members, France and the UK, hold key roles, and that the practice of sponsoring has increased over time also as a result of a greater competition. Sitting in the UNSC provides greater opportunities for sponsoring draft resolutions and inviting support. Had Italian foreign policy de-Europeanized as a result of the crisis, we should observe a reduction in the number of draft resolutions sponsored with all EU member states and a variation in Italian co-sponsoring with the main actors of the political divide on the use of austerity measures, that is Germany on the one hand, and the Southern European countries on the other.

The Europeanization of Italian foreign policy in the UNSC is not affected by the crisis (table 5.1). Before the crisis, Italy sponsored with all EU members one draft resolution, while after the crisis the number increased to 16. As it should be expected, France and the UK are the EU countries sponsoring the most with Italy in both periods, and almost all Italian draft resolutions are sponsored with them before and after the crisis. However, after the crisis Italy is closer to France than to the UK, that was not an actor in the crisis and might have been considered a better potential intra-EU alternative. This becomes even more evident when considering draft resolutions that provoked divisive votes, that is non-unanimous UNSC votes, indicat-

Table 5.1. Co-sponsors of Italian draft resolutions before and after the crisis

	2000–2008	2009–2017	2000–2008 divisive votes	2009–2017 divisive votes
Italy (2007–2008; 2017)	27	76	3	12
Germany (2003–04; 2011–2012)	6	57	2	11
Greece (2005–2006)	4	40	0	9
Spain (2003–2004; 2015–2016)	7	53	0	10
Portugal (2011–2012)	3	45	0	10
France	25	72	3	12
United Kingdom	25	67	3	12
All EU member states	1	16	0	6

Note: Among parentheses it is indicated when they served as UNSC members in the analyzed period.
Source: UNBISNET (elaboration by the author).

ing the presence of a greater political conflict on the issue. After the crisis Italy sponsored six draft resolutions on divisive votes with all the EU member states (it was zero before the crisis). That is, half of the draft resolutions Italy sponsored and that ended up being divisive votes after the crisis were sponsored with all the EU member states. This indicates that even on the most conflictual issues Italy increased its contribution to the creation and maintenance of an EU position in the UNSC.

As for variations in sponsoring coalitions along the lines of the conflict related to the economic crisis, the best comparison is the one between co-sponsoring with Germany, as representative of the austerity measures, and Spain, as representative of the Southern European countries, because they both served in the UNSC before and after the crisis. No major differences in the Italian foreign policy behavior can be detected in relation to the two countries. If anything, Italy co-sponsored with Germany after the crisis more than it did with Spain. And the same behavior can be found when considering the most politically divisive issues. This suggests that the crisis had no impact on the Europeanization of Italian foreign policy on the most politically important issues in the most authoritative forum.

The previous analysis has shown that the rise of Euroscepticism and the disenchantment toward the EU registered in Italian public opinion after the crisis has not traveled to the foreign policy domain. At least not yet. Some effects could be seen in the choice of EU preferred coalitional partners, since a little distance with Germany, a traditional coalition partner for Italy, was put in the UNGA. But overall the two countries co-sponsored more than two-thirds of Italian draft resolutions, showing the persistence of their partnership and their reliance on each other for their political initiatives. Even after the crisis Italy kept voting in the UNGA predominantly with the European formalized coalition, although the numbers lowered. Moreover, on the most important foreign policy issues, debated in the UNSC, not only no effect of the crisis could be detected, but Italy acted much more than in the previous period with its partners of the European formalized coalition, Germany included.

Overall Italian foreign policy has remained highly Europeanized after the crisis, especially on important issues. Damages to the we-feeling, signs of which were here visible, did not travel to foreign policy. But a trend of higher volatility in the choice of intra-EU coalition partners took place. Coupled with a context of greater difficulties in creating a European formalized coalition seen in the UNGA and with changes at the domestic level that promote more critical positions toward the EU, the main challenge to continuity in Italian foreign policy is that this may lead to a foreign policy behavior in which supporting the creation of the European formalized coalition is seen less as a value per se and more in purely opportunistic terms. That is, to supporting occasional alignments rather than a stable coalition.

A REDUCTION IN THE OPPORTUNITIES? CHALLENGES TO ITALIAN FOREIGN POLICY BEHAVIOR

Despite the emergence of Euroscepticism in Italian public opinion and of changes in the domestic political system that have led to the rise of Eurosceptic parties and to the growing prominence of the pro- vs. anti-EU cleavage, so far even after the crises that have hit Europe and that have had particularly harsh economic consequences on Italy, Italian foreign policy has maintained high levels of Europeanization, especially on important issues (see the UNSC). That the European crises have not had an impact on foreign policy so far, however, does not exclude that they might in the future. A recent trend toward greater volatility in the choice of intra-EU coalition partners has indeed become apparent on less important issues (see the UNGA), betraying a more utilitarian attachment to Europe. Volatility can also be associated with endogenous developments within the EU, in which the recurring crises have highlighted not only lack of intra-EU cohesion and solidarity, and limits in the capacity to provide effective solutions, but also a return to the prevalence of governments and coordination—and therefore of national instances—in European decision-making processes (Fabbrini 2015; Cotta 2017).

This represents a challenge for the foreign policy of EU member states and is causing growing difficulties in reaching a common position, as reflected in the declining trend of EU member states' cohesion visible in the UNGA (figure 5.6). Cohesion is still above 50 percent, indicating that it is still pos-

The Challenge of Crises 157

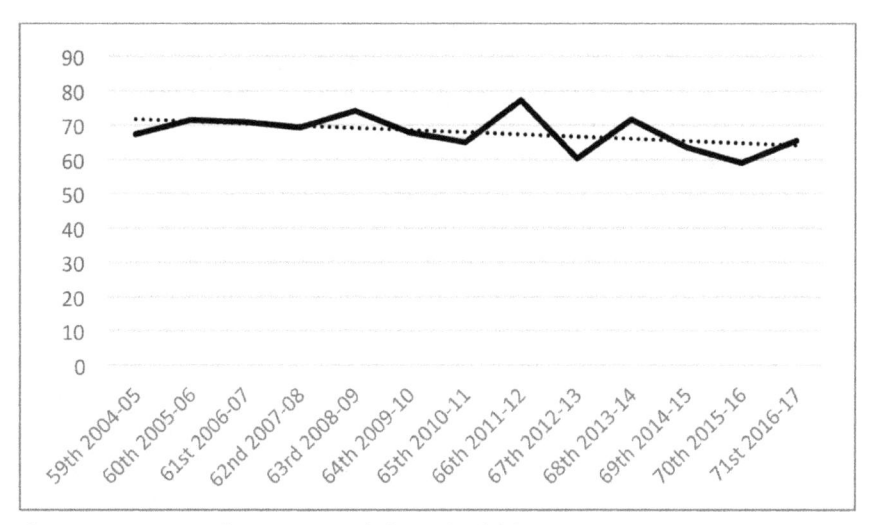

Figure 5.6. **EU member states unanimity voting in the UNGA (percentage), 2004–2017.**
Source: UNGA website and UNBISNET (elaboration by the author).

sible to create common positions. But the downward trend (the dotted line in the figure) also tells us that this is becoming increasingly difficult. Long gone are the times when percentages of EU member states unanimous voting were above 75 percent (Luif 2003: 28). More recently EU member states have voted unanimously in just above 60 percent of the votes (59 percent in the 70th session), an important drop in cohesion that has increased over time, more drastically after the crises in Europe. It is therefore more difficult for EU member states to reach a common position, encouraging higher volatility and more opportunistic foreign policy behaviors.

The Eurozone crisis and the limitations in the EU response to the migration crisis have highlighted limits in the capacity of the EU to realize and promote a global actorness model based on the use of economic instruments to reach political goals. They have also exposed weaknesses that are difficult to overcome, making the European formalized coalition less attractive and secure than before in a context of rising polarization at the international level and of a crisis of that international hegemonic order that had structured Italian foreign policy since the end of World War II.

The crisis of the international hegemonic order in a context of rising polarization and competition represents indeed another challenge to the Europeanization of Italian foreign policy, one that has become particularly evident since the Trump administration has been elected in the US. Treated as a loser after World War II, Italy's choice for European integration was part of its choice for the Western camp and a way to play its role as a member of the US-led dominant coalition in a hegemonic system and increase its status through the performance of system maintenance activities, a behavior that is typical of middle powers. Upholding the European formalized coalition was a way of supporting the hegemonic order and gaining influence through the politics of scale that uploading issues onto the European agenda allows. For middle powers competing for status, as Italy is, this could provide an important advantage.

The characteristics of the US-led hegemonic order created after World War II gave stability to the hegemonic structure, making this order easy to join and hard to overturn (Ikenberry 2010: 514). However, after the 2007 financial crisis major cracks became evident. The "rising powers" are the political subjects that have received the most attention in the analysis of the crisis of the order. At the moment, they represent the only potential (although not yet consolidated) alternative coalition to the dominant one, and they have introduced elements of greater competition and polarization in the system (Monteleone 2015). Among them, China and Russia are perceived as the greatest challenge to the current organization of the international system. They are not liberal democracies and they hold significant economic and military capabilities, that they use to support other non-democratic regimes, posing an ideological challenge to the liberal features of the existing hegemonic order. The diffusion of the so-called Beijing consensus, promoted through development and based on incremental reforms, export-led growth, state capitalism and authoritarianism, as opposed to the Washington consensus, grounded on the promotion of state models based on laissez-faire capitalism and liberal democracy, highlights the Chinese quest for the growing legitimacy of its political and economic model as a better alternative to the US one. On the one hand, this undermines the legitimacy of the US-led order; on the other hand, it presents the ideological infrastructure of a potential new one (Schweller and Pu 2011).

According to Schweller (2011), we have already entered a phase in which the current order is delegitimized, in which practices of soft balancing and criticism of the existing order are undermining the legitimacy of the US right to rule and of its order. Particularly evident after the 2007 financial crisis in the US, louder calls for reform of the main multilateral institutions of the US-led order by the rising powers and their quest to be given more power and influence within them signal dissatisfaction with the existing organization of the international system. The reforms of the main multilateral institutions already approved go in the direction of consenting some influence, but the decision-making process remains in the hands of the US and its Western allies (Woods 2010; Vestergaard and Wade 2013 and 2015; Monteleone 2018). This encourages rising powers to create their own alternative institutions in an open contestation with the existing ones. Initiatives such as the creation of the Asian Infrastructure Investment Bank have been in response to the unresponsiveness to reform calls of universal institutions such as the IMF or the World Bank, that had already been reformed (Patrick 2015). This introduces an element of challenge to the existing pecking order and to the ordering rules that define legitimacy in the current organization of the international system (Kupchan 2012), exasperating fragmentation and introducing competition on values and interests (Barma et al. 2007, 2013, and 2014).

Some scholars tend to minimize contestation, highlighting that the new institutions are an instrument in a quest for increased status within the current order (Brooks and Wohlforth 2016) and that they should be considered as little more than useful to provide forum shopping to the rising powers (Voeten 2014). Others acknowledge that contestation is relevant in the creation of the new institutions because they provide greater bargaining leverage to dissatisfied actors by indicating exit options and may help to promote a change of the existing multilateral institutions (Morse and Keohane 2014; Lipscy 2015a and 2015b; Zangl et al. 2016). The struggle for the revision of political hierarchy is taking place. However, the non-Western states that are requesting reform are also asking to operate within the existing organization of the international system, suggesting that it is not the organization of the international system promoted by the US after World War II that is contested, but the US authority (Ikenberry 2015a and 2015b).

Competition between the US, on the one hand, and China and Russia, on the other, within the existing universal multilateral institutions has dramatically increased. In the UNSC, the unreformed institution in which the US still holds substantial control of the agenda-setting and significant control of the decision-making outcomes, the number of divisive votes has risen (figure 5.7), proving that it is becoming more difficult for the US to hegemonize it. Russia and China have made increasing use of their veto power, but also the

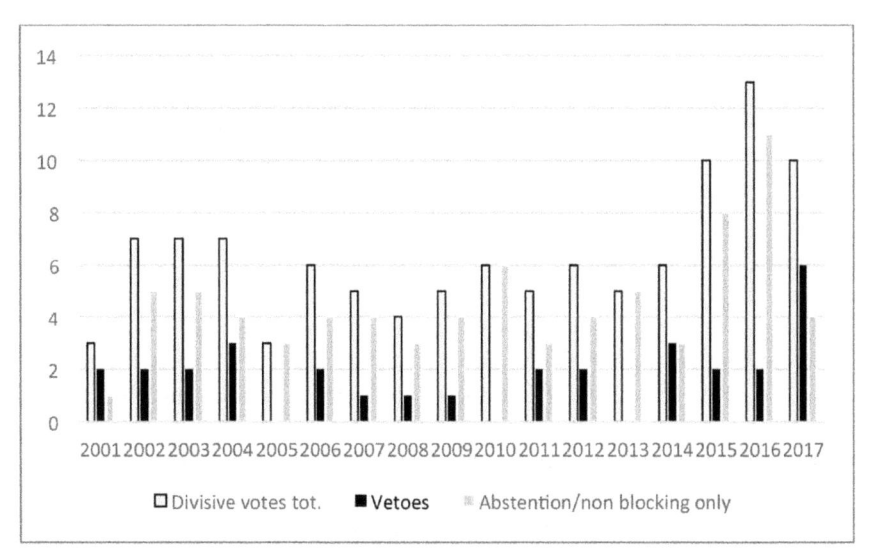

Figure 5.7. Divisive votes in the UNSC, 2001–2017.
Source: UNSC website (elaboration by the author).

US has had to use it. In the WTO, the institution in which reforms have led to a reduced distance between the influence of the US and the rising powers on decision-making processes, the stalemate reached has led the Obama administration to propose free trade agreements (the TPP and the TTIP) as alternatives, and the Trump administration to threaten US exit from the organization (BBC 2018). The US has long requested reform of the multilateral institutions acknowledging that controlling them was becoming more difficult. The request also entered the national security strategies of the Obama administration. But while the Obama administration still perceived multilateral institutions in the US interest and tried to reform them to face competition from within, building on the support of the dominant coalition but trying to widen it (Monteleone 2018), the Trump administration acknowledges that the rise of the new powers and their ability in creating supporting coalitions makes the current universal multilateral institutions too difficult to hegemonize and prefers to deal with competition outside of them, reshuffling the dominant coalition that has traditionally supported the US and calling prospective new members to stricter adherence to US authority.

In this phase, the relevance for the US of the EU and the European integration project is under question. After World War II, for Italy joining the European integration process meant joining the Western camp, because the project was strongly promoted by the US, while aspiring to be included into the dominant coalition. Supporting the European integration process and supporting the US were not contradicting goals, but mutually supporting ones. And while cracks between Americans and Europeans emerged with the end of the Cold War, especially in the economic sector, the EU and the US established a multilevel and multidimensional cooperation to maintain the existing organization of the international system and promote its rules and underlying—and shared by both partners—liberal values (Monteleone 2003, 2011, and 2012). The crises burnt out after 2007 exposed limitations of this cooperation, though. The joint declaration of the 2011 US-EU summit, after the Eurozone crisis, restricted the areas for joint action in the security field and put on top of the agenda the Eurozone crisis. This was a change in the issues composing the transatlantic agenda, but it also represented a variation of perspective: the US-EU relationship became more inward looking and the EU itself became an issue. The concentration of the transatlantic security agenda on specific areas and transnational challenges was meaningful because it represented the result of the impossibility for the EU to keep on committing globally and long term, as it used to do previously. It was also the result of the diverging strategic interests of the two actors, now interested in different areas. The crisis therefore raised the question of whether, in front of global changes that see the growth of new actors, a weakened EU could still be a useful global partner for the US, and still (aspire to) maintain and promote a global political agenda. Given the prevalence in the use of economic instruments to reach political goals, the Eurozone crisis put under strain the capacity of the EU to act internationally both in relation to its instruments (its economic component) and in relation to the political willingness of its members to continue to act together (its political component). The irregularity of US-EU summits and the decision not to hold them regularly (EU Observer 2010) is an indication of an adaptation to lower expectations of the institutional structure framed in the 1990s, due to domestic changes in Europe in relation to the Lisbon treaty, but also to changing global circumstances, among which the announced exit of the UK from the EU and the current political weakness of the EU may play an increasing role in the future.

If at the bilateral level the European crisis mainly affected a highly interdependent economy, at the global level the crisis affected the capacity of the US and European countries to control the most important global decision-making processes at a time in which the political and economic growth of new actors challenges the existing organization of the international political system, and calls abound in relation to an imminent or already realized post-Western world (among others, Acharya 2014; Barma et al. 2007, 2013, and 2014; Kupchan 2012; Layne 2012). This is all the most relevant at a time when, while the EU keeps on defining the US as its "core partner" in the security sector and points at the transatlantic trade agreement (TTIP) as a testimony of its commitment to shared values (European Union 2016: 37), the declarations of the Trump administration show signs of disengagement not just from the transatlantic partnership, but also from the world order that that partnership helped to support.

This comes at a time when the EU is undergoing an identity crisis after the Brexit vote and wonders whether it can continue along the same path or must reinvent itself proceeding at different speeds (Panebianco 2017). And it should ring an alarm bell for transatlantic relations: they are showing great resilience, but their relevance is under challenge. If previous US administrations had shown a tendency to use minilateral—when not unilateral—solutions, betraying a greater and greater difficulty in finding the political will to keep on investing in the old order, the Trump administration started adopting a revisionist outlook, disregarding the liberal values that underpinned it and challenging the organization of the international system that the US had promoted after World War II and in which the European partners played an important supporting role (Ikenberry 2017; Parsi 2018). The US has not disengaged from multilateral institutions, but the reduced support for multilateralism and the preference for bilateralism and a transactional approach make evident the change of pace (Wright 2019). The downgrading of the EU's diplomatic status in Washington without notice (Birnbaum and Hudson 2019), the identification of the EU as a "foe" on trade and the continuous calls for NATO allies to increase their contribution (CBS News 2018), all contribute to the undergoing revision of the order in a direction that values the contribution—possibly an increased one—of individual states rather than aggregates. That no major impact has been evident so far does not exclude changes in the future. The new US revisionist outlook is a challenge for the foreign policies of all the states that were recognizing the US as the global leader to follow. The significant drop in the voting cohesion between Italy and the US in the UNGA in the only year of the Trump administration for which data are available at the moment of writing confirms the difficulty of moving forward.

The combination between the crisis of the EU, reflected in the greater difficulty of EU member states to achieve common positions, and the crisis of the hegemonic order is an important challenge for Italian foreign policy. The three traditional pillars of Italian foreign policy are all affected, and they no longer necessarily support each other. The current phase of redefinition of coalitions leaves room for greater uncertainty and temporarily translates into a more volatile Italian foreign policy behavior, because there are fewer incentives to build on the European formalized coalition to perform system maintenance activities eventually useful to increase the Italian status. Under the current US administration, this is particularly evident, because it is increasingly costly to support the creation and maintenance of a European formalized coalition to perform system maintenance functions, and the current declared disinterest of the global leader toward system maintenance makes the effort scarcely appreciated. Regardless of the persistence of the revisionist outlook adopted by the current US administration, and even imagining a more resilient order than nowadays often depicted (Nye 2017; Sullivan 2018; Deudney and Ikenberry 2018), the European crises and the crisis of the order have reduced the potential EU contribution to system maintenance and have shown the need to exert attractiveness in an international system undergoing change, both widening support for it and accepting a redefinition of the rules and institutions that Americans and Europeans contributed to putting in place and that have favored them so much over time.

As a middle power obsessed with status, Italy is left with difficult choices. It may continue following the traditional foreign policy guidelines, trying to act with a more restricted European formalized coalition within multilateral institution to increase its status by performing system maintenance activities in support of the US-led hegemonic order, aware of the diminishing returns in the short-term of this behavior but betting on the future opportunity to regroup the dominant coalition that the challenge of the rising powers may provide. Or it may discontinue them and count on its own power to build occasional and flexible alignments outside of the existing universal multilateral institutions, aware that this behavior requires greater resources also of a military type and interventions that may clash with its strategic culture, that it increases the number of middle power competitors and leads to higher risks of marginalization.

NOTES

1. The question is "In general, does the European Union conjure up for you a very positive, fairly positive, neutral, fairly negative or very negative image?" Fairly positive and very positive have been summed up to create positive image and fairly negative and very negative have been summed up to create negative image. The data chart can be found at http://ec.europa.eu/commfront office/publicopinion/index.cfm/Chart/getChart/chartType/gridChart//themeKy/19/ groupKy/102/countries/IT/savFiles/555,1,54,554,880,6,11,47,2,632,702 ,867,5,184,521,663,698,805,8,37,850,33,41,3,7,49,186,190,196,646,838,9,10,187 ,197/periodStart/042000/periodEnd/032018 (accessed on 18 September 2018).

2. Data compare answers to the question "I would like to ask you a question about how much trust you have in certain media and institutions. For each of the following media and institutions, please tell me if you tend to trust it or tend not to trust it. The European Union" available at http://ec.europa.eu/commfrontoffice/publicopinion/index .cfm/Chart/getChart/chartType/gridChart//themeKy/18/groupKy/97/countries/IT/sav Files/555,54,554,880,6,11,47,2,632,702,867,5,521,698,805,8,37,850,33,41,3,7,49 ,646,838,9,10,187/periodStart/102003/periodEnd/032018 (accessed on 18 September 2018) with answers to the question "I would like to ask you a question about how much trust you have in certain media and institutions. For each of the following media and institutions, please tell me if you tend to trust it or tend not to trust it. The (NATIONALITY) government" available at http://ec.europa.eu/commfront office/publicopinion/index.cfm/Chart/getChart/chartType/gridChart//themeKy/18/ groupKy/98/countries/IT/savFiles/555,54,179,554,880,6,11,47,2,632,702,867,5,521 ,663,698,805,8,37,850,33,41,3,7,49,186,646,838,9,10,187,197/periodStart/042001/ periodEnd/032018 (accessed on 18 September 2018).

3. Data refers to the question "What is your opinion on each of the following statements? Please tell me for each statement, whether you are for it or against it. A common foreign policy of all Member States of the EU" http://ec.europa .eu/commfrontoffice/publicopinion/index.cfm/Chart/getChart/chartType/grid Chart//themeKy/29/groupKy/184/countries/IT/savFiles/555,1,129 ,179,554,880,6,47,661,632,702,867,5,137,143,191,521,663,698,805,8,37 ,662,850,33,41,3,7,49,186,190,195,196,646,838,9,10,118,187/periodStart/091992/ periodEnd/032018 and http://ec.europa.eu/commfrontoffice/publicopinion/index .cfm/Chart/getChart/chartType/gridChart//themeKy/29/groupKy/184/coun tries/EU/savFles/118,661,129,137,143,662,191,195,196,663,179,186 ,187,190,49,47,41,37,33,8,9,10,3,1,5,6,7,521,554,555,632,646,698,702,805,838,850 ,867/periodStart/091992/periodEnd/032018 (accessed on 19 September 2018).

4. Because the migration crisis develops later and builds onto the financial and economic one, dividing again Southern European states from Northern ones, and because it is the fact that the crisis is a European one that is relevant, it is considered useful to analyze the effects of both crises together and starting from the first one that manifested itself. The effects of the referendum on Brexit will not be analyzed, because the referendum took place in June 2016 and not enough data are available to make a systematic comparison.

Conclusions

The main pillars of Italian foreign policy have been set with the post–World War II choice to play the role of ally of the US and become a member of the dominant coalition in the newly established hegemonic organization of the international political system. The alliance with the US, the participation in the European integration process and multilateralism were all part of the same choice for the Western camp in support of the US-led organization of the international political system. They helped to legitimize domestic politics through foreign policy commitments and they were consonant with the Italian need to distance itself from its fascist past and redefine its own identity based on supranationalism rather than nationalism. They also helped Italy in the much longed for process of being reaccepted by the international community and regaining part of the status the country had lost.

During the Cold War, because the domestic political situation reproduced at the national level the international competition between the two superpowers, Italian foreign policy could not be an issue in the domestic political competition, it had to be low profile, and Italian foreign policy style could only be passive. But already back then Italy occasionally tried to play the self-ascribed role of coalition facilitator and to increase its status as a middle power by performing activities that could help not only to support the alliance it belonged to but also maintain the existing organization of the international political system.

Since the 1970s, a bipartisan consensus emerged on Italian foreign policy and especially on the European pillar, progressively encouraging a greater activism that became more evident with the end of the Cold War. When European states started cooperating in the field of foreign policy, this offered Italy the possibility to conduct its foreign policy in a way that was considered consistent with its identity, strategic culture, but also domestic and international opportunity structure. The Europeanization of foreign policy allowed the country to build on the politics of scale that acting with other European members granted and to amplify its influence, without running into domestic opposition and bypassing domestic controversies. The furthering of the European integration process in the field of foreign policy gave Italy also an advantage in its quest for status, because especially within multilateral institutions the country gained the possibility to exploit the leverage that the support of a coalition capable of supplying the economic and political resources and leadership needed to advance initiatives provides when performing international system maintenance activities.

At the end of the Cold War, on the one hand, Italy started a more active foreign policy with multilateral legitimation. On the other hand, its relationship with multilateralism, and the EU in particular, became part of the domestic political competition, especially when these two pillars of Italian foreign policy were in occasional dissonance with the third, the alliance with the US from which they originally derived. The traditional pillars of Italian foreign policy remained, but the now alternating domestic governing coalitions gave of them different interpretations. The presence of crises in Europe and the rise of new powers potentially challenging the organization of the international system on the basis of which Italian foreign policy had traditionally been structured gave cause for concern about the continuation of previous policies and processes. As a consequence, literature has been divided on whether Italian foreign policy was highly Europeanized or, as a result of domestic tensions and a changing international context, it had de-Europeanized.

Building on Hill and Wong's (2011: 211) definition of the characteristics of the ideal type Europeanized foreign policy, it has been proposed that the Europeanization of foreign policy leads to behavior analogous to the creation of a political coalition at the international level. States whose foreign policies are Europeanized are expected to create a political unit that acts together not just because its members share homogeneous preferences, but also because they create internal bonds and expectations on how members of the unit should behave, they develop an organizational distinctiveness and procedural norms to manage conflicts and disagreements that allow them to overcome their original preferences. But their relations are not as binding as those of an alliance and this allows defections. This European formalized coalition can be considered a subset of the US-led dominant coalition: it has traditionally acted in support of the global leader and its organization, helping the global leader to pursue the shared agenda within multilateral institutions. In this respect, the Europeanization process is not insulated from the dynamics of the international system.

It has also been proposed to assess and analyze variations in the Europeanization of Italian foreign policy by looking at Italian voting and sponsoring behavior at the UN, that represents the intersection between a pillar of Italian foreign policy and a basic tenet of the EU in which all the relevant actors are represented. Likewise, it has been proposed to focus on whether Italian coalitional behavior at the UN reflects a willingness to adapt its foreign policy to belong to the European formalized coalition and whether this behavior is used to increase Italian structural opportunities and status as a country contributing to the maintenance of the organization of the international system.

The picture that emerged in relation to the analyzed period, 2000–2017, is that, despite a context of decreasing EU cohesion, Italian foreign policy is Europeanized. This is particularly evident in the Security Council, where the most important foreign policy issues are debated. In the UNSC the traditional structure of Italian foreign policy is present, and Italy regularly acts with the US and the other EU members, especially France and the UK. But Europeanization is present also in the UNGA, where Italian behavior is more articulated and where the stakes are less high. The small Italian distance from the European formalized coalition in voting has actually reduced over time, and when distances are expressed, they are more in terms of partial disagreements to minimize distances and conflicts. Italy sponsors with the European formalized coalition around 80 percent of its draft resolutions. In all the analyzed years Italy regularly and predominantly acted with the European formalized coalition, facilitating its creation and maintenance over time, while acting without was for Italy a marginal behavior. Looking at human rights, a quintessential issue area for the identity of the EU, it emerges that Italy tends to adapt its foreign policy to converge and facilitate the creation and maintenance of the European formalized coalition, as evident in both the UNGA and the UNSC. On disarmament and nuclear issues, Italy makes efforts to adapt its foreign policy even when there is a divergence with the other EU members on the issue. The analysis of the specific case studies also showed that through the European formalized coalition the country achieves otherwise unachievable goals, as in the case of the moratorium on death penalty in the UNGA or in the case of the resolution on human trafficking from Libya in the UNSC. Europeanization for Italy changes the opportunity structure and the resulting cooperation with the European formalized coalition is consistent, across issues and over time, elements identified in the literature as necessary to identify a causal relation.

This is not to say that Italy does not ever defect or does not promote its national interest. Defections from the European formalized coalition are possible and have taken place in the UNGA. The case of the right to development resolution indicates that when the Italian dissent with the rest of the

EU countries widens, Italy prefers to be in a minority position, but does not adapt its position to the one adopted by the coalition. Likewise, on the resolution "Follow-up to nuclear disarmament obligations agreed to at the 1995, 2000 and 2010 Review Conferences of the Parties to the Treaty on the Non-Proliferation of Nuclear Weapons," in the 70th session Italy voted in isolation, distancing itself from all the other EU member states and from the US on an issue of importance for the country. Defection is less frequent in the UNSC, where the stakes are much higher. Here Italian defection can be seen in what the UNSC did not to: its reform. UNSC reform is probably one of the most important issues in Italian foreign policy since the 1990s and it is a priority national interest shared by all governments regardless of the composition. Not commanding enough support from the European states (most of which sided with Germany) nor from the US to gain a permanent seat, Italy acted mostly with non-European countries to prevent a reform that would have marginalized Italy and reduced its status.

Italy does not normally take advantage from divisions among EU members. They certainly create the opportunity to free ride, but the Italian support to the creation and maintenance of the European formalized coalition also becomes more valued. That is why in case of intra-European divisions Italy can be found facilitating the negotiated convergence to a common position of at least a majority of EU member states believing that this is in the Italian interest and that this is the appropriate behavior for an EU member. In this effort, some countries have been found to be more frequent coalition partners in the analyzed period, indicating a greater reliance on each other's support to build the wider European formalized coalition. Among the big EU members, in the UNGA Italy has been traditionally closer to Germany than to France or the UK. Otherwise, its support net is made mostly of Mediterranean and small EU countries, while it tends to share fewer initiatives with East European countries (except for Slovenia). In the Security Council, the composition changes coalitional dynamics, so nonpermanent European members like Italy tend to rely on the two European permanent members as transmission belts to promote their initiatives. This makes of France and the UK the two EU members closer to Italy. But despite the direct clash in relation to the UNSC reform, Germany is also a close member to build the European formalized coalition with, together with the original six founding members, while the East European countries are more distant.

Both the logic of appropriateness and the logic of consequences have been found at play in Italian behavior. Over time Italy has redefined its identity so that the feeling of belonging to the European "community" has led to going beyond the coordination reflex and to identifying acting with the European formalized coalition and sticking with it as the appropriate behavior, what the country is expected to do. This has led to support initiatives that are not necessarily in the national interest, as result of the internalization of specific values promoted by the EU and of the belief in the importance of a common European position. This is normally seen in relation to processes of downloading and cross-loading.

The logic of consequences can be often seen too, especially in processes of uploading of issues that are in the Italian interest onto the agenda of the EU. Indeed, Italy frequently builds on the European formalized coalition because this offers additional resources to exert influence on decision-making processes. To be clear, this is a "thinner" version of Europeanization, that as such is opportunistic, potentially more volatile and subject to variations in results.

In the Italian case, facilitating the creation and maintenance and building on the European formalized coalition was also a means to gain status. Middle powers can gain status by performing system maintenance activities and they normally act within multilateral institutions so that this behavior can be seen at the UN. The European integration project was originally strongly prompted by the US, and European states are members of the US-led dominant coalition. This has long ensured that EU foreign policy goals were consonant with the US ones and that European states at the UN acted in support of the maintenance and stability of the current organization of the international political system. For Italy supporting the creation and maintenance of the European formalized coalition also meant enabling through European political and financial resources the adoption of measures that could support the organization of the international system and that Italy acting alone would not have had. Within the current organization of the international political system, building on the European formalized coalition allowed Italy to aspire to move from a supporting position to a cabinet position, and therefore to regain the lost status and be more influential. Italy builds on the European formalized coalition not in opposition but in support of the US and its organization of the international system. Italian closeness to the US is particularly important for the country, that may exploit its freedom of maneuver when no challenger is on the horizon but remains close to the global leader on issues of importance for the US and most importantly it increases its closeness (without diminishing the one with the European formalized coalition) when potential competitors emerge. Both in the UNGA and in the UNSC it is evident that as soon as China and Russia were identified as potential challengers to the US, not only did Italy become closer to the US, but it also increased its distance from China and, despite its close partnership, from Russia.

Warnings about a de-Europeanization were not totally unfounded, though, as some traces could also be found in the context of the present work in the UNGA. If in the 1990s it had been assessed that Italian voting cohesion with the EU majority was regularly above 95 percent, in the 2000s and 2010s it diminished to between 90 percent and 95 percent, and in two sessions it even touched 80 percent or little more. A greater distance also emerges in Italian sponsoring behavior, since Italy at the beginning of the 2000s sponsored with the European formalized coalition around 90 percent of its draft resolutions while in more recent years the numbers have become closer to 80 percent. But these are not yet numbers that allow discussions about a de-Europeanization, if not in relative terms. And in the UNSC, where the most important foreign policy issues are decided upon, the opposite trend, that is an increase in actions with the European states, could be observed.

What was evident, though, was a change in the context, which made it more difficult for Italy to act with the European formalized coalition and to interpret its traditional role under changing structural conditions. EU cohesion in the UNGA has been drastically reducing over time and the occasions in which EU members are so divided as not to be able to create an EU majority have become more frequent. Moreover, the increase in Euroscepticism in Italian public opinion, the EU crises, the growing EU irrelevance and the turn of the Trump administration toward the abandonment of the international hegemonic order on the basis of which Italy had traditionally structured its foreign policy increased the political cost to act with the European formalized coalition without any guarantee that this political investment will have the same returns it had in the past. So far all of this has had no impact in the UNSC, and therefore on the most important issues, where cooperation with European states and the US after the crises has increased. But in the UNGA it has resulted in a slightly increased distance in the relationship with Germany, a traditional preferential partner, and in a more volatile Italian behavior.

In a changing opportunity structure, Italian political actors are left with a very difficult choice: following the traditional foreign policy guidelines, accepting the certain diminishing returns of this behavior; or counting on occasional alignments and limited resources in a system moving toward greater competition, coexisting with the shadow of marginalization. The choice depends on the level of awareness that political actors reach of the costs that these options imply.

Bibliography

Acharya A. (2014), *The End of American World Order*, Cambridge, Polity Press.
Adler E. and Barnett M. (eds.) (1998), *Security Communities*, Cambridge, Cambridge University Press.
Alecu de Flers N. and Müller P. (2012), Dimensions and Mechanisms of Europeanization of Member State Foreign Policy: State of the Art and New Research Avenues, *Journal of European Integration*, 34(1), 19–35.
Aliboni R. and Greco E. (1996), Foreign Policy Re-Nationalization and Internationalism in the Italian Debate, *International Affairs*, 72(1), 43–51.
Alker H. R. (1964), Dimensions of Conflict in the General Assembly, *American Political Science Review*, 58(3), 642–657.
Alker H. R. and Russett B. (1965), *World Politics in the General Assembly*, New Haven, CT, Yale University Press.
Allan B. B., Vucetic S. and Hopf T. (2018), The Distribution of Identity and the Future of International Order: China's Hegemonic Prospects, *International Organization*, 72(4), 839–869.
Allison G. (2017), *Destined for War: Can America and China Escape Thucydides's trap?* Boston and New York, Houghton Mifflin Harcourt.
Ammendola T. and Isernia P. (2005), L'Europa vista dagli italiani: i primi vent'anni, in Cotta M., Isernia P. and Verzichelli L. (eds.), *L'Europa in Italia*, Bologna, Il Mulino.
Anderson C. J. and Hecht J. D. (2018), The Preference for Europe: Public Opinion about European Integration since 1952, *European Union Politics*, Online First.
Andreatta F. (2001), Italy at a Crossroads: The Foreign Policy of a Medium Power after the End of Bipolarity, *Daedalus*, 130(2), 45–65.
Andreatta F. (2008a), La politica estera italiana. "Policy analysis" di una media potenza, in Capano G. (ed.), *Non solo potere: le altre facce della politica*, Bologna, Il Mulino.

Andreatta F. (2008b), Italian Foreign Policy: Domestic Politics, International Requirements and the European Dimension, *Journal of European Integration*, 30(1), 169–181.
Attinà F. (1979), *Diplomazia e politica estera*, Milan, Franco Angeli.
Attinà F. (1983), La formazione della politica estera italiana, *Democrazia e Diritto*, 23(5), 105–119.
Attinà F. (2003), *La sicurezza degli stati nell'era dell'egemonia americana*, Milan, Giuffrè.
Attinà F. (2008), Theories of Long-term Change and the Future of World Political Institutions, in Modelski G., Devezas T. and Thompson W. R. (eds.), *Globalization as Evolutionary Process*, London and New York, Routledge.
Attinà F. (2009), *La scelta del multilateralismo*, Milano, Giuffrè.
Attinà F. (2011), *The Global Political System*, Houndmills, Palgrave.
Attinà F. (2016), L'Europa alle prese con la crisi migratoria, in Panebianco S. (ed.), *Sulle onde del Mediterraneo*, Milan, Egea.
Bailey M., Strezhnev A. and Voeten E. (2017), Estimating Dynamic State Preferences from United Nations Voting Data, *Journal of Conflict Resolution*, 61(2), 430–456.
Bailey S. D. and Daws S. (1998), *The Procedure of the Security Council*, Oxford, Clarendon Press.
Baldini A. (2016), Italy and the Netherlands to Split Term at UNSC, Agreement Is Sign of European Unity, ItalyUN.it, http://www.onuitalia.com/eng/2016/06/28/italy-netherlands-agree-split-term-unsc-italian-creativity-leads-solution/ (accessed on 24 August 2018).
Barbulescu R. and Beaudonnet, L. (2014), Protecting Us, Protecting Europe? Public Concern about Immigration and Declining Support for European Integration in Italy, *Perspectives on European Politics and Society*, 15(2), 216–237.
Barma N., Ratner E. and Weber S. (2007), A World Without the West, *The National Interest*, N. 90, July/August, 23–30.
Barma N., Ratner E. and Weber S. (2013), The Mythical Liberal Order, *The National Interest*, N. 124, March/April, 56–67.
Barma N., Ratner E. and Weber S. (2014), Welcome to the World Without the Rest, *The National Interest*, November 12, http://nationalinterest.org/feature/welcome-the-world-without-the-west-11651 (accessed on 23 September 2018).
Baxter P., Jordan J. and Rubin L. (2018), How Small States Acquire Status: A Social Network Analysis, *International Area Studies Review*, First Published May 22, 2018, https://doi.org/10.1177/2233865918776844.
BBC (2018), Trump Threatens to Pull US out of World Trade Organization, 31 August, https://www.bbc.com/news/world-us-canada-45364150 (accessed on 23 September 2018).
Bellucci P. and Conti N. (2012), *Gli italiani e l'Europa*, Rome, Carocci.
Bially Mattern J. and Zarakol A. (2016), Hierarchies in World Politics, *International Organization*, 70(3), 623–654.
Bicchi F. (2014), Information Exchanges, Diplomatic Networks and the Construction of European Knowledge in European Union Foreign Policy, *Cooperation and Conflict*, 49(2), 239–259.

Birnbaum M. and Hudson J. (2019), The Trump Administration Downgraded the E.U. Ambassador—and Didn't Tell Him, *Washington Post*, 8 January 2019, https://www.washingtonpost.com/world/europe/the-trump-administration-down graded-the-eu-ambassador—and-didnt-tell-him/2019/01/08/94aa81e4-1357 -11e9-ab79-30cd4f7926f2_story.html?utm_term=.9347d6b11906 (accessed on 8 January 2019)

Blavoukos S. and Bourantonis D. (2011), The EU's Performance in the United Nations Security Council, *Journal of European Integration*, 33(6), 731–742.

Blavoukos S. and Bourantonis D. (eds.) (2017), *The EU in UN Politics*, London, Palgrave Macmillan.

Blavoukos S., Bourantonis D., Galariotis I. and Gianniou M. (2016), The European Union's Visibility and Coherence at the United Nations General Assembly, *Global Affairs*, 2(1), 35–45.

Börzel T. A. and Risse T. (2003), Conceptualizing the Domestic Impact of Europe, in Featherstone K. and Radaelli C. M. (eds.), *The Politics of Europeanization*, Oxford, Oxford University Press.

Börzel T. A. and Risse T. (2012), When Europeanisation Meets Diffusion: Exploring New Territory, *West European Politics*, 35(1), 192–207.

Bourantonis D. (2005), *The History and Politics of UN Security Council Reform*, London and New York, Routledge.

Bressanelli E. and De Candia M. (2018), Love, Convenience, or Respectability? Understanding the Alliances of the Five Star Movement in the European Parliament, *Italian Political Science Review*, Online first, 30 April 2018, 1–24.

Brighi E. (2006), One Man Alone'? A Longue Durée Approach to Italy's Foreign Policy under Berlusconi, *Government and Opposition*, 41(2), 278–297.

Brighi E. (2007), Europe, the USA and the "Policy of the Pendulum": The Importance of Foreign Policy Paradigms in the Foreign Policy of Italy (1989–2005), *Journal of Southern Europe and the Balkans*, 9(2), 99–115.

Brighi E. (2011), Resisting Europe? The Case of Italy's Foreign Policy, in Wong R. and Hill C. (eds.) (2011), *National and European Foreign Policies. Towards Europeanization*, Milton Park and New York, Routledge.

Brighi E. (2013), *Foreign Policy, Domestic Politics and International Relations: The Case of Italy*, Milton Park and New York, Routledge.

Brighi E. (2017), Italian Foreign Policy after the Cold War. Crisis and the Limits of a Post-Ideological Foreign Policy, in Evangelista M. (ed.), *Italy from Crisis to Crisis*, London and New York, Routledge.

Brighi E. and Giugni L. (2016), Foreign Policy and the Ideology of Post-Ideology: The Case of Matteo Renzi's Partito Democratico, *International Spectator*, 51(1), 13–27.

Brooks S. G. and Wohlforth W. C. (2016), The Once and Future Superpower. Why China Won't Overtake the United States, *Foreign Affairs*, 95(3), 91–104.

Buchanan A. and Keohane R. O. (2006), The Legitimacy of Global Governance Institutions, *Ethics & International Affairs*, 20(4), 405–437.

Bull M. J. (2018), In the Eyes of the Storm: The Italian Economy and the Eurozone Crisis, *South European Society and Politics*, 23(1), 13–28.

Bull M. J. and Pasquino G. (2018), Italian Politics in an Era of Recession: The End of Bipolarism? *South European Society and Politics*, 23(1), 1–12.

Burmester N. and Jankowski M. (2014), Reassessing the European Union in the United Nations General Assembly, *Journal of European Public Policy*, 21(10), 1491–1508.

Burmester N. and Jankowski M. (2018), One Voice or Different Choice? Vote Defection of European Union Member States in the United Nations General Assembly, *The British Journal of Politics and International Relations*, 20(3), 652–673.

Caffarena A. and Gabusi G. (2017), Making Sense of a Changing World: Foreign Policy Ideas and Italy's National Role Conceptions after 9/11, *Italian Political Science Review*, 47(2), 125–147.

Caiani M. and Conti N. (2014), In the Name of the People: The Euroscepticism of the Italian Radical Right, *Perspectives on Politics and Society*, 15(2), 183–197.

Carbone M. (2011), Italy as a Development Actor: A Tale of Bipartisan Failure, in Carbone M. (eds.), *Italy in the Post-Cold War Order: Adaptation, Bipartisanship, Visibility*, Lanham, MD Lexington Books.

Carbone M. and Quartapelle L. (2016), Italy's Development Policy and the Domestic Politics of Europeanisation: Why Europe Matters So Little, *European Politics and Society*, 17(1), 42–57.

Carlassare L. (2013), L'articolo 11 della Costituzione nella visione dei Costituenti, in Ronzitti N. (ed.), *L'articolo 11 della costituzione*, Naples, Editoriale Scientifica.

CBS News (2018), "I Think the European Union Is a Foe," Trump Says ahead of Putin Meeting in Helsinki, 15 July 2018, https://www.cbsnews.com/news/donald-trump-interview-cbs-news-european-union-is-a-foe-ahead-of-putin-meeting-in-helsinki-jeff-glor/ (accessed on 6 January 2019).

Charalambous G., Conti N. and Pedrazzani A. (2018), The Political Contestation of European Integration in Southern Europe: Friction Among and Within Parties, *Party Politics*, 24(1), 39–51.

Chiaramonte A. and Emanuele V. (2018), L'onda sismica non si arresta. Il mutamento del sistema partitico italiano dopo le elezioni del 2018, in Emanuele V. and Paparo A. (eds.), *Gli sfidanti al governo*, Rome, LUISS University Press.

Cladi L. and Webber M. (2011), Italian Foreign Policy in the Post-Cold War Period: A Neoclassical Realist Approach, *European Security*, 20(2), 205–219.

Clementi M., Pisciotta B. and Dian M. (eds.) (2018), *US Foreign Policy in a Challenging World*, Cham, Springer.

Coleman J. M. (1970), The Benefits of Coalition, *Public Choice*, 8(1), 45–61.

Coleman J. S. (1973), Loss of Power, *American Sociological Review*, 38(1), 1–17.

Coleman J. S. (1986), Control of Collectivities and the Power of a Collectivity to Act, in Coleman J. S., *Individual Interests and Collective Action*, Cambridge, Cambridge University Press

Conti N. (2017), The Italian Political Elites and Europe: Big Move, Small Change? *International Political Science Review*, 38(5), 534–548.

Conti N., Di Mauro D. and Memoli V. (2018), The European Union Under Threat of a Trend Toward National Sovereignty, *Journal of Contemporary European Research*, 14(3), 231–252.

Conti N. and Memoli V. (2015), Show the Money First! Recent Public Attitudes towards the EU in Italy, *Italian Political Science Review*, 45(2), 203–222.
Cooper A. F., Higgott R. A. and Nossal K (eds.) (1993), *Relocating Middle Powers*, Vancouver, University of British Columbia Press.
Cooper A. F. (1997), Niche Diplomacy: A Conceptual Overview, in Cooper A. F. (ed), *Niche Diplomacy*, Houndmills and New York, Macmillan Press.
Coralluzzo V. (1994), La politica europea dell'Italia: antichi vizi e opinabili virtù, *Teoria politica*, 10(2), 121–126.
Coralluzzo V. (2000), *La politica estera dell'Italia repubblicana (1946–1992)*, Milan, Franco Angeli.
Corbetta R., Volgy T. J., Baird R. G. and Grant K. A. (2011), Status and the Future of International Politics, in Volgy T. J., Corbetta R., Grant K. A. and Baird R. G. (eds.), *Major Powers and the Quest for Status in International Politics*, New York, Palgrave Macmillan.
Costa Bona E. and Tosi L. (2007), *L'Italia e la sicurezza collettiva*, Perugia, Morlacchi.
Coticchia F. (2013), *Qualcosa è cambiato? L'evoluzione della politica di difesa italiana dall'Iraq alla Libia (1991–2011)*, Pisa, Pisa University Press.
Cotta M. (2017), *Un'altra Europa è possibile*, Bologna, Il Mulino.
Cotta M., Isernia P. and Verzichelli L. (2005), Introduzione, in Cotta M., Isernia P. and Verzichelli L. (eds.), *L'Europa in Italia*, Bologna, Il Mulino.
Council of the European Union (2017), *EU Priorities at the United Nations and the 72nd United Nations General Assembly (September 2017—September 2018)*, Brussels, 17 July 2017.
Cox M. (2005), Beyond the West: Terrors in Transatlantia, *European Journal of International Relations*, 11(2), 119–127.
Cox R. W. (1983), Gramsci, Hegemony and International Relations: An Essay in Method, *Millennium*, 12(2), 162–175.
Cox R. W. (1992), Towards a Post-Hegemonic Conceptualization of World Order: Reflections on the Relevancy of Ibn Khaldun, in Rosenau J. N. and Czempiel E.-O. (eds.), *Governance Without Government: Order and Change in World Politics*, Cambridge, Cambridge University Press.
Croci O. (2005), The 'Americanization' of Italian Foreign Policy? *Journal of Modern Italian Studies*, 10(1), 10–26.
Croci O. (2008), Not a Zero-Sum Game: Atlanticism and Europeanism in Italian Foreign Policy, *The International Spectator*, 43(4), 137–155.
Cronin B. (2001), The Paradox of Hegemony: America's Ambiguous Relationship with the United Nations, *European Journal of International Relations*, 7(1), 103–130.
D'Argenio A. (2015), Ban Ki-moon: "Con l'Italia contro i trafficanti," *La Repubblica*, 28 April 2015, http://ricerca.repubblica.it/repubblica/archivio/repubblica/2015/04/28/ban-ki-moon-con-litalia-contro-i-trafficanti09.html?ref=search (accessed on 2 September 2018).
De Giovannangeli U. (2018), L'Italia il "paesino" preferito di Trump, *HuffingtonPost.it,* 30 July 2018, https://www.huffingtonpost.it/2018/07/30/litalia-il-paesino-preferito-di-trump_a_23492541/ (accessed on 5 January 2019).

De Marchis G. (2015), "Subito il sì dell'Onu e blocchiamo i barconi," *La Repubblica*, 21 April 2015, http://ricerca.repubblica.it/repubblica/archivio/repubblica/2015/04/21/subito-il-si-dellonu-e-blocchiamo-i-barconi08.html?ref=search (accessed on 2 September 2018).

Dedring J. (2004), Reflection on the Coordination of the EU Member States in Organs of the United Nations, *CFSP Forum*, 2(1), 1–3.

Dee M. (2017), The EU in UN Disarmament Forums, in Blavoukos S. and Bourantonis D. (eds.), *The EU in UN Politics*, London, Palgrave Macmillan.

Della Porta D. and Caiani M. (2006), *Quale Europa? Europeizzazione, identità e conflitti*, Bologna, Il Mulino.

Deudney D. and Ikenberry G. J. (2018), Liberal World. The Resilient Order, *Foreign Affairs*, 97(4), 16–24.

Di Mauro D. (2014), Is the Honeymoon Over? Explaining Italy's Mass Support and Opposition Towards Europe, *Perspectives on European Politics and Society*, 15(2), 143–164.

Diodato E. and Niglia F. (2017), *Italy in International Relations*, Palgrave.

DISPOC/LAPS and IAI (2017), *Gli italiani e la politica estera*, October 2017, http://www.iai.it/sites/default/files/laps-iai_2017.pdf (accessed on 19 September 2018).

Dobrescu M., Schumacher T. and Stavridis S. (2017), Southern Europe. Portugal, Spain, Italy, Malta, Greece, Cyprus, in Hadfield A., Manners I., Whitman R. (eds.), *Foreign Policies of EU Member States*, Abingdon and New York, Routledge.

Drezner D. W. (2012), Praised Be the Glorious Sovereigntists Who Protect the U.S.A. from. . . . from. . . . Wait, What? *Foreign Policy*, 5 December 2012, http://foreignpolicy.com/2012/12/05/praised-bethe-glorious-sovereigntists-who-protect-the-u-s-a-from-from-wait-what/ (accessed on 3 December 2016).

Drieskens E. (2009), Walking on Eggshells: Non-Permanent Members Searching for an EU Perspective at the UN Security Council, in Drieskens E. and Wouters J. (eds.), *Belgium in the UN Security Council. Reflections on the 2007–2008 Membership*, Antwerp, Intersentia.

Drieskens E., Marchesi D. and Kerremans B. (2007), In Search of a European Dimension in the UN Security Council, *The International Spectator*, 42(3), 421–430.

Duque M. G. (2018), Recognizing International Status: A Relational Approach, *International Studies Quarterly*, 62(3), 577–592.

Easton D. (1965), *A Systems Analysis of Political Life*, New York, Wiley.

EU Observer (2010), EU-US summits to take place 'only when necessary,' 27 March 2010, http://euobserver.com/foreign/29782 (accessed on 23 September 2019).

European External Action Service (2017), *The European Union at the United Nations, Fact Sheet*, https://eeas.europa.eu/headquarters/headquarters-homepage/9875/european-union-united-nations_en (accessed on 4 August 2018).

European Union (2003), *European Security Strategy. A Secure Europe in a Better World*.

European Union (2016), *Shared Vision, Common Action: A Stronger Europe. A Global Strategy for the European Union's Foreign and Security Policy*.

Fabbrini S. (2015), *Which European Union?* Cambridge, Cambridge University Press.

Fabbrini S. and Piattoni S. (2008), Introduction: Italy in the EU, in Fabbrini S. and Piattoni S. (eds.), *Italy in the European Union*, Lanham, Rowman & Littlefield.

Featherstone K. (2003), Introduction: In the Name of Europe, in Featherstone K. and Radaelli C. M. (eds.), *The Politics of Europeanization*, Oxford, Oxford University Press.

Ferraris L.V. (ed.) (1998), *Manuale della politica estera italiana*, Roma-Bari, Laterza.

Ferrera M. (2016), *Rotta di collisione?* Roma-Bari, Laterza.

Finnemore M. and Jurkovic M. (2014), Getting a Seat at the Table: The Origins of Universal Participation and Modern Multilateral Conferences, *Global Governance*, 20(3), 361–373.

Fois G. A. and Pagani F. (2008), A Wolf in Sheep's Clothing? Italy's Policies toward International Organizations, *Journal of Modern Italian Studies*, 13(1), 75–88.

Foot R., MacFarlane S. N. and Mastanduno M (eds.) (2003), *US Hegemony and International Organizations*, Oxford, Oxford University Press.

Foradori P. (2017), Protecting Cultural Heritage During Armed Conflict: The Italian Contribution to 'Cultural Peacekeeping,' *Modern Italy*, 22(1), 1–17.

Foradori P. and Rosa P. (2008), Italy and Defense and Security Policy, in Fabbrini S. and Piattoni S. (eds.), *Italy in the European Union*, Lanham, Rowman & Littlefield.

Fulci F. P. (1999), Italy and the Reform of the UN Security Council, *International Spectator*, 34(2), 7–16.

Galariotis I. and Gianniou M. (2017), Evidence from the EU Presence at UNGA: In Pursuit of Effective Performance, in Blavoukos S. and Bourantonis D. (eds.), *The EU in UN Politics*, London, Palgrave Macmillan.

Gharekhan C. R. (2006), *The Horseshoe Table. An Inside View of the UN Security Council*, New Delhi, Pearson Longman.

Giacomello G. and Verbeek B. (2011), "It's the Perception, Stupid!" The Hard Life of Italy as a Middle Power, in Giacomello G. and Verbeek B. (eds.), *Italy's Foreign Policy in the Twenty-First Century*, Lanham, Lexington Books.

Giannetti D., Pedrazzani A. and Pinto L. (2017), Party System Change in Italy: Politicising the EU and the Rise of Eccentric Parties, *South European Society and Politics*, 22(1), 21–42.

Gilley B. (2009), *The Right to Rule*, New York, Columbia University Press.

Gilpin R. (1981), *War and Change in World Politics*, Cambridge, Cambridge University Press.

Ginsberg R. (1989), *Foreign Policy Actions of the European Community: The Politics of Scale*, Boulder, Lynne Rienner.

Ginsberg R. (2001), *The European Union in International Politics: Baptism by Fire*, Lanham, Rowman & Littlefield.

Giuliani M. (1992), Il processo decisionale italiano e le politiche comunitarie, *Polis*, 6(2), 307–342.

Goldstein J. (1988), *Long Cycles: Prosperity and War in the Modern Age*, New Haven, Yale University Press.

Government of the Netherlands (2016), Netherlands and Italy to work in concert on Security Council, News Item, 22 September 2016, https://www.government.nl/lat

est/news/2016/09/22/netherlands-and-italy-to-work-in-concert-on-security-council (accessed on 24 August 2018).
Hadfield A., Manners I. and Whitman R. G. (2017a), Introduction, in Hadfield A., Manners I. and Whitman R. G. (eds.), *Foreign Policies of EU Member States*, Abingdon and New York, Routledge.
Hadfield A., Manners I. and Whitman R. G. (2017b), Conclusion, in Hadfield A., Manners I. and Whitman R. G. (eds.), *Foreign Policies of EU Member States*, Abingdon and New York, Routledge.
Hansler J. (2017), Nikki Haley: The US Is "Taking names" on Jerusalem Resolution, 10 December 2017, https://edition.cnn.com/2017/12/20/politics/nikki-haley-taking-names-on-jerusalem/index.html (accessed on 21 August 2018).
Henrikson A. K. (1997), Middle Powers as Managers: International Mediation Within, Across and Outside Institutions, in Cooper A. F. (ed), *Niche Diplomacy*, Houndmills and New York, Macmillan Press.
Higgott R. (1997), Issues, Institutions and Middle Power Diplomacy: Action and Agendas in the Post-Cold War Era, in Cooper A. F. (ed), *Niche Diplomacy*, Houndmills and New York, Macmillan Press.
Hill C. (2006), The European Powers in the Security Council: Differing Interests, Differing Arenas, in Laatikainen K. and Smith K. E. (eds.), *The European Union at the United Nations. Intersecting Multilateralisms*, Houndmills and New York, Palgrave.
Hill C. (2011), Foreword, in Carbone M. (ed.), *Italy in the Post-Cold War Order*, Lanham, Lexington Books.
Hill C. and Andreatta F. (2001), Struggling to Change: the Italian State and the New Order, in Wallace W. and Niblett R. (eds.), *Rethinking European Order: West European Responses, 1989–97*, Basingstoke, Palgrave Macmillan.
Hill C. and Wong R. (2011), Many Actors, One Path? The Meaning of Europeanization in the Context of Foreign Policy, in Wong R. and Hill C. (eds.), *National and European Foreign Policies. Towards Europeanization*, Milton Park and New York, Routledge.
Holsti K. J. (1970), National Role Conceptions in the Study of Foreign Policy, *International Studies Quarterly*, 14(3), 233–309.
Hosli M. O., Moody R., O'Donovan B., Kaniovski S., Little A. G. H. (2011), Squaring the Circle? Collective and Distributive Effects of United Nations Security Council Reform, *Review of International Organizations*, 6(2), 163–187.
Hulton S. C. (2004), Council Working Methods and Procedure, in Malone D. (ed.), *The UN Security Council*, Boulder and London, Lynne Rienner.
Hurd I. (2002), Legitimacy, Power and the Symbolic Life of the UN Security Council, *Global Governance*, 8(1), 35–51.
Hurd I. (2007), *After Anarchy*, Princeton, Princeton University Press.
Iakovidis I. (2017), The EU Performance in the Case of the International Moratorium on Death Penalty, in Blavoukos S. and Bourantonis D. (eds.), *The EU in UN Politics*, London, Palgrave Macmillan.
Ignazi P. (2004), Al di là dell'Atlantico, al di qua dell'Europa. Dove va la politica estera italiana, *Il Mulino*, 53(2), 267–277.

Ignazi P., Giacomello G. and Coticchia F. (2012), *Italian Military Operations Abroad*, Houndmills and New York, Palgrave Macmillan.

Ikenberry G. J. (1998), Constitutional Politics in International Relations, *European Journal of International Relations*, 4(2), 147–177.

Ikenberry G. J. (2001), *After Victory: Institutions, Strategic Restraint and the Rebuilding of Order After Major Wars*, Princeton, Princeton University Press.

Ikenberry G. J. (2003), State Power and the Institutional Bargain: America's Ambivalent Economic and Security Multilateralism, in Foot R., MacFarlane S. N. and Mastanduno M. (eds.), *US Hegemony and International Organizations*, Oxford, Oxford University Press.

Ikenberry G. J. (2010), The Liberal International Order and its Discontents, *Millennium*, 38(3), 509–521.

Ikenberry G. J. (2011), *Liberal Leviathan*, Princeton, Princeton University Press.

Ikenberry G. J. (2015a), The Future of Multilateralism: Governing the World in a Post-Hegemonic Era, *Japanese Journal of Political Science*, 16(3), 399–413.

Ikenberry G. J. (2015b), The Future of Liberal World Order, *Japanese Journal of Political Science*, 16(3), 450–455.

Ikenberry G. J. (2017), The Plot Against American Foreign Policy, *Foreign Affairs*, 96(3), 2–9.

Ikenberry G. J. and Kupchan C. A. (1990), Socialization and Hegemonic Power, *International Organization*, 44(3), 283–315.

Isernia P. (1996), Bandiera e risorse: la politica estera negli anni Ottanta, in Cotta M. and Isernia P. (eds.), *Il gigante dai piedi di argilla*, Bologna, Il Mulino.

Isernia P. (2008), Present at Creation: Italian Mass Support for European integration in the Formative Years, *European Journal of Political Research*, 47(3), 383–410.

Isernia P. (2017), Italia malato d'Europa: quattro ragioni per cui è forse vero, *Affarinternazionali*, http://www.affarinternazionali.it/2017/11/italia-malato-europa-ragioni/ (accessed on 19 September 2018).

Isernia P. and Longo F. (2017), The Italian Foreign Policy: Challenges and Continuities, *Italian Political Science Review*, 47(2), 107–124.

Italian Ministry of Foreign Affairs (2007), *Italy in the Security Council (2007–2008)*, 23 October 2007, https://www.esteri.it/mae/en/sala_stampa/archivionotizie/approfondimenti/20071023_italiaconsiglio.html (accessed on 23 August 2018).

ItalyUN.it (2016), UNSC, Lambertini: "Italy Supports the Statement by the Netherlands in Sign of Split-term Cooperation," http://www.onuitalia.com/eng/2016/09/14/unsc-lambertini-italy-supports-statement-netherlands-sign-split-term-cooperation/ (accessed on 24 August 2018).

Jin X. and Hosli M. O. (2013), Pre- and Post-Lisbon: European Union Voting in the United Nations General Assembly, *West European Politics*, 36(6), 1274–1291.

Johansson-Nogués E. (2004), The Fifteen and the Accession States in the UN General Assembly: What Future for European Foreign Policy in the Coming Together of the 'Old' and 'New' Europe? *European Foreign Affairs Review*, 9(1), 67–92.

Jones E. (2018), Italy's Revolt Against the EU. Populism Reaches Rome, *Foreign Affairs*, 24 May 2018, https://www.foreignaffairs.com/articles/italy/2018-05-24/italys-revolt-against-eu (accessed on 17 September 2018).

Junn R. S. (1983), Voting in the United Nations Security Council, *International Interactions*, 9(4), 315–352.

Kagan R. (2003), *Of Paradise and Power*, New York, Random House.

Karns M. P. and Mingst K. A. (2013), International Organizations and Diplomacy, in Cooper A. F., Heine J. and Thakur R. C. (eds.), *The Oxford Handbook of Modern Diplomacy*, Oxford, Oxford University Press.

Kaufmann J. (1980), *United Nations Decision Making*, Alphen aan den Rijn, Sijthoff & Noordhoff.

Kaye D. (2013), Stealth Multilateralism. U.S. Foreign Policy without Treaties—or the Senate, *Foreign Affairs*, 92(5), 113–124.

Keohane R. O. (2006), The Contingent Legitimacy of Multilateralism, in Newman E., Thakur R. e Tirman J. (eds.), *Multilateralism Under Challenge? Power, International Order and Structural Change*, Tokyo and New York, United Nations University Press.

Kim S. Y. and Russett B. (1996), The New Politics of Voting Alignments in the United Nations General Assembly, *International Organization*, 50(4), 629–652.

Kissack R. (2008), Outreach, Overstretch or Underhand? Strategies for Crossregional Consensus in Support of a UN General Assembly Resolution on a Moratorium on the Use of the Death Penalty, *European Foreign Policy Unit Working Paper 2008–2*, London, London School of Economics EFPU.

Kissack R. (2012), The EU in the Negotiations of a UN General Assembly Resolution on a Moratorium on the Use of the Death Penalty, in Wouters J., Bruyninckx H., Basu S., Schunz S. (eds.) (2012), *The European Union and Multilateral Governance*, Basingstoke, Palgrave Macmillan.

Kissack R. (2017), The EU in the World. From Multilateralism to Global Governance, in Hadfield A., Manners I. and Whitman R. G. (eds.), *Foreign Policies of EU Member States*, Abingdon and New York, Routledge.

Kolinovsky S. (2017), Nikki Haley Warns 'US Will Be Taking Names' of Countries Against Jerusalem Embassy Move, 20 December 2017, https://abcnews.go.com/Politics/nikki-haley-warns-us-taking-names-countries-jerusalem/story?id=51905360 (accessed on 21 August 2018).

Kupchan C. A, (2012), *No One's World. The West, The Rising Rest, and the Coming Global Turn*, New York, Oxford University Press.

La Repubblica (2015), Immigrazione, vertice al Viminale con Regioni e Comuni. Ban Ki-moon arriva in Italia, 26 April 2015, https://www.repubblica.it/politica/2015/04/26/news/immigrazione_vertice_al_viminale_con_regioni_e_comuni_ban_ki_moon_arriva_in_italia-112909382/?ref=search (accessed on 2 September 2018).

La Repubblica (2018), Manovra, l'Italia taglia i fondi all'Onu per 32 milioni all'anno, 24 December 2018), https://www.repubblica.it/politica/2018/12/24/news/manovra_taglio_fondi_onu-215011836/?ref=RHPPBT-BH-I0-C4-P13-S1.4-T1 (accessed on 24 December 2018).

Laatikainen K. (2004), Assessing the EU as an Actor at the UN: Authority, Cohesion, Recognition and Autonomy, *CFSP Forum*, 2(1), 4–9.

Laatikainen K. (2015), The EU and the United Nations, in Jørgensen K. E., Aarstad Å. K., Drieskens E., Laatikainen K. and Tonra B. (eds), *The SAGE Handbook of European Foreign Policy*, London, SAGE.

Laatikainen K. (2017), Conceptualizing Groups in UN Multilateralism: The Diplomatic Practice of Group Politics, *The Hague Journal of Diplomacy*, 12(2–3), 113–137.

Laatikainen K. and Smith K. E. (2006a), Introduction—The European Union at the United Nations: Leader, Partner or Failure? in Laatikainen K. and Smith K. E. (eds.), *The European Union at the United Nations. Intersecting Multilateralisms*, Houndmills and New York, Palgrave.

Laatikainen K. and Smith K. E. (eds.) (2006b), *The European Union at the United Nations. Intersecting Multilateralisms*, Houndmills and New York, Palgrave.

Laatikainen K. and Smith K. E. (2017), Introduction: The Multilateral Politics of UN Diplomacy, *The Hague Journal of Diplomacy*, 12(2–3), 95–112.

Ladrech R. (1994), The Europeanization of Domestic Politics and Institutions: The Case of France, *Journal of Common Market Studies*, 32(1), 69–88.

Ladrech R. (2000), *Europeanization and National Politics*, Houndmills and New York, Palgrave.

Lake D. A. (2009), *Hierarchy in International Relations*, Ithaca, Cornell University Press.

Lake D. A. (2013), Legitimating Power. The Domestic Politics of U.S. International Hierarchy, *International Security*, 38(2), 74–111.

Lake D. A. (2017), Hierarchy and International Relations: Theory and Evidence, *Oxford Research Encyclopedia of Politics*.

Landler M. (2017), Trump Threatens to End American Aid: 'We're Watching Those Votes' at the U.N., 20 December 2017, https://www.nytimes.com/2017/12/20/world/middleeast/trump-threatens-to-end-american-aid-were-watching-those-votes-at-the-un.html (accessed on 21 August 2018).

Larsen H. (2009), A Distinct FPA for Europe? Towards a Comprehensive Framework for Analysing the Foreign Policy of EU Member States, *European Journal of International Relations*, 15(3), 537–566.

Layne C. (2012), This Time it's Real: The End of Unipolarity and the Pax Americana, *International Studies Quarterly*, 56(1), 203–213.

Lipscy P. Y. (2015a), Explaining Institutional Change: Policy Areas, Outside Options, and the Bretton Woods Institutions, *American Journal of Political Science*, 59(2), 341–356.

Lipscy P. Y. (2015b), Who's Afraid of the AIIB. Why the United States Should Support China's Asian Infrastructure Investment Bank, *Foreign Affairs*, May 7, https://www.foreignaffairs.com/articles/china/2015-05-07/whos-afraid-aiib (accessed on 23 September 2018).

Lucarelli S. (2015), Italy and the EU: From True Love to Disenchantment? *Journal of Common Market Studies*, 53(1), 40–60.

Lugato M. (2013), L'articolo 11 della Costituzione e le Nazioni Unite, in Ronzitti N. (ed.), *L'articolo 11 della costituzione*, Napoli, Editoriale Scientifica.

Luif P. (2003), *EU Cohesion in the UN General Assembly*, EU Institute of Security Studies Occasional Paper n. 49.

Major C. (2005), Europeanisation and Foreign and Security Policy—Undermining and Rescuing the Nation State? *Politics*, 25(3), 175–190.

Malone D. (2000), Eyes on the Prize: The Quest for Nonpermanent Seats of the UN Security Council, *Global Governance*, 6(1), 3–23.

Mammarella G. and Cacace P. (2010), *La politica estera dell'Italia*, Bari-Roma, Laterza.

Manners I. (2002), Normative Power Europe: A Contradiction in Terms? *JCMS: Journal of Common Market Studies*, 40(2), 235–258.

Manners I. and Whitman R. G. (2000), Introduction, in Manners I. and Whitman R. G. (eds.), *The Foreign Policies of European Union Member States*, Manchester and New York, Manchester University Press.

Manners I. and Whitman R. G. (eds.) (2000), *The Foreign Policies of European Union Member States*, Manchester and New York, Manchester University Press.

Marchesi D. (2010), The EU Common Foreign and Security Policy in the UN Security Council: Between Representation and Coordination, *European Foreign Affairs Review*, 15(1), 97–114.

Maull H. W. (2009), Germany and the Art of Coalition Building, *Journal of European Integration*, 30(1), 131–152.

Mazzoni M. and Barbieri G. (2014), Grasshoppers against Ants or Malfunctions of Capitalism? The Representation of the European Economic Crisis in the Main Italian Newspapers, *Perspectives on European Politics and Society*, 15(2), 238–253.

McDonald P. J. (2015), Great Powers, Hierarchy, and Endogenous Regimes: Rethinking the Domestic Causes of Peace, *International Organization*, 69(3), 557–588.

Meijers M. J. (2017), Contagious Euroscepticism: The impact of Eurosceptic support on mainstream party positions on European integration, *Party Politics*, 23(4), 413–423.

Menzione E. (2017), *La sfida di New York*, Soveria Mannelli, Rubbettino.

Miller J. L., Cramer J., Volgy T. J., Bezerra P., Hauser M. and Sciabarra C. (2015), Norms, Behavioral Compliance, and Status Attribution in International Politics, *International Interactions*, 41(5), 779–804.

Ministero degli affari esteri (2007), *L'Italia nel Consiglio di sicurezza (2007–08)*, Dossier Farnesina, n. 46.

Ministero degli affari esteri (2008), *Rapporto 2020*.

Modelski G. (1987) (ed.), *Exploring Long Cycles*, Boulder, Lynne Rienner.

Modelski G. (1990), Is World Politics Evolutionary Learning? *International Organization*, 44(1), 1–24.

Modelski G. (1999), From Leadership to Organization: The Evolution of Global Politics, in Bornschier V. and Chase-Dunn C. (eds.), *The Future of Global Conflict*, London, SAGE.

Modelski G. (2008), Globalization as evolutionary process, in Modelski G., Devezas T. and Thompson W. R. (eds.), *Globalization as Evolutionary Process*, London and New York, Routledge.

Modelski G. and Perry G. (2002), "Democratization in Long Perspective" Revisited, *Technological Forecasting and Social Change*, 69(4), 359–376.

Modelski G. and Thompson W. R. (1999), The Long and Short of Global Politics in the Twenty-First Century: An Evolutionary Approach, *International Studies Review*, 1(2), 109–140.

Monteleone C. (2003), The New Transatlantic Agenda: Transatlantic Security Relations between Post-Hegemonic Cooperation and Interdependence, *Journal of Transatlantic Studies*, 1(1), 87–107.

Monteleone C. (2007), The Evolution of the Euro-Atlantic Pluralistic Security Community: Impact and Perspectives of the Presence of American Bases in Italy, *Journal of Transatlantic Studies*, 5(1), 63–87.

Monteleone C. (2011), The Enabling Factor: The Influence of US-EU Cooperation on UN Peace Operations, *European Security*, 20(2), 265–289.

Monteleone C. (2012), Multilateral Security and the Transatlantic Coalition at the UN Security Council, in Laursen F. (ed.), *The EU, Security, and Transatlantic Relations*, Brussels, PIE Peter Lang.

Monteleone C. (2015), Coalition Building in the UN Security Council, *International Relations*, 29(1), 45–68.

Monteleone C. (2018), Spatial Fragmentation of, and US Support for, the Main Multilateral Institutions of the Western Order, in Clementi M., Pisciotta B. and Dian M. (eds.), *US Foreign Policy in a Challenging World*, Cham, Springer.

Morlino L. and Raniolo F. (2017), *The Impact of the Economic Crisis on South European Democracies*, Cham, Palgrave Macmillan.

Morse J. C. and Keohane R. O. (2014), Contested Multilateralism, *Review of International Organizations*, 9(4), 385–412.

Moumoutzis K. (2011), Still Fashionable Yet Useless? Addressing Problems with Research on the Europeanization of Foreign Policy, *Journal of Common Market Studies*, 49(3), 607–629.

Neack L. (1995), UN Peace-keeping: In the Interest of Community or Self? *Journal of Peace Research*, 32(3), 181–196.

Neack L. (2014), *The New Foreign Policy: Complex Interactions, Competing Interests* (3d ed.), Lanham, MD, Rowman & Littlefield.

Neack L. (2017), Searching for Middle Powers, *Oxford Research Encyclopedia of Politics*.

Newman E. (2007), *A Crisis of Global Institutions?* London and New York, Routledge.

Nexon D. H. and Neumann I. B. (2018), Hegemonic-order Theory: A Field-theoretic Account, *European Journal of International Relations*, 24(3), 662–686.

Norloff C. (2017), Hegemony, Hierarchy, and Unipolarity: Theoretical and Empirical Foundations of Hegemonic Order Studies, *Oxford Research Encyclopedia of Politics*.

Nuti L. (1993a), "Me Too, Please": Italy and the Politics of Nuclear Weapons, 1945–1975, *Diplomacy & Statecraft*, 4(1), 114–148.

Nuti L. (1993b), US Forces in Italy, 1945–63, in Duke S. and Krieger W. (eds.), *US Military Forces in Europe: The Early Years, 1945–1970*, Boulder, Westview.

Nuti L. (1999), *Gli Stati Uniti e l'apertura a sinistra: importanza e limiti della presenza americana in Italia*, Bari-Roma, Laterza.

Nuti L. (2003), The Role of the US in Italy's Foreign Policy, *The International Spectator*, 38(1), 91–101.

Nuti L. (2007), *La sfida nucleare*, Bologna, Il Mulino.

Nuti L. (2011a), Italian Foreign Policy in the Cold War: A Constant Search for Status, in Carbone M. (ed.), *Italy in the Post-Cold War Order*, Lanham, Lexington Books.

Nuti L. (2011b), Italy's Nuclear Choices, *UNISCI Discussion Papers*, N. 25.

Nuti L. (2017), *Italy as a Hedging State? The Problematic Ratification of the Non-proliferation Treaty*, EUT Edizioni Università di Trieste.

Nye J. S. (2017), Will the Liberal Order Survive? The History of an Idea, *Foreign Affairs*, 96(1), 10–16.

O'Neill B. (1996), Power and Satisfaction in the United Nations Security Council, *Journal of Conflict Resolution*, 40(2), 219–237.

Obama B. (2007), Renewing American leadership, *Foreign Affairs*, 86(4), 2–16.

Obama B. (2008), Announcement of National Security Team, http://www.gwu.edu/*action/2008/chrntran08/obama120108st.html (accessed on 3 December 2016).

Orsini F. G. (2005), *Il mito dell'ONU*, Rome, Fondazione Liberal.

Paasivirta E. and Porter D. (2006), EU Coordination at the UN General Assembly and ECOSOC: A View from Brussels, a View from New York, in Wouters J., Hoffmeister F. and Ruys T. (eds.), *The United Nations and the European Union: An Ever Stronger Partnership*, The Hague, T.M.C. Asser Press.

Panebianco A. (1977), La politica estera italiana: un modello interpretativo, *Il Mulino*, 26(6), 845–879.

Panebianco A. (1982), Le cause interne del "basso profilo," *Politica internazionale*, *10*(2), 15–21.

Panebianco A. (1986), La dimensione internazionale dei processi politici, in Pasquino G. (ed.), *Manuale di Scienza Politica*, Bologna, Il Mulino.

Panebianco A. (1997), *Guerrieri democratici*, Bologna, Il Mulino.

Panebianco A. (2015), La politica estera italiana fra continuità e discontinuità, in Galli della Loggia E. (ed.), *Questo diletto almo paese*, Bologna, Il Mulino.

Panebianco S. (ed.) (2016), *Sulle onde del Mediterraneo*, Milan, Egea.

Panebianco S. (2017), The 60th Anniversary of the EU: A New Élan for the EU . . . or Maybe Not, *Global Affairs*, 3(1), 1–3.

Panke D. (2013), Regional Power Revisited: How to Explain Differences in Coherency and Success of Regional Organizations in the United Nations General Assembly, *International Negotiation*, 18(2), 265–291.

Panke D. (2017a), The Institutional Design of the United Nations General Assembly: An Effective Equalizer? *International Relations*, 31(1), 3–20.

Panke D. (2017b), Speaking with One Voice: Easier Said than Done? The EU in the UNGA, in Blavoukos S. and Bourantonis D. (eds.), *The EU in UN Politics*, Palgrave Macmillan, London.

Parsi V. E. (2011), Conclusion: After the Cold War, A World of Opportunity and Greater Responsibility for Italy Too, in Carbone M. (ed.), *Italy in the Post-Cold War Order*, Lanham, Lexington Books.

Parsi V. E. (2018), *Titanic*, Bologna, Il Mulino.

Pasquino G. (1974), Pesi internazionali e contrappesi nazionali, in Cavazza F. L. and Grubard S. R. (eds.), *Il caso italiano*, Milan, Garzanti.

Patrick S. (2014), The Unruled World. The Case for Good Enough Global Governance, *Foreign Affairs*, 93(1), 58–73.

Patrick S. (2015), World Order: What, Exactly, Are the Rules? *The Washington Quarterly*, 39(1), 7–27.

Pirozzi N. (2009), Italy's Mandate at the UN Security Council (2007–2008): A Missed Opportunity, in Drieskens E. and Wouters J. (eds.), *Belgium in the UN Security Council. Reflections on the 2007–2008 Membership*, Antwerp, Intersentia.

Pouliot V. (2016), *International Pecking Orders*, Cambridge, Cambridge University Press.

Pouliot V. and Thérien J. P. (2015), The Politics of Inclusion: Changing Patterns in the Governance of International Security, *Review of International Studies*, 41(2), 211–237.

Puchala D. (1982–83), American Interests and the United Nations, *Political Science Quarterly*, 97(4), 571–588.

Puchala D. (2005), World Hegemony and the United Nations, *International Studies Review*, 7(4),571–584.

Putnam R. D. (1988), Diplomacy and Domestic Politics: The Logic of Two-Level Games, *International Organization*, 42(3), 427–460.

Radaelli C. M. (2003), The Europeanization of Public Policy, in Featherstone K. and Radaelli C. M. (eds.), *The Politics of Europeanization*, Oxford, Oxford University Press.

Rampini F. (2015), Migranti, battaglia europea sulle quote Mogherini: uso della forza, l'Onu dirà sì, *La Repubblica*, 12 May 2015, http://ricerca.repubblica.it/repubblica/archivio/repubblica/2015/05/12/migranti-battaglia-europea-sulle-quote-mogherini-uso-della-si01.html?ref=search and http://ricerca.repubblica.it/repubblica/archivio/repubblica/2015/05/12/mogherini-allonu-per-il-piano-migrantianche-cina-e-russia-libera10.html?ref=search (accessed on 2 September 2018).

Rappresentanza Permanente (2017), Statement Delivered by Ambassador Sebastiano Cardi, Permanent Representative of Italy to the United Nations, at the Security Council Meeting on the Cooperation Between the United Nations and Regional and Subregional Organizations in Maintaining International Peace and Security: European Union, https://italyun.esteri.it/rappresentanza_onu/en/comunicazione/archivio-news/2017/05/consiglio-di-sicurezza-meeting_15.html (accessed on 24 August 2018).

Ratti L. (2011), Italy as a Multilateral Actor: The Inescapable Destiny of a Middle Power, in Carbone M. (ed.), *Italy in the Post-Cold War Order*, Lanham, Lexington Books.

Ravenhill J. (1998), Cycles of Middle Power Activism: Constraint and Choice in Australian and Canadian foreign policies, *Australian Journal of International Affairs*, 52(3), 309–327.

Reus-Smit C. (1997), The Constitutional Structure of International Society and the Nature of Fundamental Institutions, *International Organization*, 51(4), 555–589.

Risse T., Caporaso J. and Green Cowles M. (2001), Introduction, in Green Cowles M., Caporaso J. and Risse T. (eds.), *Transforming Europe: Europeanization and Domestic Change*, Ithaca, Cornell University Press.

Robertson J. (2017), Middle-Power Definitions: Confusion Reigns Supreme, *Australian Journal of International Affairs*, 71(4), 355–370.

Romano S. (2006), Berlusconi's Foreign Policy: Inverting Traditional Priorities, *The International Spectator*, 41(2), 101–107.

Romero F. (2016), Rethinking Italy's Shrinking Place in the International Arena, *The International Spectator*, 51(1), 1–12.

Ronzitti N. (2008), US Military Bases in Italy: In Keeping with International Law? Still Needed? *The International Spectator*, 43(2), 79–94.

Rosa P. (2003), L'europeizzazione della politica estera: tra sovranazionalismo e transgovernativismo, in Fabbrini S. (ed.), *L'europeizzazione dell'Italia*, Rome, Laterza.

Rosa P. (2014), The Accommodationist State: Strategic Culture and Italy's Military Behaviour, *International Relations*, 28(1), 88–115.

Rosa P. (2016), *Strategic Culture and Italy's Military Behavior*, Lanham, Lexington Books.

Rosa P. (2018), Patterns of Strategic Culture and the Italian Case, *International Politics*, 55(2), 316–333.

Ruggie J. G. (1993), Multilateralism: The Anatomy of an Institution, in Ruggie J. G. (ed.), *Multilateralism Matters*, New York, Columbia University Press.

Salleo F. and Pirozzi N. (2008), Italy and the United Nations Security Council, *The International Spectator*, 43(2), 95–111.

Santoro C. M. (1991), *La politica estera di una media potenza*, Bologna, Il Mulino.

Scharpf F. W. (1999), *Governing in Europe: Effective and Democratic?* Oxford, Oxford University Press.

Schweller R. L. (2011), The Future is Uncertain and the End is Always Near, *Cambridge Review of International Affairs*, 24(2), 175–184.

Schweller R. L. and Pu X. (2011), After Unipolarity. China's Visions of International Order in an Era of U.S. Decline, *International Security*, 36(1), 41–72.

Security Council Report (2017), Security Council Elections 2017, Research Report 2017, https://www.securitycouncilreport.org/atf/cf/%7B65BFCF9B-6D27-4E9C-8CD3-CF6E4FF96FF9%7D/unsc_elections_2017.pdf (24 August 2018).

Sengupta S. (2017), Nikki Haley Puts U.N. on Notice: U.S. Is 'Taking Names,' *New York Times*, 27 January 2017, https://www.nytimes.com/2017/01/27/world/americas/nikki-haley-united-nations.html?rref=collection%2Ftimestopic%2FHaley%2C%20Nikki (accessed on 3 August 2018).

Serricchio F., Tsakatika M. and Quaglia L. (2013), Euroscepticism and the Global Financial Crisis, *Journal of Common Market Studies*, 51(1), 51–64.

Skidmore D. (2005), Understanding the Unilateralist Turn in U.S. Foreign Policy, *Foreign Policy Analysis*, 1(2), 207–228.

Skidmore D. (2012), The Obama Presidency and US Foreign Policy: Where's the Multilateralism? *International Studies Perspectives*, 13(1), 43–64.

Smadja D. (2006), The European Union and the Reform of the United Nations, in Wouters J., Hoffmeister F. and Ruys T. (eds.), *The United Nations and the European Union: An Ever Stronger Partnership*, The Hague, T.M.C. Asser Press.

Smith C. B. (2006), *Politics and Process at the United Nations. The Global Dance*, Boulder, and London, Lynne Rienner.

Smith K. E. (2015), The EU as a Diplomatic Actor in the Field of Human Rights, in Koops J. A. and Macaj G. (eds.), *The European Union as a Diplomatic Actor*, Houndmills, Palgrave.

Smith K. E. (2017), EU Member State at the UN: Europeanization Arrested? *Journal of Common Market Studies*, 55(3), 628–644.

Smith M. E. (2000), Conforming to Europe: The Domestic Impact of EU Foreign Policy Co-operation, *Journal of European Public Policy*, 7(4), 613–631.

Stephen M. D. (2014), Rising Powers, Global Capitalism and Liberal Global Governance: A Historical Materialist Account of the BRICs Challenge, *European Journal of International Relations*, 20(4), 912–938.

Stephen M. D. (2017), Emerging Powers and Emerging Trends in Global Governance, *Global Governance*, 23(3), 483–502.

Sullivan J. (2018), The World After Trump, *Foreign Affairs*, 97(2), 10–19.

Tardy T. and Zaum D. (2016), France and the United Kingdom in the Security Council, in von Einsiedel S., Malone D. M. and Stagno Ugarte B. (eds.), *The UN Security Council in the 21st Century*, Boulder and London, Lynne Rienner.

Tercovich G. (2016), Italy and UN Peacekeeping: Constant Transformation, *International Peacekeeping*, 23(5), 681–701.

Thompson W. R. (2001), *Evolutionary Interpretations of World Politics*, New York and London, Routledge.

Thompson W. R. and Zakhirova L. (2017), Systemic Leadership, Energy Considerations, and the Leadership Long-Cycle Perspective, *Oxford Research Encyclopedia of Politics*.

Todd J. E. (1966), An Analysis of Security Council Voting Behavior, *The Western Political Quarterly*, 22(1), 61–78.

Tonra B. (2000), Denmark and Ireland, in Manners I. and Whitman R. (eds.), *The Foreign Policies of European Union Member States*, Manchester, Manchester University Press.

Tonra B. (2001), *The Europeanisation of National Foreign Policy*, Aldershot, Ashgate.

Tonra B. (2003), Constructing the CFSP: The Utility of a Cognitive Approach, *Journal of Common Market Studies*, 41(4): 731–756.

Tonra B. (2015), Europeanization, in Jørgensen K.E., Aarstad Å. K., Drieskens E., Laatikainen K. and Tonra B. (eds.), *The SAGE Handbook of European Foreign Policy*, London, SAGE.

Tosi L. (2010), *Sulla scena del mondo*, Napoli, Editoriale Scientifica

Tronconi F. (2018), The Italian Five Star Movement During the Crisis: Towards Normalisation? *South European Society and Politics*, 23(1), 163–180.

Tsakaloyannis P. and Bourantonis D. (1997), The European Union's Common Foreign and Security Policy and the Reform of the Security Council, *European Foreign Affairs Review*, 2(2), 197–209.

Tsardanidis C. and Stavridis S. (2005), The Europeanization of Greek Foreign Policy: A Critical Appraisal, *Journal of European Integration*, 27(2), 217–239.

United Nations (2016), General Assembly Elects 4 New Non-permanent Members to Security Council, as Western and Others Group Fails to Fill Final Vacancy,

GA/11796, https://www.un.org/press/en/2016/ga11796.doc.htm (accessed on 24 August 2018).
United Nations General Assembly (1993a), Question of the Equitable Representation on and Increase in the Membership of the Security Council, 20 July 1993, A/48/264.
United Nations General Assembly (1993b), Question of the Equitable Representation on and Increase in the Membership of the Security Council, 26 July 1993, A/48/264/Add.1.
United Nations General Assembly (1998a), Question of Equitable Representation on and Increase in the Membership of the Security Council and Related Matters, Amendments to Draft Resolution A/53/L.16, 18 November 1998, A/53/L.42.
United Nations General Assembly (1998b), Question of Equitable Representation on and Increase in the Membership of the Security Council and Related Matters, 20 November 1998, A/53/L.16/Rev.1.
United Nations General Assembly (2015), Implementation of General Assembly Resolutions 55/235 and 55/236, A/70/331/Add.1.
United Nations General Assembly (2016), 108th Plenary Meeting, Thursday, 30 June 2016, 3 p.m., Official Records, A/70/PV.108.
United Nations General Assembly (2017a), 37th Meeting, Thursday, 21 December 2017, 10 a.m., Emergency Special Session, Official Records, A/ES-10/PV.37.
United Nations General Assembly (2017b), 107th Plenary Meeting, Tuesday, 28 June 2016, 3 p.m., Official Records, A/70/PV.107.
United Nations Secretariat (2017), Assessment of Member States' Advances to the Working Capital Fund for the Biennium 2018–2019 and Contributions to the United Nations Regular Budget for 2018, ST/ADM/SER.B/973.
United Nations Security Council (2007), 5805th Meeting, Monday, 17 December 2007, 10 a.m., S/PV.5805.
United Nations Security Council (2008a), 5987th Meeting, Tuesday, 7 October 2008, 10 a.m., S/PV.5987.
United Nations Security Council (2008b), 6020th Meeting, Thursday, 20 November 2008, 10.30 a.m., S/PV.6020.
United Nations Security Council (2012), 6729th Meeting, Monday, 5 March 2012, 10 a.m., S/PV.6729.
United Nations Security Council (2015), 7439th Meeting, Monday, 11 May 2015, 10 a.m., S/PV.7439.
United Nations Security Council (2017a), 8139th Meeting, Monday, 18 December 2017, 12.25 p.m., S/PV.8139.
United Nations Security Council (2017b), 7857th Meeting Tuesday, 10 January 2017, 10 a.m., S/PV.7857.
United Nations Security Council (2017c), Letter Dated 17 November 2017 from the Permanent Representative of Italy to the United Nations Dddressed to the Secretary-General, S/2017/972.
United States Department of State (1984), *Report to Congress on Voting Practices in the United Nations*, https://archive.org/search.php?query=%28collection%3Ausde

ptofstateunreports+OR+mediatype%3Ausdeptofstateunreports%29+AND+-media type%3Acollection&sort=date&page=1 (accessed on 2 August 2018).
United States Department of State (1987), *Report to Congress on Voting Practices in the United Nations*, https://archive.org/search.php?query=%28collection%3Ausde ptofstateunreports+OR+mediatype%3Ausdeptofstateunreports%29+AND+-media type%3Acollection&sort=date&page=1 (accessed on 2 August 2018).
United States Department of State (1990), *Report to Congress on Voting Practices in the United Nations 1989,* https://archive.org/search.php?query=%28collection%3 Ausdeptofstateunreports+OR+mediatype%3Ausdeptofstateunreports%29+AND+ -mediatype%3Acollection&sort=date&page=1 (accessed on 2 August 2018).
United States Department of State (1993), *Voting Practices in the United Nations 1992*, https://archive.org/details/votingpracticesi1992unit/page/n0 (accessed 30 September 2018).
United States Department of State (1996), *Voting Practices in the United Nations 1995*, https://archive.org/details/votingpracticesi1995unit/page/n0 (accessed 30 September 2018).
United States Department of State (1999), *Voting Practices in the United Nations 1998*, https://archive.org/details/votingpracticesi1998unit/page/14 (accessed 30 September 2018).
United States Department of State (2002), *Voting Practices in the United Nations 2001*, https://www.state.gov/p/io/rls/rpt/2001/vtg/index.htm (accessed 30 September 2018).
United States Department of State (2004), *Voting Practices in the United Nations 2004*, https://www.state.gov/p/io/rls/rpt/c14622.htm (accessed 30 September 2018).
United States Department of State (2007), *Voting Practices in the United Nations 2007*, https://www.state.gov/p/io/rls/rpt/c25867.htm (accessed 30 September 2018).
United States Department of State (2011), *Report to Congress on Voting Practices in the United Nations 2010*, https://www.state.gov/p/io/rls/rpt/c44269.htm (accessed 30 September 2018).
United States Department of State (2014), *Report to Congress on Voting Practices in the United Nations 2013*, https://www.state.gov/p/io/rls/rpt/2013/2013/index.htm (accessed 30 September 2018).
United States Department of State (2017), *Report to Congress on Voting Practices in the United Nations 2016*, https://www.state.gov/p/io/rls/rpt/2016/practices/index .htm (accessed 30 September 2018).
United States Department of State (2018), *Report to Congress on Voting Practices in the United Nations 2017*, https://www.state.gov/p/io/rls/rpt/2017/practices/index .htm (accessed 30 September 2018).
Usherwood S. and Startin N. (2013), Euroscepticism as a Persistent Phenomenon, *Journal of Common Market Studies*, 51(1), 1–16.
Vaccara S. and Nobis C. (2018), All'ONU Conte accontenta tutti: l'Italia è multilaterale e sovranista, *La voce di New York*, 26 September 2018, https://www .lavocedinewyork.com/onu/2018/09/26/allonu-conte-accontenta-tutti-litalia-e -multilaterale-e-sovranista/ (accessed on 27 September 2018).

Valbruzzi M. (2018), *Chi ha vinto la partita del governo?* http://www.cattaneo.org/wp-content/uploads/2018/05/Analisi-Istituto-Cattaneo-Il-governo-M5s-e-Lega-23-maggio-2018-1.pdf (accessed on 21 September 2018).
Valbruzzi M. and Vignati R. (eds.) (2018), *Il vicolo cieco*, Bologna, Il Mulino.
Valigi M. (2017), *Le medie potenze*, Milan, Vita e Pensiero.
Varsori A. (2010), *La Cenerentola d'Europa?* Soveria Mannelli, Rubbettino.
Varsori A. (2015), The Foreign Policy of First Republic Italy: New Approaches, *Journal of Modern Italian Studies*, 20(3), 292–297.
Verbeke J. (2006), EU Coordination on Security Council matters, in Wouters J., Hoffmeister and Ruys T. (eds.), *The United Nations and the European Union: An Ever Stronger Partnership*, The Hague, T.M.C. Asser Press.
Vestergaard J. and Wade R. H. (2013), Protecting Power: How Western States Retain the Dominant Voice in the World Bank's Governance, *World Development*, 46, 153–164.
Vestergaard J. and Wade R. H. (2015), Still in the Woods: Gridlock in the IMF and the World Bank Puts Multilateralism at Risk, *Global Policy*, 6(1), 1–12.
Voeten E. (2000), Clashes in the Assembly, *International Organization*, 54(2), 182–215.
Voeten E. (2004), Resisting the Lonely Superpower: Responses of States in the United Nations to US Dominance, *Journal of Politics*, 66(3), 729–754.
Voeten E. (2005), The Political Origins of the UN Security Council's Ability to Legitimize the Use of Force, *International Organization*, 59(3), 527–557.
Voeten E. (2013), Data and Analyses of Voting in the United Nations General Assembly, in Reinalda B. (ed.), *Routledge Handbook of International Organization*, London, Routledge.
Voeten E. (2014), A World without the West? Not so Fast, *The Washington Post*, 14 November 2014, https://www.washingtonpost.com/blogs/monkey-cage/wp/2014/11/14/a-world-without-the-west-not-so-fast/ (accessed on 23 September 2018).
Volgy T. J., Corbetta R., Grant K. A. and Baird R. G. (2011), Major Power Status in International Politics, in Volgy T. J., Corbetta R., Grant K. A. and Baird R. G. (eds.), *Major Powers and the Quest for Status in International Politics*, New York, Palgrave Macmillan.
Walston J. (2004), The Shift in Italy's Euro-Atlantic policy. Partisan or Bipartisan? *The International Spectator*, 39(4), 115–125.
Walston J. (2007), Italian Foreign Policy in the "Second Republic." Changes of Form and Substance, *Modern Italy*, 12(1), 91–104.
Welch Larson D., Paul T. V. and Wohlforth W. C. (2014), Status and World Order, in Paul T. V., Welch Larson D. and Wohlforth W. C. (eds.), *Status in World Politics*, New York, Cambridge University Press.
White B. (2001), *Understanding European Foreign Policy*, Basingstoke, Palgrave.
White House (2015), *National Security Strategy*.
Winter E. (1996), Voting and Vetoing, *American Political Science Review*, 90(4), 813–823.

Wohlforth W. C., de Carvalho B., Leira H. and Neumann I. B. (2018), Moral Authority and Status in International Relations: Good States and the Social Dimension of Status Seeking, *Review of International Studies*, 44(3), 526–546.

Wong R. (2005), The Europeanization of Foreign Policy, in Hill C and Smith M. (eds.), *International Relations and the European Union*, Oxford, Oxford University Press.

Wong R. and Hill C. (2011), Introduction, in Wong R. and Hill C. (eds.), *National and European Foreign Policies. Towards Europeanization*, Milton Park and New York, Routledge.

Woods N. (2010), Global Governance after the Financial Crisis: A New Multilateralism or the Last Gasp of the Great Powers? *Global Policy*, 1(1), 51–63.

Wright T. (2019), Trump's Foreign Policy Is No Longer Unpredictable, *Foreign Affairs*, 18 January 2019, https://www.foreignaffairs.com/articles/world/2019-01-18/trumps-foreign-policy-no-longer-unpredictable?cid=int-flb&pgtype=hpg (accessed on 19 January 2019)

Young H. and Rees N. (2005), EU Voting Behaviour in the UN General Assembly, 1990–2002: The EU's Europeanising Tendencies, *Irish Studies in International Affairs*, 16, 193–207.

Zangl B., Heußner F., Kruck A. and Lanzendörfer X. (2016), Imperfect Adaptation: How the WTO and the IMF Adjust to Shifting Power Distributions among their Members, *Review of International Organizations*, 11(2), 171–196.

Zarakol A. (ed.) (2017), *Hierarchies in World Politics*, Cambridge, Cambridge University Press.

Index

Page references for figures are italicized.

adaptation, national, 2, 3, 24, 26–29, 34, 36, 41, 45–47, 55, 57, 64, 66–68, 71, 74–75, 97, 99–102, 116, 142, 151, 167–68
Afghanistan, 8, *112*, 138n7, 138n9
Africa, *113*, 125, 129–33
agenda setting, 17–18, 38, 52–54, 56, 61, 63, 66, 70, 110, 115, 119, 124–25, 127, 132–33, 135–38, 141, 144–45, 158–61, 166, 169
Asian Infrastructure Investment Bank (AIIB), 22, 158
Austria, 75, *84*, *90*, 98, 100–101, 105–7, 116, *117*, *120*, 134, 138n9, 153

Belgium, 75, *84*, *90–91*, 102, 106–7, *112–13*, *117*, *120*, 122, 127–28, 131, 133–34, 138n9, 153
Berlusconi government, 23, 54, 79–81, 91–93, 143
blue helmets of culture, 51, 124–25
Brazil, 3, 11, 22, 47, 63, 71n4, 93–94, *117*, 130, 132, 138n9
Brazil, Russia, India, and China (BRIC), 11, 22, 40, 47, 62–63, 68–70, 84–87, 92–94, 107n3, 110

Bulgaria, 58, *90*, 101, 106–7, *117*, *120*, 131, 134, 138n6, 138n9
Bush (George W.) administration, 19, 54, 92–93

Cardi, Sebastiano, 123–24, 139n15
China, 3, 11, 22, 47, 54, 61–63, 71, 71n4, 93–94, 110–14, 116, *117*, 118, 120–21, 126, 130, 132, 136, 138n9, 158–59, 169
coalition building, 13–14, 17–18, 23, 42n14, 60, 66, 68–70, 86–90, 102, 110, 134, 142, 160, 162–63, 168–69
coalition facilitator, 2–4, 10, 14, 23, 29, 36–41, 47, 62, 64, 66–67, 71, 73, 77, 79, 81–82, 84, 88, 109, 118, 132, 138, 142, 165, 167–69
Coffee Club, 129–30
Common Foreign and Security Policy (CFSP), 26, 34, 55
contributions to the UN budget, 9, 46, 49–50, 61, 128–29
coordination reflex, 27–28, 30, 141–42, 168–69
crises: Brexit, 22, 62, 123, 142, 161, 164n4; Eurozone, 142–44, 147, 151,

157, 160–61; hegemonic order, 3–4, 10, 16, 19–20, 22, 40–41, 54, 63–65, 68–68, 75, 109, 142, 149, 157–62, 170; migration, 8, 22, 62, 97, 124, 135–36, 142–45, 148, 157, 164n4

Croatia, *84*, 101, *113*, 114, *117*, *120*, 134, 138n4

Cyprus, 55, *84*, *90*, 98, 100–101, 105–7, *120*, 131, 134, 136–37

Czech Republic, *90*, 101, 106–7, 114, *120*, 124, 131, 138n9

de-Europeanization, 1, 11–12, 24, 28, 31, 35–36, 43, 63, 68–69, 71, 75, 77, 79, 82, 84–85, 87–88, 93–94, 116, 141–42, 151, 154, 166, 169–70

defection, 3, 8–9, 31, 37–40, 43–46, 53, 57–59, 65–66, 74, 78, 82–83, 94, 98–99, 101, 107, 114–15, 119, 125, 136–37, 166–68

Democratic party, 148

Denmark, 58, 75, 83–84, 90, *91*, 101, *120*, 127, 131, 133–34, 136, 138n9

disarmament, 11, 58, 73–74, *76*, 83, 89, 95, 102–7, 142, 167–68

dominant coalition, 1–2, 10, 17, 21–23, 38–41, 52, 63–64, 68, 81, 85–86, 94, 109, 118, 120–21, 132, 142, 157–58, 160, 162, 165–66, 169

Estonia, 58, *90*, 101, 107, *120*, 131, 138n9

EUNAVFORMED, 135

European formalized coalition: definition, 2, 38–41, 64, 68, 70; how to analyze membership at the UN, 64–71

European Political Cooperation (EPC), 26, 55

European Union (EU): security strategy, 44–45

Europeanization of foreign policy ideal type, 2, 31, 37–39, 43, 65, 74, 83, 86, 98, 166

Europeanization of foreign policy logics: appropriateness, logic of, 25, 27, 36–37, 62, 141, 168–69; consequences, logic of, 25, 27, 36–37, 62, 141, 168–69

Europeanization of foreign policy methodological problems, 27–29, 43

Europeanization of foreign policy modes, 31–32, 73–74

Europeanization of foreign policy processes: cross-loading, 30, 71, 99–100, 169; downloading, 11, 29, 71, 136–38, 169; uploading, 11, 29–30, 36, 71, 95, 99, 106, 133–36, 138, 141, 144, 158, 169

Europeanization of foreign policy theories, 24–29

Europeanization of Italian foreign policy at the UN: operationalization, 64–66, 75–77, 110

Euroscepticism, 8, 32–33, 62–63, 142–49, 155–56, 170

F35, 9, 12n8

Finland, 75, *90–91*, 100, 106, *120*, 131, 153

France, 9, 21, 48, 57–59, 71n4, 78, 83–84, 90, 98, 100, 106, 110–18, *120*, 123–35, 138n9, 154, *155*, 167–68

Fulci, Francesco Paolo, 128–30

G4, 130–31

General Assembly, UN: committees, 67, 69, 73, 88–89, 100–101, 106; plenary, 69, 73, 88–89, 127

Gentiloni, Paolo, *80*, 92, 97, 123

Germany, 9, 19, 21, 50–51, 58, 71n4, 75, 83–84, 90, *91*, 94, 100–102, 105–7, *117*, 119–20, 126–32, 134, 138n9, 144, 150–56, 168, 170

Greece, 75, 90, *91*, 98–101, 107, *120*, 127, 131, 133–34, 144, 148, 151–54, *155*

Haley, Nikki, 62
hegemony: hegemonic theories, 16–20; hegemonic war, 16–18, 42n15; phases, 17–18, 22–23, 39–41, 41n3, 63, 68, 75, 81, 85, 94, 160–62
Human Rights Council, 59, 62
human rights in the General Assembly: cloning, 83, 100; the girl child, 101; moratorium on the use of the death penalty, 50, 95, 99, 141, 167; right to development, 97–98, 102, 167; right to food, 98, 100–101
human rights in the Security Council: children and armed conflict, 136–37; protection of civilians in armed conflicts, 136–37; sexual violence against civilians in armed conflicts, 119, 137; women, peace, and security, 137
human smuggling and trafficking, 124, 132–33, 135–36, 141, 167
Hungary, *90*, 100, 107, 114, *120*, 138n9, 153

Iraq, 8, 21, 54, 78, *112*
Ireland, *84*, *90*, 98, 100–101, 105, *117*, *120*, 137, 138n9, 139n19
Italian Christian Democratic party, (DC), 5, 49
Italian cohesion with EU member states at the UN: coordination among EU member states, 23, 43–46, 50, 55–59, 62–63, 73–78; voting, 73–86, 95–100, 102–6, 112–14, 151–53, 156–57; sponsoring, 86–94, 100–102, 106–7, 114–21, 132–38, 153–56
Italian Communist party, (PCI), 5–6, 32, 49
Italian foreign policy: membership of the dominant coalition, 1, 10, 22–23, 40–41, 63–64, 68, 81, 85–86, 94, 109, 118, 120–21, 132, 142, 157–58, 160, 162, 165, 169; myths, 9, 32–33, 46, 145–46; pillars, 1, 7–9, 12n3, 15, 23, 35, 40, 48–59, 60, 143, 162, 165–66
Italian foreign policy partners: Brazil, 92–94; BRIC, 84–85, 92–94; China, 92–94, 114, *117*, 121; India, 92–94; regular partners among EU member states, 83–84, 90–91, 116, *117*, 119–20, 152–56; Russia, 92–94, 114, *117*, 121; US, 84–86, 92–94, 112–14, *117*, 118
Italian governments: center-left, 7, 23, 51, 79, 82, 91–93, 97, 143; center-right, 7, 23, 35, 51, 54, 79, 81, 91–93, 143; M5S-League coalition, 8–9, 12n9, 143, 149
Italian Socialist party (PSI), 12n2, 49

Latvia, *84*, 89, *90*, 106, 114, *120*, 131, 137
League (Northern), 8, 143, 148–49
learning, process, 27
Lebanon, 35, *117*, 138n9
Letta, Enrico, *80*
Libya, 11, 51, 124, 133, 135–36, 138, 138n9, 141, 144, 167
Lithuania, 58, *90*, 106–7, 116, *117*, *120*, 131, 135
Luxembourg, 58, 75, 83–84, 90, *91*, 98, 101–2, 106–7, 116, *120*, 127, 131, 134–35, 138n9, 153

M5S, Five-Star Movement, 8, 143, 147–49
Malta, 83, *84*, *90*, 98, 100, 106, *120*, 130–31, 136–37, 138n9
Mediterranean, 5, 35, 49, 90, 124–25, 135–36, 144–45, 168
Middle East, 21, 35, 58, 74, *76*, 105, 107n8, *112–13*, 114
middle power, 2–3, 10, 13–15, 16, 23–24, 35, 37, 41, 46–48, 62, 64–66, 129, 131, 158, 162–63, 165, 169
ministry of foreign affairs, Italian, 33–34, 122, 139n11

Mogherini, Federica, 44, 135
Monti, Mario, *80*, 143
MUOS, 9, 12n8
multilateralism and multilateral institutions, 1, 3–4, 6–10, 13–15, 18–24, 31, 37–38, 40–41, 42n9, 43–47, 48–52, 53–55, 60–65, 74, 81–82, 91–92, 102, 104, 158–63, 165–66, 169

Netherlands, 11, 51, 70, 75, 90, *91*, 101–2, 106–7, 112, *117*, *120*, 123–24, 127, 131, 133–34, 136, 138n7, 138n9
Non-Aligned Movement (NAM), 97, 126, 130
nationalism, 6–9, 33, 165
North Atlantic Treaty Organization (NATO), 5, 8, 22, 102, 133, 162
nuclear issues, 5, 11, 54, 57, 83, 89, 102–7, 142, 167–68

Obama administration, 54, 61, 92–93, 160

peacekeeping, 7–10, 13, 14–15, 23, 46, 49–52, 53, 60–61, 63, 125, 128–29, 133
Poland, *90*, 100–101, 107, 114, *120*, 131, 137, 138n9
Portugal, 75, 83–84, 90, *91*, 98, 100, *117*, *120*, 125, 127–28, 131, 133–34, 138n9, 148, 152–53, *155*
Prodi, Romano, 23, 79, *80*, 82, 91
public opinion polls, Italy: EU image, *145*, 146, 163n1; support for a common foreign policy, *150*, 151; trust in the EU, *146*, 147, 149, 151, 163n2

Renzi, Matteo, *80*, 92, 97, 143
Romania, *90*, 101, 114, *117*, *120*, 131, 134

Russia, 3, 8–9, 11, 22–23, 35, 47, 54, 61–63, 71, 71n4, 93–94, 110–14, 116, *117*, 118, 120–21, 123, 126, 130, 132, 136, 138n9, 158–59, 169

Security Council, UN: Italy as a European member, 121–25; processes of Europeanization, 132–38; reform, 11, 23, 45–46, 49–50, 52, 59–63, 122, 125–32, 139n12, 139n13, 139n14, 141, 168
Slovakia, 58, 83–84, *90*, 100, *112*, *117*, *120*, 131, 137
Slovenia, 58, 83–84, 90, *91*, 98, 100, 107, *120*, 131, 153, 168
socialization, process of, 24, 27–30, 33, 52
Somalia, 11, *113*, 132–35, 138, 139n16
Spain, 75, 84, 90, *91*, 98, 100–101, 106–7, *117*, 119, *120*, 128, 130–31, 133–34, 139n9, 148, 152–53, *155*
split term, 11, 51, 70, 112, 121–25, 138n7
sponsoring behavior: how to analyze coalition membership, 68–71, 114–16
status, 3–4, 6, 10–11, 13–15, 16, 23–24, 35, 37, 41, 44, 46–49, 51–52, 59–60, 62–66, 69–70, 73, 75, 78, 87, 92, 94, 102, 110, 125–29, 132, 141–42, 157–59, 162, 165–69
strategic culture, 3, 9–10, 17, 24, 28, 37, 40, 46, 48, 64, 102, 163, 165
Sweden, *84*, 107, *113*, 114, *117*, *120*, 123, 131, 134

Trans Adriatic Pipeline (TAP), 9, 12n8
Trump administration, 9, 12n9, 19, 22, 54–55, 61–62, 157–58, 160–62, 170

unilateralism, 9, 19, 21, 54, 161
United Kingdom, 48, 57–59, 71n4, 78, 83–84, 90, 94, 101, 106–7, 110, *112*,

113, 115–16, *117*, 118, 120, 123–24, 126–35, 138n9, 154–55, 161, 167–68
United States: Italian sponsoring cohesion with at the UN, 92–94, 116–18, 120; Italian voting cohesion with at the UN, 52–55, 84–86, 112–14; military bases in Italy, 5, 17, 22, 102; National Security Strategy, 61
Uniting for Consensus (UfC), 52, 130–32, 139n15
US-led order, 1–4, 10, 13–22, 24, 39–41, 47, 52, 54, 62–65, 68–71, 73, 75, 92, 109, 116, 121, 142, 149, 157–62, 165–66, 169–70

veto, 52, 63, 110–14, 120–21, 127–28, 130, 138n3, *159*, 160
vincolo esterno (external constraint), 4–6, 11, 24, 32–33, 63, 143–44
vote changes, 67–68
voting behavior at the UN: absence, 67–68, 83, 105, 111, 134; abstention, 67, 105, 113, 135; how to analyze coalition membership, 67–68; vote changes, 67–68

Western European and Others Group (WEOG), 51, 55, 122–23

About the Author

Carla Monteleone is associate professor of political science and international relations at the University of Palermo, Italy. Her main research interests are in the field of international security, transatlantic relations, multilateralism (particularly the UN), IR theory, and Italian foreign policy. She has been a visiting scholar at Columbia University and Georgetown University, and she was awarded a Fulbright Schuman scholarship. She has contributed to several national and international research projects, including on Italian foreign policy, on the impact of the Eurozone crisis on the Europeanization of the foreign policy of Southern EU member states, on the role of the United States in the contemporary spatially fragmented international system, and on American military bases in Europe. She is currently on the editorial board of the *Journal of Transatlantic Studies*. This book is part of her research agenda on coalitional behavior and changes in the organization of the international system.

Ingram Content Group UK Ltd.
Milton Keynes UK
UKHW021359280423
420938UK00022B/131